AP CHEMISTRY
Power Practice Workbook

AP Chemistry
Power Practice Workbook

발 행 2024년 12월 20일

저 자 유현정
발행인 최영민
발행처 피앤피북
주 소 경기도 파주시 신촌로 16
전 화 031-8071-0088
팩 스 031-942-8688
전자우편 hermonh@naver.com
출판등록 2015년 3월 27일
등록번호 제406-2015-31호

ⓒ 유현정 2024, Printed in Korea.

ISBN 979-11-94085-26-3 (53740)

- 책 값은 뒤 표지에 있습니다.
- 헤르몬하우스는 피앤피북의 임프린트 출판사입니다.
- 이 책의 어느 부분도 저작권자나 발행인의 승인 없이 무단 복제하여 이용할 수 없습니다.

AP CHEMISTRY

Power Practice Workbook

Hyunjung Yoo, M.S.

AP Chemistry의 특징

유현정 선생님의 《AP Chemistry Power Practice Workbook》은 AP Chemistry의 주요 개념을 완벽하게 정리하고 연습할 수 있는 보조 문제집으로, 개념 이해와 문제 해결 능력을 체계적이고 꼼꼼하게 탄탄히 다져 주어, 학생들이 화학을 깊이 이해하고 자신감을 갖추며 학습 목표를 성공적으로 달성할 수 있도록 돕습니다. 또한 이 책은 College Board 의 가이드라인에 맞추어 구성되어 있어, AP Chemistry 시험에서 다루어지는 주제를 체계적으로 연습할 수 있습니다. 이 교재를 통해 AP Chemistry 시험을 준비하는 많은 학생들이 자기주도적으로 공부하는 데 도움이 되기를 바랍니다.

● Regular Chemistry 복습

AP Chemistry 에서 기본이 되는 Regular Chemistry 의 Mole calculation, Stoichiometry, Molarity 관련된 응용 문제들을 Review 파트에 수록하여 학생들이 틈틈이 복습할 수 있도록 구성하였습니다.

● Topic Key Point Review

각 토픽에는 "Key Point Review" 섹션이 마련되어 있어, 토픽 별 핵심 개념을 간단하고 명료하게 정리하여 학생들이 반드시 이해하고 넘어가야 할 사항들을 절대로 놓치지 않도록 돕습니다.

● **3단계 문제 구성**

《AP Chemistry Power Practice Workbook》의 문제 유형은 학습자의 개념 이해와 문제 해결 능력을 체계적으로 강화할 수 있도록 세 가지 단계로 구성되어 있습니다.

⇒ True/False 문제: 개념을 포함한 문장을 단순히 읽고 넘어가는 것이 아니라 각 문장에서 틀린 부분을 찾아냄으로써 개념에 대한 정확하고 깊이 있는 이해를 확인할 수 있습니다.

⇒ Concept Check 문제: Free response 문제로 구성되어, 문제를 단계별로 해결해 나가는 사고력과 문제 해결 능력을 길러줍니다.

⇒ Multiple Choice 문제: 각 주제별로 개념을 최종적으로 복습할 수 있는 객관식 문제로, 학습한 내용을 종합적으로 점검할 수 있습니다.

● **친절하고 상세한 문제풀이**

⇒ 각 토픽마다 Worked Solution 이 포함되어 있어, 학생들이 혼자서도 스스로 학습할 수 있도록 지원합니다. 복잡한 AP Chemistry 문제들을 체계적으로 접근하는 방법을 제시하여, 학생들이 문제를 단계별로 이해하고 해결해 나갈 수 있도록 돕습니다.

⇒ 특히, 자기주도 학습을 하는 학생들이 개념과 풀이 과정을 차근차근 따라가며 깊이 있는 이해를 할 수 있도록 설계되었습니다.

《AP Chemistry Power Practice Workbook》은 AP Chemistry 개념 정리와 실전 대비에 필요한 필수 학습 도구로, 본격적인 시험 대비 문제풀이 전에 사용하기에 최적화되어 있습니다. 이 책을 통해 학생들이 AP Chemistry 의 기본기를 탄탄히 다지고, 시험에서 원하는 성과를 이루길 바랍니다.

AP Chemistry 시험을 잘 보기 위한 꿀 Tip

▶ 개념정리의 완성 (겨울방학까지) - 나만의 단권화 노트 만들기

기본적인 개념 정리는 빠를수록 좋아요. 겨울방학까지 각 단원 별 주요 개념을 꼼꼼하게 정리해 나만의 단권화 노트를 완성하세요. 이 노트는 시험 직전에 빠르게 복습할 때 큰 도움이 될 거예요. 중요한 포인트나 헷갈리기 쉬운 부분을 시각적으로 강조하여 기억하기 쉽게 만들어 보세요.

▶ 개념정리 3 회독

3 회독은 단순히 눈으로 읽고 지나가는 것이 아니라, 적극적으로 개념을 이해하고 내 것으로 만드는 과정이에요. 내가 친구나 가족에게 선생님이 되어 설명한다고 생각하고, 어려운 개념도 쉽게 풀어낼 수 있을 정도로 공부하세요. 말로 설명하며 학습하면 자신의 이해도를 점검할 수 있고, 기억에 오래 남게 돼요.

▶ 문제풀이와 함께

개념 정리만으로는 충분한 실력을 쌓기 어려워요. 개념을 3 회독하면서 응용 문제도 꼭 풀어보세요. 문제를 풀면서 이해한 개념이 실제로 적용되는지 확인하고, 다양한 문제 유형에 익숙해져야 합니다. 처음부터 문제를 책에 직접 풀지 말고, 패드나 노트를 활용해 문제 풀이 과정을 정리해보세요. 이렇게 정리한 풀이 과정을 복습할 때 참고 자료로 활용할 수 있어요. 처음에 헷갈리거나 틀린 문제, 풀이과정이 명쾌하지 않은 문제는 문제 번호 옆에 체크표시를 하여 혼자 풀어낼 수 있을 때까지 연습하세요.

예시) ·헷갈린 것 : △ 세모 또는 ☆ 별   ·틀린 것 : ×

▶ 실전 문제풀이는 늦어도 2월에 시작

AP Chemistry 시험은 5월에 있지만, 4월에 실전 문제 풀이를 시작하면 시간이 부족해요. 실전 문제를 풀면서 시험 스타일과 문제 유형에 익숙해지는 것은 필수입니다. 따라서 늦어도 2월부터는 실전 문제 풀이를 시작해 시험 직전에 충분히 대비할 수 있도록 하세요. 실전 문제 풀이를 통해 시간 관리 능력도 키울 수 있어요.

▶ 오답노트 만들기

실수를 되풀이하지 않기 위해서는 오답 노트를 활용하는 것이 좋습니다. 단원별로 오답 노트를 만들어 틀린 문제와 헷갈렸던 문제를 기록하고, 왜 틀렸는지 분석하세요. 이러한 과정을 통해 약점을 파악하고, 반복해서 틀리는 문제 유형을 개선할 수 있어요. 시험 전에는 오답 노트를 통해 마지막으로 약점을 점검하세요.

위의 꿀 Tip 들을 차근차근 실천해 나가면, AP Chemistry 시험에서 좋은 결과를 얻을 수 있을 거예요!

저자 소개

유현정 선생님은 열정적이고 타이트하며 꼼꼼하고 섬세한, 체계적인 접근으로 학생들에게 완성도 높은 학습 경험을 제공합니다.

서강대학교에서 화학과 생명과학을 복수 전공하며 수석으로 조기 졸업하였고, 서울대학교에서 유기화학 석사 학위를 취득하였습니다. 또한 국제 저명 저널인 JACS에 연구 논문을 게재하며 학문적 깊이를 인정받았습니다.

이후 10여 년간 압구정동과 대치동에서 수많은 학생들을 지도하며, Chemistry와 Biology 분야에서 학생들이 깊이 있는 이해와 학문적 자신감을 키울 수 있도록 이끄는 교육 전문가로 자리매김하였습니다.

아울러 단순한 강의자가 아닌, 학생 맞춤형 성장 트레이너로서, 학생 개개인의 학습 스타일과 이해의 어려움을 세심하게 파악하고 그에 맞는 피드백과 체계적인 학습 계획을 제공하는 것으로 잘 알려져 있습니다. 특히, 학생들이 어려워하는 개념을 쉽고 명확하게 설명하고, 스스로 학습의 즐거움을 느낄 수 있도록 차근차근 지도하여 학생들이 주도적으로 학습에 참여할 수 있도록 돕고 있습니다. 학생들과의 적극적인 소통과 피드백을 통해 단순한 시험 준비 이상의 성장을 이끌어내며, Chemistry와 Biology를 깊이 이해하고 흥미를 갖도록 하는 데 주력하고 있습니다.

유현정 선생님의 Chemistry 커리큘럼은 Regular Chemistry, AP Chemistry, IB Chemistry, Olympiad Chemistry까지 아우르며, 다양한 수준의 학생들을 위한 맞춤형 학습이 가능합니다. 저학년 학생들이 Regular Chemistry로 기초를 튼튼히 다진 후 AP/IB Chemistry에서 좋은 성과를 거둘 수 있도록 하고, 나아가 Olympiad와 같은 최고 수준의 시험에 도전할 수 있는 실력을 길러줍니다.

Contents

AP Chemistry Exam Information   10

AP Chemistry Equations and Constants   10

PERIODIC TABEL OF THE ELEMENTS   13

Review of Regular Chemistry   15

Worked solution with answer for Review   39

Topic _1 Atomic structure & Properties 51

Topic _2 Compounds Sturcture & Properties 69

Topic _3 Properties of Substances & Mixtures 89

Topic _4 Chemical Reactions 117

Topic _5 Kinetics 135

Topic _6 Thermochemistry 153

Topic _7 Equilibrium 203

Topic _8 Acids and Bases 245

Topic _9 Thermodynamics and Electrochemistry 297

AP Chemistry Exam Information

Section	Question Type	Number of Questions	Exam Weighting
I	Multiple choice questions	60	50%
II	Free response questions	3 Long (10 points each) 4 Short (4 points each)	
Total 3 hours 15 minutes long			
A scientific or graphing calculator is recommended for use on both sections of the exam.			

AP Chemistry Equations and Constants

Unit symbols
gram, g
mole, mol
liter, L
meter, m
second, s
hertz, Hz
atmosphere, atm
millimeter of mercury, mm Hg
degree Celsius, °C
kelvin, K
joule, J
volt, V
coulomb, C
ampere, A

Unit conversions
1 hertz = $1s^{-1}$
1 atm = 760 mmHg = 760 torr
K = °C + 273.15
1 volt = $\dfrac{1\ joule}{1\ coulomb}$
1 ampere = $\dfrac{1\ coulomb}{1\ second}$

METRIC PREFIXES		
Factor	Prefix	Symbol
10^9	Giga	G
10^6	Mega	M
10^3	Kilo	k
10^{-2}	Centi	c
10^{-3}	Milli	m
10^{-6}	Micro	μ
10^{-9}	Nano	n
10^{-12}	pico	p

ATOMIC STRUCTURE $E = h\nu$ $c = \lambda\nu$ $F_{coulombic} \propto \frac{q_1 q_2}{r^2}$	E = energy ν = frequency λ = wavelength F = force q = charge r = separation Planck's constant, $h = 6.626 \times 10^{-34}$ J s Speed of light, $c = 2.998 \times 10^8$ m s^{-1} Avogadro's number, $= 6.022 \times 10^{23}$ mol^{-1}
GASES, LIQUIDS, AND SOLUTIONS $\frac{P_1 V_1}{T_1} = \frac{P_2 V_2}{T_2}$ $PV = nRT$ $P_A = P_{total} \times X_A$, where $X_A = \frac{moles\ A}{total\ moels}$ $P_{total} = P_A + P_B + P_C + \ldots$ $n = \frac{m}{M}$ $D = \frac{m}{V}$ $KE = \frac{1}{2} mv^2$ $M = \frac{n_{solute}}{L_{solution}}$ $A = \varepsilon\ b\ c$	P = pressure V = volume T = temperature n = number of moles X = mole fraction m = mass **M** = molar mass D = density KE = kinetic energy v = velocity M = molarity A = absorbance ε = molar absorptivity b = path length c = concentration Gas constant, R = 8.314 J mol^{-1} K^{-1} = 0.08206 L atm K^{-1} mol^{-1} STP = 273.15 K and 1.0 atm Ideal gas at STP = 22.4 L mol^{-1}
Kinetics $[A]_t - [A]_0 = -kt$ $\ln[A]_t - \ln[A]_0 = -kt$ $\frac{1}{[A]_t} - \frac{1}{[A]_0} = kt$ $t_{1/2} = \frac{0.693}{k}$	k = rate constant t = time $t_{1/2}$ = half-life
Equilibrium $K_c = \frac{[C]^c[D]^d}{[A]^a[B]^b}$, where $aA + bB \rightleftarrows cC + dD$ $K_p = \frac{(P_C)^c(P_D)^d}{(P_A)^a(P_B)^b}$ $K_w = [H_3O^+][OH^-] = 1.0 \times 10^{-14}$ at 25 °C $pK_w = 14 = pH + pOH$ at 25 °C $pH = -\log[H_3O^+]$ $pOH = -\log[OH^-]$	**Equilibrium Constants** K_c (Molar concentrations) K_p (gas pressure) K_w (water) K_a (acid) K_b (base)

$K_a = \frac{[H_3O^+][A^-]}{[HA]}$ $K_b = \frac{[OH^-][HB^+]}{[B]}$ $pK_a = -\log K_a$ $pK_b = -\log K_b$ $K_w = K_a \times K_b$ $pK_w = pK_a + pK_b$ $pH = pK_a + \log \frac{[A^-]}{[HA]}$	
Thermodynamics/Electrochemistry $q = c\, m\, \Delta T$ $\Delta H°_{reaction} = \Sigma \Delta H°_{f\,products} - \Sigma \Delta H°_{f\,reactants}$ $\Delta S°_{reaction} = \Sigma S°_{products} - \Sigma S°_{reactants}$ $\Delta G°_{reaction} = \Sigma \Delta G°_{f\,products} - \Sigma \Delta G°_{f\,reactants}$ $\Delta G° = \Delta H° - T\Delta S° = -RT \ln K = -nFE°$ $I = q/T$ $E_{cell} = E°_{cell} - \frac{RT}{nF} \ln Q$	q = heat m = mass c = specific heat capacity T = temperature S° = standard entropy H° = standard enthalpy G° = standard Gibbs free energy R = gas constant K = equilibrium constant n = number of moles of electrons E° = standard potential I = current (amperes) q = charge (coulombs) t = time (seconds) Q = reaction quotient Faraday's constant, F = 96,486 coulombs/ 1 mol e-

PERIODIC TABEL OF THE ELEMENTS

1 H Hydrogen 1.008																	2 He Helium 4.0026
3 Li Lithium 6.94	4 Be Beryllium 9.0122											5 B Boron 10.81	6 C Carbon 12.011	7 N Nitrogen 14.007	8 O Oxygen 15.999	9 F Fluorine 18.998	10 Ne Neon 20.180
11 Na Sodium 22.990	12 Mg Magnesium 24.305											13 Al Aluminium 26.982	14 Si Silicon 28.085	15 P Phosphorus 30.974	16 S Sulfur 32.06	17 Cl Chlorine 35.45	18 Ar Argon 39.948
19 K Potassium 39.098	20 Ca Calcium 40.078	21 Sc Scandium 44.956	22 Ti Titanium 47.867	23 V Vanadium 50.942	24 Cr Chromium 51.996	25 Mn Manganese 54.938	26 Fe Iron 55.845	27 Co Cobalt 58.933	28 Ni Nickel 58.693	29 Cu Copper 63.546	30 Zn Zinc 65.38	31 Ga Gallium 69.723	32 Ge Germanium 72.630	33 As Arsenic 74.922	34 Se Selenium 78.971	35 Br Bromine 79.904	36 Kr Krypton 83.798
37 Rb Rubidium 85.468	38 Sr Strontium 87.62	39 Y Yttrium 88.906	40 Zr Zirconium 91.224	41 Nb Niobium 92.906	42 Mo Molybdenum 95.95	43 Tc Technetium 98	44 Ru Ruthenium 101.07	45 Rh Rhodium 102.91	46 Pd Palladium 106.42	47 Ag Silver 107.87	48 Cd Cadmium 112.41	49 In Indium 114.82	50 Sn Tin 118.71	51 Sb Antimony 121.76	52 Te Tellurium 127.60	53 I Iodine 126.90	54 Xe Xenon 131.29
55 Cs Caesium 132.91	56 Ba Barium 137.33	57-71	72 Hf Hafnium 178.49	73 Ta Tantalum 180.95	74 W Tungsten 183.84	75 Re Rhenium 186.21	76 Os Osmium 190.23	77 Ir Iridium 192.22	78 Pt Platinum 195.08	79 Au Gold 196.97	80 Hg Mercury 200.59	81 Tl Thallium 204.38	82 Pb Lead 207.2	83 Bi Bismuth 208.98	84 Po Polonium 209	85 At Astatine 210	86 Rn Radon 222
87 Fr Francium 223	88 Ra Radium 226	89-103	104 Rf Rutherfordium 267	105 Db Dubnium 268	106 Sg Seaborgium 269	107 Bh Bohrium 270	108 Hs Hassium 277	109 Mt Meitnerium 278	110 Ds Darmstadtium 281	111 Rg Roentgenium 282	112 Cn Copernicium 285	113 Nh Nihonium 286	114 Fl Flerovium 289	115 Mc Moscovium 290	116 Lv Livermorium 293	117 Ts Tennessine 294	118 Og Oganesson 294

57 La Lanthanum 138.91	58 Ce Cerium 140.12	59 Pr Praseodymium 140.91	60 Nd Neodymium 144.24	61 Pm Promethium 145	62 Sm Samarium 150.36	63 Eu Europium 151.96	64 Gd Gadolinium 157.25	65 Tb Terbium 158.93	66 Dy Dysprosium 162.50	67 Ho Holmium 164.93	68 Er Erbium 167.26	69 Tm Thulium 168.93	70 Yb Ytterbium 173.05	71 Lu Lutetium 174.97
89 Ac Actinium 227	90 Th Thorium 232.04	91 Pa Protactinium 231.04	92 U Uranium 238.03	93 Np Neptunium 237	94 Pu Plutonium 244	95 Am Americium 243	96 Cm Curium 247	97 Bk Berkelium 247	98 Cf Californium 251	99 Es Einsteinium 252	100 Fm Fermium 257	101 Md Mendelevium 258	102 No Nobelium 259	103 Lr Lawrencium 266

Review of Regular Chemistry

Mole calculation

1
Calculate the number of moles in 25 grams of water (H_2O).
(Molar mass of H_2O = 18 g/mol)

2
Calculate the mass of 3.0 moles of carbon dioxide (CO_2).
(Molar mass of CO_2 = 44 g/mol)

3
Determine the number of moles in 51 grams of sodium chloride (NaCl).
(Molar mass of NaCl = 58.5 g/mol)

4
Find the mass of 2.5 moles of glucose ($C_6H_{12}O_6$).
(Molar mass of $C_6H_{12}O_6$ = 180 g/mol)

5
Calculate the number of moles in 46 grams of methane (CH_4).
(Molar mass of CH_4 = 16 g/mol)

6
Determine the number of moles in 123 grams of ethanol (C_2H_5OH).

7
Find the mass of 4.5 moles of aluminum oxide (Al_2O_3).

8
Calculate the number of moles in 86 grams of potassium bromide (KBr).

9
Calculate the mass of 5.2 moles of ammonia (NH_3).

10
Determine the number of moles in 16 grams of sodium bicarbonate ($NaHCO_3$).

11
Calculate the mass of 0.57 moles of phosphoric acid (H_3PO_4).

Simple stoichiometry

12

How many moles of water (H_2O) are produced when 2 moles of hydrogen gas (H_2) react with oxygen gas (O_2) according to the following balanced equation?

$$2\ H_2(g) + O_2(g) \rightarrow 2\ H_2O(l)$$

13

How many grams of carbon dioxide (CO_2) are produced when 3 moles of glucose ($C_6H_{12}O_6$) react with oxygen (O_2) according to the following balanced equation?

$$C_6H_{12}O_6 + 6\ O_2 \rightarrow 6\ CO_2 + 6\ H_2O$$

14

How many grams of sodium chloride (NaCl) are produced when 4.00 moles of sodium (Na) react with chlorine gas (Cl_2) according to the following balanced equation?
(Molar mass of NaCl = 58.5 g/mol)

$$2\ Na + Cl_2 \rightarrow 2\ NaCl$$

15
How many moles of nitrogen gas (N_2) are required to produce 8.2 moles of ammonia (NH_3) according to the following balanced equation?

$$N_2 + 3H_2 \rightarrow 2NH_3$$

16
Calculate the number of moles of carbon dioxide (CO_2) produced when 9.3 moles of methane (CH_4) react with excess oxygen (O_2).

17
Determine how many grams of sodium chloride (NaCl) are produced when 12.4 moles of sodium (Na) react with chlorine gas (Cl_2).

18
Find out how many grams of calcium oxide (CaO) are produced when 17.3 moles of calcium carbonate ($CaCO_3$) decompose.

19
Calculate the number of moles of ammonia (NH_3) produced when 28 moles of nitrogen gas (N_2) react with excess hydrogen gas (H_2).

Complex stoichiometry (Limiting)
20
$$N_2 + 3 H_2 \rightarrow 2 NH_3$$

If you start with 5 moles of nitrogen gas (N_2) and 12 moles of hydrogen gas (H_2), determine the limiting reactant, the amount of ammonia (NH_3) produced, and the amount of excess reactant remaining.

21
$$2 H_2(g) + O_2(g) \rightarrow 2 H_2O(l)$$

If you start with 8 moles of hydrogen gas (H_2) and 3 moles of oxygen gas (O_2), determine the limiting reactant, the amount of water (H_2O) produced, and the amount of excess reactant remaining.

22
$$C_3H_8(g) + 5 O_2(g) \rightarrow 3 CO_2(g) + 4 H_2O(l)$$

If you start with 2 moles of propane (C_3H_8) and 10 moles of oxygen gas (O_2), determine the limiting reactant, the amount of carbon dioxide (CO_2) produced, and the amount of excess reactant remaining.

23

Solid zinc (Zn) reacts with hydrochloric acid (HCl) to produce hydrogen gas (H$_2$) and zinc chloride (ZnCl$_2$).
If you start with 5.00 grams of zinc and 10.0 grams of hydrochloric acid, determine the limiting reactant, the amount of hydrogen gas produced, and the amount of excess reactant remaining.
(Molar mass of Zn = 65.38 g/mol, HCl = 36.46 g/mol, H$_2$ = 2.000 g/mol)

24

When aluminum (Al) reacts with oxygen gas (O$_2$), aluminum oxide (Al$_2$O$_3$) is formed.
If you start with 15.00 grams of aluminum and 15.00 grams of oxygen gas, determine the limiting reactant, the amount of aluminum oxide produced, and the amount of excess reactant remaining.
(Molar mass of Al = 26.98 g/mol, O$_2$ = 32.00 g/mol, Al$_2$O$_3$ = 101.96 g/mol)

25

Calcium carbonate (CaCO$_3$) reacts with hydrochloric acid (HCl) to produce carbon dioxide (CO$_2$), water (H$_2$O), and calcium chloride (CaCl$_2$).
If you start with 28.00 grams of calcium carbonate and 25.00 grams of hydrochloric acid, determine the limiting reactant, the amount of carbon dioxide produced, and the amount of excess reactant remaining.
(Molar mass of CaCO$_3$ = 100.0 g/mol, HCl = 36.46 g/mol, CO$_2$ = 44.00 g/mol)

26
Magnesium (Mg) reacts with nitrogen gas (N_2) to form magnesium nitride (Mg_3N_2).
If you start with 3.50 grams of magnesium and 7.00 grams of nitrogen gas, determine the limiting reactant, the amount of magnesium nitride produced, and the amount of excess reactant remaining.
(Molar mass of Mg = 24.31 g/mol, N_2 = 28.00 g/mol, Mg_3N_2 = 100.95 g/mol)

27
Sulfuric acid (H_2SO_4) reacts with sodium hydroxide (NaOH) to produce water (H_2O) and sodium sulfate (Na_2SO_4).
If you start with 38.5 grams of sulfuric acid and 53.7 grams of sodium hydroxide, determine the limiting reactant, the amount of water produced, and the amount of excess reactant remaining.
(Molar mass of H_2SO_4 = 98.00 g/mol, NaOH = 40.00 g/mol, H_2O = 18.00 g/mol)

28
Phosphorus (P_4) reacts with chlorine gas (Cl_2) to form phosphorus trichloride (PCl_3).
If you start with 21.5 grams of phosphorus and 33.8 grams of chlorine gas, determine the limiting reactant, the amount of phosphorus trichloride produced, and the amount of excess reactant remaining.
(Molar mass of P_4 = 123.9 g/mol, Cl_2 = 70.90 g/mol, PCl_3 = 137.33 g/mol)

29
Iron (Fe) reacts with sulfur (S_8) to form iron(II) sulfide (FeS).
If you start with 18.3 grams of iron and 27.0 grams of sulfur, determine the limiting reactant, the amount of iron(II) sulfide produced, and the amount of excess reactant remaining.
(Molar mass of Fe = 55.85 g/mol, S_8 = 256.0 g/mol, FeS = 87.91 g/mol)

Percent yield
30

$$2\ H_2(g) + O_2(g) \rightarrow 2\ H_2O(l)$$

Suppose you start with 10.0 grams of H_2 and 30.0 grams of O_2.
Assuming H_2 is the excess reactant, calculate the theoretical yield of H_2O in grams.
If the actual yield of H_2O obtained from the reactions is 12.0 grams, what is the percent yield of the reaction?

31

$$2\ KClO_3 \rightarrow 2\ KCl + 3\ O_2$$

Suppose you start with 25.0 grams of $KClO_3$.
Calculate the theoretical yield of O_2 in grams.
If the actual yield of O_2 obtained from the reaction is 7.00 grams, what is the percent yield of the reaction?

32

$$C_3H_8 + 5\ O_2 \rightarrow 3\ CO_2 + 4\ H_2O$$

Suppose you start with 44.0 grams of C_3H_8 and 160.0 grams of O_2.
Calculate the theoretical yield of CO_2 in grams.
If the actual yield of CO_2 obtained from the reaction is 66.0 grams, what is the percent yield of the reaction?

33

$$CaCO_3 + 2\ HCl \rightarrow CaCl_2 + H_2O + CO_2$$

Suppose you start with 50.0 grams of $CaCO_3$ and 73.0 grams of HCl.
Identify the limiting reactant and calculate the theoretical yield of CO_2 in grams.
If the actual yield of CO_2 obtained from the reaction is 18.0 grams, what is the percent yield of the reaction?

34

$$4\ Fe + 3\ O_2 \rightarrow 2\ Fe_2O_3$$

Suppose you start with 112.0 grams of Fe and 64.0 grams of O_2.
Identify the limiting reactant and calculate the theoretical yield of Fe_2O_3 in grams.
If the actual yield of Fe_2O_3 obtained from the reaction is 120.0 grams, what is the percent yield of the reaction?

Net ionic equations

Number	Net Ionic Equation
35	$AgNO_3(aq) + KCl(aq) \rightarrow AgCl(s) + KNO_3(aq)$ Net ionic equation :
36	$Mg(NO_3)_2(aq) + Na_2CO_3(aq) \rightarrow MgCO_3(s) + NaNO_3(aq)$ Net ionic equation :
37	$K_3PO_4(aq) + Al(NO_3)_3(aq) \rightarrow KNO_3(aq) + AlPO_4(s)$ Net ionic equation :
38	manganese(II)chloride(aq) + ammonium carbonate(aq) $\rightarrow$ manganese(II)carbonate(s) + ammonium chloride(aq) Net ionic equation :
39	strontium bromide(aq) + potassium sulfate(aq) $\rightarrow$ strontium sulfate(s) + potassium bromide(aq) Net ionic equation :
40	barium nitrate (aq) + ammonium phosphate (aq) $\rightarrow$ barium phosphate (s) + ammonium nitrate (aq) Net ionic equation :

41	Ni(NO₃)₂(aq) + 2NaOH (aq) → Ni(OH)₂ (s) + 2NaNO₃ (aq) Net ionic equation :
42	Pb(NO₃)₂(aq) + Na₂SO₄ (aq) → PbSO₄(s) + 2NaNO₃ (aq) Net ionic equation :
43	3KOH (aq) + Fe(NO₃)₃ (aq) → 3KNO₃ (aq) + Fe(OH)₃ (s) Net ionic equation :
44	2 Al(s) + 6HBr (aq) → 2AlBr₃ (aq) + 3 H₂(g) Net ionic equation :
45	Write the net ionic equation for the reaction between aqueous solutions of silver nitrate (AgNO₃) and sodium chloride (NaCl).
46	Write the net ionic equation for the reaction between aqueous solutions of barium chloride (BaCl₂) and sulfuric acid (H₂SO₄).
47	Write the net ionic equation for the reaction between aqueous solutions of potassium carbonate (K₂CO₃) and hydrochloric acid (HCl).

Challenge Questions

48

Which compound contains the lowest percentage of nitrogen by mass?

A) NH_2OH (M=33.0)
B) NH_4NO_2 (M=64.1)
C) N_2O_3 (M=76.0)
D) $NH_4NH_2CO_2$ (M=78.1)

49

Enzymes convert glucose (M = 180.2) to ethanol (M = 46.1) according to the equation:

$$C_6H_{12}O_6 \rightarrow 2\ C_2H_5OH + 2\ CO_2$$

What is the maximum mass of ethanol that can be made from 12.3 kg of glucose?

A) 0.170 kg
B) 0.280 kg
C) 2.58 kg
D) 6.29 kg

50

Commercial vinegar is a 3.58 % by mass aqueous solution of acetic acid, CH_3CO_2H (M = 60.0). What is the molarity of acetic acid in vinegar?
(Density of vinegar = 1.00 g/mL)

A) 0.597 M
B) 1.28 M
C) 2.75 M
D) 3.24 M

51

A 47.35 g sample of CuSO$_4$·5 H$_2$O (M = 249.7) is dissolved in enough water to make 0.650 L of solution. What volume of this solution must be diluted with water to make 1.00 L of 0.100 M CuSO$_4$?

A) 2.18 mL
B) 70.6 mL
C) 215 mL
D) 342 mL

52

What is the concentration of nitrate ion in a solution made by mixing 300. mL of a 0.400 M HNO$_3$ solution with 200. mL of a 0.300 M solution of Mg(NO$_3$)$_2$?

A) 0.125 M
B) 0.350 M
C) 0.480 M
D) 0.500 M

53

How many moles of sulfate ions are in 200. mL of a solution of 0.0020 M Fe$_2$(SO$_4$)$_3$?

A) 1.2×10^{-3}
B) 6.0×10^{-3}
C) 2.0×10^{-1}
D) 6.0×10^{-1}

54

A solution of Ba(OH)₂ is standardized with potassium acid phthalate (abbreviated KHP), $KHC_8H_4O_4$ (M = 204). If 1.375 g of KHP is titrated with 27.40 mL of the Ba(OH)₂ solution, what is the molarity of Ba(OH)₂?

A) 0.0170 M
B) 0.0325 M
C) 0.123 M
D) 0.275 M

55

15.0 mL of 0.20 M Ca(NO₃)₂ and 30.0 mL of 0.40 M Li₃PO₄ solutions are mixed. After the reaction is complete, which of these ions has the highest concentration in the final solution?

A) Li^+
B) NO_3^-
C) Ca^{2+}
D) PO_4^{3-}

56

A mixture is prepared by adding 75.0 mL of 0.200 M NaOH to 25.0 mL of 0.100 M NaOH. What is the [OH⁻] in the mixture?

A) 0.0700 M
B) 0.0900 M
C) 0.175 M
D) 0.245 M

57
Which compound contains the highest percentage of magnesium by mass?

A) $MgNH_4PO_4$
B) $Mg(H_2PO_4)_2$
C) $Mg_2P_4O_7$
D) $Mg_3(PO_4)_2$

58
Vanillin, $C_8H_8O_3$ (M = 152 g/mol), is the molecule responsible for the vanilla flavor in food. How many oxygen atoms are present in a 26.0 mg sample of vanillin?

A) 1.23×10^{20}
B) 3.09×10^{20}
C) 2.78×10^{23}
D) 6.18×10^{23}

59
What is the molarity of sodium ions in a solution prepared by diluting 350. mL of 0.650 M Na_2SO_4 to 1.75 L?

A) 0.115 M
B) 0.130 M
C) 0.240 M
D) 0.260 M

60

A 10.00 g sample of a soluble barium salt is treated with an excess of sodium sulfate to precipitate 11.21 g $BaSO_4$ (M = 233.4). Which barium salt is it?

A) $BaCl_2$ (M = 208.2)
B) $Ba(O_2CH)_2$ (M = 227.3)
C) $Ba(NO_3)_2$ (M = 261.3)
D) $BaBr_2$ (M = 297.1)

61

What is the concentration of nitrate ion in a 375 mL solution containing 18.0 g of $Mg(NO_3)_2$ (M = 148.3)?

A) 0.228 M
B) 0.324 M
C) 0.648 M
D) 1.73 M

62

A 125 mL sample of 0.15 M silver nitrate, $AgNO_3$, is reacted with a 2.73 g sample of calcium chloride, $CaCl_2$ (M = 111.0). Which of the following statements is true?

A) Silver nitrate is the limiting reactant and calcium nitrate precipitates.
B) Silver nitrate is the limiting reactant and silver chloride precipitates.
C) Calcium chloride is the limiting reactant and calcium nitrate precipitates.
D) Calcium chloride is the limiting reactant and silver chloride precipitates.

63

When 45.0 mL of 0.20 M $AgNO_3$ is added to 40.0 mL of 0.20 M NaCl, aqueous $NaNO_3$ and solid AgCl are formed. How much solid AgCl is produced?

A) 0.0040 mol
B) 0.0080 mol
C) 0.040 mol
D) 0.080 mol

64

How much $Sr(OH)_2 \cdot 8 H_2O$ (M = 265.76) is needed to prepare 350.0 mL of solution in which $[OH^-]$ = 0.500M?

A) 3.27 g
B) 9.30 g
C) 23.3 g
D) 30.5 g

65

A 10.00 g sample of a compound containing only carbon, hydrogen, and oxygen forms 23.98 g CO_2 and 4.91 g H_2O upon complete combustion. What is the empirical formula of the compound?

A) C_2HO
B) C_3H_3O
C) $C_6H_3O_2$
D) C_6H_6O

66
Unknown organic compound consists of 41.4% C, 3.5% H, and 55.1% O by mass. What is the empirical formula of this compound?

A) CHO
B) CH_2O
C) CH_2O_2
D) $C_{12}HO_{16}$

67
In a sample consisting of 1.00 mol NaCl and 0.300 mol LiI, what is the mass percent of iodine?

A) 15.8 %
B) 25.3 %
C) 38.6 %
D) 49.3 %

68
What is the concentration of chloride ions in a solution formed by mixing 250. mL of a 1.80 M NaCl solution with 135 mL of a 0.630 M $MgCl_2$ solution?

A) 1.61 M
B) 1.83 M
C) 1.97 M
D) 2.18 M

69

Barium chloride reacts with sodium sulfate. A student mixes a solution containing 5.00 g $BaCl_2$ (M = 208.2) with a solution containing 7.00 g Na_2SO_4 (M = 142.1) and obtains 12.0 g $BaSO_4$ (M = 233.2). What is the percent yield of this reaction?

A) 60.0%
B) 73.1%
C) 93.3%
D) The isolated barium sulfate is most likely wet, since the yield would otherwise be greater than 100%.

70

Calcium chloride reacts with sodium carbonate. A student mixes a solution containing 15.0 g of $CaCl_2$ (M = 110.98) with a solution containing 12.0 g of Na_2CO_3 (M = 105.99) and obtains 10.5 g of $CaCO_3$ (M = 100.09). What is the percent yield of this reaction?

A) 48.0 %
B) 67.3 %
C) 92.7 %
D) The isolated calcium carbonate is most likely impure, as the yield would otherwise be less than 100%.

Answer Key for Review of Regular Chemistry

#	Ans	#	Ans	#	Ans	#	Ans
1	1.4	11	56	21	2 mol H_2	31	71.5
2	1.3×10^2	12	2	22	None	32	50.0
3	0.87	13	792	23	0.121	33	81.8
4	450	14	234	24	1.664	34	74.9
5	2.9	15	4.1	25	4.59		
6	2.7	16	9.3	26	5.66		
7	459	17	719	27	22.3		
8	0.72	18	969	28	11.7		
9	88	19	56	29	16.4		
10	0.19	20	1 mol N_2	30	35.5		

35	$Ag^+(aq) + Cl^-(aq) \rightarrow AgCl(s)$
36	$Mg^{2+}(aq) + CO_3^{2-}(aq) \rightarrow MgCO_3(s)$
37	$PO_4^{3-}(aq) + Al^{3+}(aq) \rightarrow AlPO_4(s)$
38	$Mn^{2+}(aq) + CO_3^{2-}(aq) \rightarrow MnCO_3(s)$
39	$Sr^{2+}(aq) + SO_4^{2-}(aq) \rightarrow SrSO_4(s)$
40	$3\ Ba^{2+}(aq) + 2\ PO_4^{3-}(aq) \rightarrow Ba_3(PO_4)_2(s)$
41	$Ni^{2+}(aq) + 2\ OH^-(aq) \rightarrow Ni(OH)_2(s)$
42	$Pb^{2+}(aq) + SO_4^{2-}(aq) \rightarrow PbSO_4(s)$
43	$Fe^{3+}(aq) + 3\ OH^-(aq) \rightarrow Fe(OH)_3(s)$
44	$2\ Al(s) + 6\ H^+(aq) \rightarrow 2\ Al^{3+}(aq) + 3\ H_2(g)$
45	$Ag^+(aq) + Cl^-(aq) \rightarrow AgCl(s)$
46	$Ba^{2+}(aq) + SO_4^{2-}(aq) \rightarrow BaSO_4(s)$
47	$CO_3^{2-}(aq) + 2\ H^+(aq) \rightarrow H_2O(l) + CO_2(g)$

#	Ans	#	Ans	#	Ans
48	D	56	C	64	C
49	D	57	D	65	B
50	A	58	B	66	A
51	D	59	D	67	C
52	C	60	A	68	A
53	A	61	C	69	D
54	C	62	B	70	C
55	A	63	B		

Worked solution with answer for Review

A1

$$25 \text{ g } H_2O \times \frac{1 \text{ mol H2O}}{18 \text{ g H2O}} = 1.4 \text{ mol } H_2O$$

A2

$$3.0 \text{ mol } CO_2 \times \frac{44 \text{ g CO2}}{1 \text{ mol CO2}} = 1.3 \times 10^2 \text{ g } CO_2$$

A3

$$51 \text{ g NaCl} \times \frac{1 \text{ mol NaCl}}{58.5 \text{ g NaCl}} = 0.87 \text{ mol NaCl}$$

A4

$$2.5 \text{ mol } C_6H_{12}O_6 \times \frac{180 \text{ g C6H12O6}}{1 \text{ mol C6H12O6}} = 450 \text{ g } C_6H_{12}O_6$$

A5

$$46 \text{ g } CH_4 \times \frac{1 \text{ mol CH4}}{16 \text{ g CH4}} = 2.9 \text{ mol } CH_4$$

A6

Molar mass of $C_2H_5OH = (2 \times 12) + (1 \times 6) + (1 \times 16) = 46$ g/mol

$$123 \text{ g } C_2H_5OH \times \frac{1 \text{ mol } C_2H_5OH}{46 \text{ g } C_2H_5OH} = 2.7 \text{ mol } CH_4$$

A7

Molar mass of $Al_2O_3 = (2 \times 27) + (3 \times 16) = 54$ g/mol

$$4.5 \text{ mol } Al_2O_3 \times \frac{54 \text{ g } Al_2O_3}{1 \text{ mol } Al_2O_3} = 459 \text{ g } Al_2O_3$$

A8

Molar mass of KBr = 119 g/mol

$$86 \text{ g } C_2H_5OH \times \frac{1 \text{ mol KBr}}{119 \text{ g KBr}} = 0.72 \text{ mol } CH_4$$

A9

Molar mass of $NH_3 = (1 \times 14) + (3 \times 1) = 17$ g/mol

$$5.2 \text{ mol } NH_3 \times \frac{17 \text{ g } NH_3}{1 \text{ mol } NH_3} = 89 \text{ g } NH_3$$

A10

Molar mass of $NaHCO_3 = (1 \times 23) + (1 \times 1) + (1 \times 12) + (3 \times 16) = 84$ g/mol

$$16 \text{ g } C_2H_5OH \times \frac{1 \text{ mol KBr}}{84 \text{ g KBr}} = 0.19 \text{ mol } CH_4$$

A11

Molar mass of H_3PO_4 = (3 x 1) + (1 x 31) + (4 x 16) = 98 g/mol

0.57 mol H_3PO_4 x $\dfrac{98 \text{ g } H_3PO_4}{1 \text{ mol } H_3PO_4}$ = 56 g NH_3

A12

2 mol H_2 x $\dfrac{2 \text{ mol } H_2O}{2 \text{ mol } H_2}$ = 2 mol H_2

A13

3 mol $C_6H_{12}O_6$ x $\dfrac{6 \text{ mol } CO_2}{1 \text{ mol } C_6H_{12}O_6}$ x $\dfrac{44 \text{ g } CO_2}{1 \text{ mol } CO_2}$ = 792 mol CO_2

A14

4.00 mol Na x $\dfrac{2 \text{ mol NaCl}}{2 \text{ mol Na}}$ x $\dfrac{58.5 \text{ g NaCl}}{1 \text{ mol NaCl}}$ = 234 g NaCl

A15

8.2 mol NH_3 x $\dfrac{1 \text{ mol } N_2}{2 \text{ mol } NH_3}$ = 4.1 mol NH_3

A16

Balanced equation: CH_4 + 2 O_2 → CO_2 + 2 H_2O

9.3 mol CH_4 x $\dfrac{1 \text{ mol } CO_2}{1 \text{ mol } CH_4}$ = 9.3 mol CO_2

A17

Balanced equation: 2 Na + Cl_2 → 2 NaCl
Molar mass of NaCl = 58 g/mol

12.4 mol Na x $\dfrac{2 \text{ mol NaCl}}{2 \text{ mol Na}}$ x $\dfrac{58 \text{ mol NaCl}}{1 \text{ mol Na}}$ = 725 g NaCl

A18

$CaCO_3(s) \rightarrow CaO(s) + CO_2(g)$

17.3 mol $CaCO_3$ x $\dfrac{1 \text{ mol CaO}}{1 \text{ mol } CaCO_3}$ x $\dfrac{56 \text{ mol CaO}}{1 \text{ mol CaO}}$ = 970 g CaO

A19

$N_2(g) + 3 H_2(g) \rightarrow 2 NH_3(g)$

28 mol N_2 x $\dfrac{2 \text{ mol } NH_3}{1 \text{ mol } N_2}$ = 56 mol NH_3

A20

Step 1 : Determining the limiting reactant

Calculate the amount of hydrogen required to react with the nitrogen available

= 5 moles of N_2 × $\dfrac{3 \text{ mol } H_2}{1 \text{ mol } N_2}$ = 15 mol H_2

Comparing this to the amount of hydrogen provided:

Required: 15 moles of H_2

Provided: 12 moles of H_2

Since only 12 moles of H_2 are available (less than the required 15 moles), hydrogen is the limiting reactant.

Or
Compare $\frac{5 \text{ mol } N_2}{1}$ vs. $\frac{12 \text{ mol } H_2}{3}$
Smaller one (H_2) is limiting reactant.

Step 2 : Determining the amount of NH_3 produced.
12 mol $H_2 \times \frac{2 \text{ mol } NH_3}{3 \text{ mol } H_2}$ = 8 mol NH_3

Step 3 : Determining the amount of excess reactant remaining.
12 mol $H_2 \times \frac{1 \text{ mol } N_2}{3 \text{ mol } H_2}$ = 4 mol N_2 reacted
Initial 5 mol N_2 – 4 mol N_2 consumed = 1 mol N_2 remained

A21

Step 1 : Determining the limiting reactant
Calculate the amount of hydrogen required to react with the oxygen available
= 3 moles of $O_2 \times \frac{2 \text{ mol } H_2}{1 \text{ mol } O_2}$ = 6 mol H_2
Comparing this to the amount of oxygen provided:
Required: 6 moles of H_2
Provided: 8 moles of H_2
Required H_2 < Provided H_2
Oxygen is the limiting reactant.
or
Compare $\frac{8 \text{ mol } H_2}{2}$ vs. $\frac{3 \text{ mol } O_2}{1}$
Smaller one (O_2) is limiting reactant.

Step 2 : Determining the amount of H_2O produced.
3 mol $O_2 \times \frac{2 \text{ mol } H_2O}{1 \text{ mol } O_2}$ = 6 mol H_2O

Step 3 : Determining the amount of excess reactant remaining.
3 mol $O_2 \times \frac{2 \text{ mo } H_2}{1 \text{ mol } O_2}$ = 6 mol H_2 reacted
Initial 8 mol H_2 – 6 mol H_2 consumed = 2 mol H_2 remained

A22

Step 1 : Determining the limiting reactant
Calculate the amount of oxygen required to react with the propane available
= 2 moles of $C_3H_8 \times \frac{5 \text{ mol } O_2}{1 \text{ mol } C_3H_8}$ = 10 mol O_2
Comparing this to the amount of oxygen provided:
Required: 10 moles of O_2
Provided: 10 moles of O_2
Required H_2 = Provided H_2
Since the required amount of O_2 to react completely with the propane is exactly the amount available (10 moles), we start with just enough oxygen to consume all the propane without any excess. Thus, there is no limiting reactant in the typical sense as both reactants will be completely consumed.

Step 2 : Determining the amount of CO_2 produced.

$2 \text{ mol } C_3H_8 \times \dfrac{3 \text{ mol } CO_2}{1 \text{ mol } C_3H_8} = 6 \text{ mol } CO_2$

Step 3 : Determining the amount of excess reactant remaining.
None

A23

Step 1 : Calculating moles of reactants
Mole of Zn = $5.00 \text{ g} \times \dfrac{1 \text{ mol Zn}}{65.38 \text{ g Zn}} = 0.0765 \text{ mol Zn}$

Mole of HCl = $10.0 \text{ g} \times \dfrac{1 \text{ mol HCl}}{36.46 \text{ g HCl}} = 0.274 \text{ mol HCl}$

Step 2 : Determining the limiting reactant
Required moles of HCl for 0.0765 moles of Zn
= $0.0765 \text{ mol Zn} \times \dfrac{2 \text{ mol HCl}}{1 \text{ mol Zn}} = 0.153 \text{ moles of HCl}$
Since 0.2742 moles of HCl are available and only 0.153 moles of HCl are needed to react with all the zinc provided, HCl is in excess and Zn is the limiting reactant.

Step 3 : Determining the amount of H_2 produced.
$0.0765 \text{ mol Zn} \times \dfrac{1 \text{ mol } H_2}{1 \text{ mol Zn}} = 0.0765 \text{ mol H2}$

Step 4 : Determining the amount of excess reactant remaining.
$0.0765 \text{ mol Zn} \times \dfrac{2 \text{ mo HCl}}{1 \text{ mol Zn}} = 0.153 \text{ mol HCl reacted}$
Remaining moles of HCl
= Initial 0.274 mol − 0.153 mol consumed = 0.122 mol of HCl

A24

$4 \text{ Al} + 3 \text{ O}_2 \rightarrow 2 \text{ Al}_2O_3$
Step 1 : Calculating moles of reactants
Mole of Al = $15.00 \text{ g} \times \dfrac{1 \text{ mol Al}}{26.98 \text{ g Al}} = 0.556 \text{ mol Al}$

Mole of O_2 = $15.00 \text{ g} \times \dfrac{1 \text{ mol } O_2}{32.00 \text{ g } O_2} = 0.469 \text{ mol } O_2$

Step 2 : Determining the limiting reactant
Required moles of O_2 for 0.556 mol Al
= $0.556 \text{ mol Al} \times \dfrac{3 \text{ mol } O_2}{4 \text{ mol Al}} = 0.417 \text{ moles of } O_2$

Since 0.417 moles of O_2 are needed and 0.469 moles are available, aluminum (Al) is the limiting reactant because the required oxygen can be fully provided by the available oxygen.

Step 3 : Determining the amount of Al_2O_3 produced.
$0.556 \text{ mol Al} \times \dfrac{2 \text{ mol } Al_2O_3}{4 \text{ mol Al}} = 0.278 \text{ mol } Al_2O_3$

Step 4 : Determining the amount of excess reactant remaining.
$0.556 \text{ mol Al} \times \dfrac{3 \text{ mol } O_2}{4 \text{ mol Al}} = 0.417 \text{ mol } O_2 \text{ reacted}$
Remaining moles of O_2
= Initial 0.469 mol − 0.417 mol consumed = 0.052 mol of O_2 remained

Mass of O_2 remained = 0.052 mol of $O_2 \times \frac{32.00 \text{ g } O_2}{1 \text{ mol } O_2}$ = 1.664 g O_2

A25

$CaCO_3(s) + 2 \text{ HCl(aq)} \rightarrow CO_2(g) + H_2O(l) + CaCl_2(aq)$
Step 1 : Calculating moles of reactants
Mole of $CaCO_3$ = 28.00 g × $\frac{1 \text{ mol } CaCO_3}{100.0 \text{ g } CaCO_3}$ = 0.2800 mol $CaCO_3$
Mole of HCl = 25.00 g × $\frac{1 \text{ mol HCl}}{36.46 \text{ g HCl}}$ = 0.686 mol HCl

Step 2 : Determining the limiting reactant
Required moles of HCl for 0.2800 mol $CaCO_3$
= 0.2800 mol $CaCO_3 \times \frac{2 \text{ mol HCl}}{1 \text{ mol } CaCO_3}$ = 0.5600 moles of HCl

Since 0.686 moles of HCl are available, which is more than the required 0.56moles, hydrochloric acid is in excess and calcium carbonate is the limiting reactant.

Step 3 : Determining the amount of CO_2 produced.
0.2800 mol $CaCO_3 \times \frac{1 \text{ mol } CO_2}{1 \text{ mol } CaCO_3}$ = 0.2800 mol CO_2
0.2800 mol $CO_2 \times \frac{44.00 \text{ g } CO_2}{1 \text{ mol } CO_2}$ = 12.32 g CO_2

Step 4 : Determining the amount of excess reactant remaining.
0.2800 mol $CaCO_3 \times \frac{2 \text{ mol HCl}}{1 \text{ mol } CaCO_3}$ = 0.5600 mol HCl reacted
Remaining moles of HCl
= Initial 0.686 mol − 0.5600 mol consumed = 0.126 mol of HCl remained
Mass of HCl remained = 0.126 mol of HCl × $\frac{36.46 \text{ g HCl}}{1 \text{ mol HCl}}$ = 4.59 g HCl

A26

$3 \text{ Mg} + N_2 \rightarrow Mg_3N_2$
Step 1 : Calculating moles of reactants
Mole of Mg = 3.50 g × $\frac{1 \text{ mol Mg}}{24.31 \text{ g Mg}}$ = 0.144 mol Mg
Mole of N_2 = 7.00 g × $\frac{1 \text{ mol } N_2}{28.00 \text{ g } N_2}$ = 0.250 mol N_2

Step 2 : Determining the limiting reactant
$\frac{0.144 \text{ mol Mg}}{3}$ vs. $\frac{0.250 \text{ mol } N_2}{1}$
Smaller Mg is limiting reactant.

Step 3 : Determining the amount of Mg_3N_2 produced.
0.144 mol Mg × $\frac{1 \text{ mol } Mg_3N_2}{3 \text{ mol Mg}}$ = 0.0480 mol Mg_3N_2
0.0480 mol Mg_3N_2 × $\frac{100.95 \text{ g } Mg_3N_2}{1 \text{ mol } Mg_3N_2}$ = 4.85 g Mg_3N_2

Step 4 : Determining the amount of excess reactant remaining.
0.144 mol Mg × $\frac{1 \text{ mol } N_2}{3 \text{ mol Mg}}$ = 0.0480 mol N_2 reacted

Remaining moles of N_2
= Initial 0.250 mol − 0.0480 mol consumed = 0.202 mol of N_2 remained
Mass of HCl remained = 0.202 mol of $N_2 \times \dfrac{28.00 \text{ g HCl}}{1 \text{ mol HCl}}$ = 5.66 g HCl

A27

$H_2SO_4 + 2\ NaOH \rightarrow Na_2SO_4 + 2\ H_2O$
Step 1 : Calculating moles of reactants
Mole of H_2SO_4 = 38.5 g × $\dfrac{1 \text{ mol } H_2SO_4}{98.00 \text{ g } H_2SO_4}$ = 0.393 mol H_2SO_4
Mole of NaOH = 53.7 g × $\dfrac{1 \text{ mol NaOH}}{40.00 \text{ g NaOH}}$ = 1.342 mol NaOH

Step 2 : Determining the limiting reactant
$\dfrac{0.393 \text{ mol } H_2SO_4}{1}$ vs. $\dfrac{1.342 \text{ mol NaOH}}{2}$
Smaller H_2SO_4 is limiting reactant.

Step 3 : Determining the amount of H_2O produced.
0.393 mol H_2SO_4 × $\dfrac{2 \text{ mol } H_2O}{1 \text{mol } H_2SO_4}$ × $\dfrac{18.00 \text{ g } H_2O}{1 \text{mol } H_2O}$ = 14.2 g H_2O

Step 4 : Determining the amount of excess reactant remaining.
0.393 mol H_2SO_4 × $\dfrac{2 \text{ mol NaOH}}{1 \text{ mol } H_2SO_4}$ = 0.786 mol NaOH reacted
Remaining moles of NaOH
= Initial 1.342 mol − 0.786 mol consumed = 0.556 mol of NaOH remained
Mass of NaOH remained = 0.556 mol of NaOH × $\dfrac{40.00 \text{ g NaOH}}{1 \text{ mol NaOH}}$ = 22.2 g HCl

A28

$P_4 + 6\ Cl_2 \rightarrow 4\ PCl_3$
Step 1 : Calculating moles of reactants
Mole of P_4= 21.5 g × $\dfrac{1 \text{ mol } P_4}{123.9 \text{ g } P_4}$ = 0.174 mol P_4
Mole of Cl_2= 33.8 g × $\dfrac{1 \text{ mol } Cl_2}{70.90 \text{ g } Cl_2}$ = 0.477 mol Cl_2

Step 2 : Determining the limiting reactant
$\dfrac{0.174 \text{mol } P_4}{1}$ vs. $\dfrac{0.477 \text{ mol } Cl_2}{6}$
Smaller Cl_2 is limiting reactant.

Step 3 : Determining the amount of PCl_3 produced.
0.477 mol Cl_2 × $\dfrac{4 \text{ mol } PCl_3}{6 \text{mol } Cl_2}$ × $\dfrac{137.33 \text{ g } PCl_3}{1 \text{mol } PCl_3}$ = 43.6 g PCl_3

Step 4 : Determining the amount of excess reactant remaining.
0.477 mol Cl_2 × $\dfrac{1 \text{ mol } P_4}{6 \text{mol } Cl_2}$ = 0.0795 mol P_4 reacted
Remaining moles of NaOH
= Initial 0.174 mol − 0.0795 mol consumed = 0.0945 mol of P_4 remained
Mass of P_4 remained 0.0945 mol of P_4 × $\dfrac{123.9 \text{ g NaOH}}{1 \text{ mol NaOH}}$ = 11.7 g P_4

A29

$8 \text{ Fe} + S_8 \rightarrow 8 \text{ FeS}$

Step 1 : Calculating moles of reactants

Mole of Fe = 18.3 g × $\frac{1 \text{ mol Fe}}{55.85 \text{ g Fe}}$ = 0.328 mol Fe

Mole of S_8 = 27.0 g × $\frac{1 \text{ mol } S_8}{256.0 \text{ g } S_8}$ = 0.106 mol S_8

Step 2 : Determining the limiting reactant

$\frac{0.328 \text{ mol Fe}}{8}$ vs. $\frac{0.106 \text{ mol } S_8}{1}$

Smaller Fe is limiting reactant.

Step 3 : Determining the amount of FeS produced.

0.328 mol Fe × $\frac{8 \text{ mol FeS}}{8 \text{ mol Fe}}$ × $\frac{87.91 \text{ g FeS}}{1 \text{ mol FeS}}$ = 28.8 g FeS

Step 4 : Determining the amount of excess reactant remaining.

0.328 mol Fe × $\frac{1 \text{ mol } S_8}{8 \text{ mol Fe}}$ = 0.0410 mol S_8 reacted

Remaining moles of NaOH
= Initial 0.106 mol − 0.0410 mol consumed = 0.065mol of S_8 remained

Mass of P_4 remained 0.065 mol of S_8 × $\frac{256.0 \text{ g } S_8}{1 \text{ mol } S_8}$ = 16.6 g S_8

A30

Step 1 : Calculating moles of reactants

Mole of H_2 = 10.0 g × $\frac{1 \text{ mol } H_2}{2.016 \text{ g } H_2}$ = 4.96 mol H_2

Mole of O_2 = 30.0 g × $\frac{1 \text{ mol } O_2}{32.00 \text{ g } O_2}$ = 0.938 mol O_2

Step 2 : Determining the limiting reactant

$\frac{4.96 \text{ mol } H_2}{2}$ vs. $\frac{0.938 \text{ mol } O_2}{1}$

Smaller O_2 is limiting reactant.

Step 3 : Calculating the theoretical yield

0.938 mol O_2 × $\frac{2 \text{ mol } H_2O}{1 \text{ mol } O_2}$ × $\frac{18.02 \text{ g } H_2O}{1 \text{ mol } H_2O}$ = 33.8 g H_2O

Step 4 : Calculating the percent yield

% yield = $\frac{\text{Actual yield}}{\text{Theoretical yield}}$ × 100

= $\frac{12.0 \text{ g } H_2O}{33.8 \text{ g } H_2O}$ × 100

= 35.5 %

A31

Step 1 : Calculating moles of reactants

Mole of $KClO_3$ = 25.0 g × $\frac{1 \text{ mol } KClO_3}{122.55 \text{ g } KClO_3}$ = 0.204 mol $KClO_3$

Step 2 : Calculating the theoretical yield

$$0.204 \text{ mol KClO}_3 \times \frac{3 \text{ mol O}_2}{2 \text{ mol KClO}_3} \times \frac{32.00 \text{ g O}_2}{1 \text{ mol O}_2} = 9.79 \text{ g H}_2\text{O}$$

Step 3 : Calculating the percent yield

% yield = $\frac{\text{Actual yield}}{\text{Theoretical yield}} \times 100$

$= \frac{7.00 \text{ g H}_2\text{O}}{9.79 \text{ g H}_2\text{O}} \times 100$

$= 71.5\ \%$

A32

Step 1 : Calculating moles of reactants

Mole of C_3H_8 = 44.0 g × $\frac{1 \text{ mol } C_3H_8}{44.10 \text{ g } C_3H_8}$ = 0.998 mol C_3H_8

Mole of O_2 = 162 g × $\frac{1 \text{ mol } O_2}{32.00 \text{ g } O_2}$ = 5.06 mol O_2

Step 2 : Determining the limiting reactant

$\frac{0.998 \text{ mol } C_3H_8}{5}$ vs. $\frac{5.06 \text{ mol } O_2}{5}$

Smaller C_3H_8 is limiting reactant.

Step 3 : Calculating the theoretical yield

0.998 mol C_3H_8 × $\frac{3 \text{ mol } CO_2}{1 \text{ mol } C_3H_8}$ × $\frac{44.01 \text{ g } CO_2}{1 \text{ mol } CO_2}$ = 132 g CO_2

Step 3 : Calculating the percent yield

% yield = $\frac{\text{Actual yield}}{\text{Theoretical yield}} \times 100$

$= \frac{66.0 \text{ g } CO_2}{132 \text{ g } CO_2} \times 100$

$= 50.0\ \%$

A33

$CaCO_3 + 2\ HCl \rightarrow CaCl_2 + H_2O + CO_2$

Step 1 : Calculating moles of reactants

Mole of $CaCO_3$ = 50.0 g × $\frac{1 \text{ mol } CaCO_3}{100.09 \text{ g } CaCO_3}$ = 0.500 mol $CaCO_3$

Mole of HCl = 73.0 g × $\frac{1 \text{ mol HCl}}{36.36 \text{ g HCl}}$ = 2.00 mol HCl

Step 2 : Determining the limiting reactant

$\frac{0.500 \text{ mol } CaCO_3}{1}$ vs. $\frac{2.00 \text{ mol HCl}}{2}$

Smaller $CaCO_3$ is limiting reactant.

Step 3 : Calculating the theoretical yield

0.500 mol $CaCO_3$ × $\frac{1 \text{ mol } CO_2}{1 \text{ mol } CaCO_3}$ × $\frac{44.01 \text{ g } CO_2}{1 \text{ mol } CO_2}$ = 22.0 g CO_2

Step 3 : Calculating the percent yield

% yield = $\frac{\text{Actual yield}}{\text{Theoretical yield}} \times 100$

$= \frac{18.0 \text{ g } CO_2}{22.0 \text{ g } CO_2} \times 100$

= 81.8 %

A34

Step 1 : Calculating moles of reactants
Mole of Fe = 112.0 g x $\frac{1 \text{ mol Fe}}{55.85 \text{ g Fe}}$ = 2.005 mol Fe
Mole of O$_2$ = 64.0 g x $\frac{1 \text{ mol O}_2}{32.00 \text{ g O}_2}$ = 2.00 mol O$_2$

Step 2 : Determining the limiting reactant
$\frac{2.005 \text{ mol Fe}}{4}$ vs. $\frac{2.00 \text{ mol O}_2}{3}$
Smaller Fe is limiting reactant.

Step 3 : Calculating the theoretical yield
2.005 mol Fe x $\frac{2 \text{ mol Fe}_2\text{O}_3}{4 \text{ mol Fe}}$ x $\frac{159.7 \text{ g Fe}_2\text{O}_3}{1 \text{ mol Fe}_2\text{O}_3}$ = 160.2 g Fe$_2$O$_3$

Step 3 : Calculating the percent yield
% yield = $\frac{\text{Actual yield}}{\text{Theoretical yield}}$ x 100
= $\frac{120.0 \text{ g Fe}_2\text{O}_3}{160.2 \text{ g Fe}_2\text{O}_3}$ x 100
= 74.9 %

A48 (D)

A) $\frac{14}{33}$ x 100 = 42.4 %
B) $\frac{2 \times 14}{64}$ x 100 = 43.6 %
C) $\frac{2 \times 14}{76}$ x 100 = 36.8 %
D) $\frac{2 \times 14}{78}$ x 100 = 35.9 %

A49 (D)

12.3 kg glucose x $\frac{1 \text{ mol glucose}}{180.2 \text{ g glucose}}$ x $\frac{2 \text{ mol ethanol}}{1 \text{ mol glucose}}$ x $\frac{46.1 \text{ g ethanol}}{1 \text{ mol ethanol}}$ = 6.29 kg

A50 (A)

$\frac{3.58 \text{ g vinegar} \times \frac{1 \text{ mol}}{60.0 \text{ g}}}{100 \text{g solution} \times \frac{1 \text{ mL}}{1.00 \text{ g}} \times \frac{1 \text{ L}}{1000 \text{ mL}}}$ = 0.597 M

A51 (D)

$\frac{47.35 \text{ g} \times \frac{1 \text{ mol}}{249.7 \text{ g}}}{0.650 \text{ L}}$ = 0.292 M
(0.292 M) (x mL) = (0.100 M) (1.00 L)
x = 342 mL

A52 (C)

[NO$_3^-$] from HNO$_3$ = (0.400 M)(0.300 L) = 0.120 mol
[NO$_3^-$] from Mg(NO$_3$)$_2$ = (0.300 M)(0.200 L) = 0.120 mol
$\frac{0.240 \text{ mol}}{0.500 \text{ L}}$ = 0.480 M

A53 (A)

$Fe_2(SO_4)_3 \rightarrow 2\ Fe^{3+} + 3\ SO_4^{2-}$
$[Fe_2(SO_4)_3] = (0.0020M)(0.200L) = 0.0004$ mol
$[SO_4^{2-}] = 3 \times 0.0004$ mol $= 0.0012$ mol $= 1.2 \times 10^{-3}$ mol

A54 (C)

Mole of KHP $= 1.375$ g $\times \dfrac{1\ mol}{204\ g} = 0.00674$ mol

Mole of $Ba(OH)_2 = \dfrac{1}{2} \times 0.00674 = (0.0274L)(x\ M)$

$x = 0.123$ M

A55 (A)

$3\ Ca(NO_3)_2 + 2\ Li_3PO_4 \rightarrow 6\ LiNO_3 + Ca_3(PO_4)_2$

$\dfrac{(15.0\ mL)\ (0.20\ M)}{1}\ Ca(NO_3)_2$ vs $\dfrac{(30.0\ mL)\ (0.40\ M)}{2}\ Li_3PO_4$

$Ca(NO_3)_2 \rightarrow$ limiting

I	3 mmol	12 mmol		
C	- 3 mmol	- 2 mmol	+ 6 mmol	+ 1 mmol
E	0	10 mmol	6 mmol	1 mmol

Remained in the solution = 10 mmol Li_3PO_4 + 6 mmol $LiNO_3$ + 1 mmol $Ca_3(PO_4)_2$
$[Li^+] = 30$ mmol
$[PO_4^{3-}] = 12$ mmol
$[Ca^{2+}] = 3$ mmol
$[NO_3^-] = 6$ mmol
Highest concentration = Li^+

A56 (C)

$[OH^-]$ from 0.200 M NaOH = (0.200 M)(75.0 mL) = 15.0 mmol
$[OH^-]$ from 0.100 M NaOH = (0.100 M)(25.0 mL) = 2.5 mmol

$\dfrac{17.5\ mmol}{(75.0+25.0)\ mL} = 0.175$ M

A57 (D)

A) $\dfrac{24.3}{137.3} \times 100 = 17.7\ \%$

B) $\dfrac{24.3}{218.3} \times 100 = 11.1\ \%$

C) $\dfrac{(2)(24.3)}{222.6} \times 100 = 21.9\ \%$

D) $\dfrac{(3)(24.3)}{262.9} \times 100 = 27.7\ \%$

A58 (B)

$\dfrac{26.0}{1000}$ g vanillin $\times \dfrac{1\ mol\ Vanillin}{152\ g\ Vanillin} \times \dfrac{3\ mol\ O\ atoms}{1\ mol\ Vanillin} \times \dfrac{6.02*10^{23}\ O\ atoms}{1\ mol\ O\ atom}$
$= 3.09 \times 10^{20}$ atoms

A59 (D)

(0.350 L)(0.650 M) = (1.75 L) (x M)
x = 0.130 M
moles of Na^+ ions = 2 $\times$ 0.130 M = 0.260 M

A60 (A)

Mole of $BaSO_4$ = 11.21 g × $\frac{1 \text{ mol}}{233.4 \text{ g}}$ = 0.048 mol
Moles of barium in salt = 0.048 mol
For $BaCl_2$, 0.048 mol × 208.2 g/mol = 9.99 g

A61 (C)

$$\frac{(18.0 \text{ g})(\frac{1 \text{ mol}}{148.3 \text{ g}})}{0.375 \text{ L}} = 0.648 \text{ M}$$

A62 (B)

2 $AgNO_3$ + $CaCl_2$ → 2 AgCl(s) + $Ca(NO_3)_2$
Moles of $AgNO_3$ = (0.15 M)(0.125 L) = 0.01875 mol
Moles of $CaCl_2$ = 2.73g × $\frac{1 \text{ mol}}{111.0 \text{ g}}$ = 0.0246 mol
Silver nitrate is limiting reactant.

A63 (B)

Moles of $AgNO_3$ = (0.045 L)(0.20 M) = 0.009 mol
Moles of NaCl = (0.040 L)(0.20 M) = 0.008 mol
NaCl is limiting reactant.
Moles of AgCl formed = 0.008 mol

A64 (C)

0.250 M = $\frac{(x \text{ g})(\frac{1 \text{ mol}}{265.76 \text{ g}})}{0.350 \text{ L}}$
x = 23.3 g

A65 (B)

Moles of C = $\frac{23.98 \text{ g } CO_2}{44.01 \text{ g/mol}}$ = 0.545 mol
Moles of H = $\frac{4.91 \text{ g } H_2O}{18.02 \text{ g/mol}}$ × 2 = 0.545 mol
Total mass of C and H = (0.545 mol)(12.01 g/mol) + (0.545 mol)(1.008 g/mol) = 7.87 g
Mass of O = 10.00 – 7.87 = 2.13 g
Moles of O = $\frac{2.13 \text{ g O}}{16.00 \text{ g/mol}}$ = 0.133 mol
Empirical formula = C_3H_3O

A66 (A)

Moles of C = $\frac{41.4 \text{ g C}}{12.01 \text{ g/mol}}$ = 3.45 mol
Moles of H = $\frac{3.5 \text{ g H}}{1.008 \text{ g/mol}}$ = 3.47 mol
Moles of O = $\frac{55.1 \text{ g O}}{16.00 \text{ g/mol}}$ = 3.44 mmol
Ratio = 1 : 1 : 1

A67 (C)

$$\frac{126.91 * 0.300}{(22.99+35.45)+(6.94+126.91)(0.300)} \times 100 = 38.6 \%$$

A68 (A)

[Cl⁻] from NaCl = (1.80 M)(250 mL) = 450 mmol
[Cl⁻] from MgCl$_2$ = (0.630 M)(135 mL) x 2 = 170 mmol
$\frac{(450+170) \text{ mmol}}{(250+135) \text{ mL}}$ = 1.61 M

A69 (D)

BaCl$_2$ + Na$_2$SO$_4$ → BaSO$_4$ + 2 NaCl
Moles of BaCl$_2$ = 5.0 g x $\frac{1 \, mol}{208.2 \, g}$ = 0.0240 mol → limiting
Moles of Na$_2$SO$_4$ = 7.0 g x $\frac{1 \, mol}{142.1 \, g}$ = 0.0493 mol
Mass of BaSO$_4$ produced = 0.0240 mol x $\frac{233.2 \, g}{1 \, mol}$ = 5.59 g = Theoretical yield.
% yield = $\frac{12.0 \, g}{5.59 \, g}$ x 100 = 214.3 %
The isolated barium sulfate is most likely wet, since the yield would otherwise be greater than 100%.

A70 (C)

CaCl$_2$ + Na$_2$CO$_3$ → CaCO$_3$ + 2 NaCl
Moles of CaCl$_2$ = 15.0 g x $\frac{1 \, mol}{110.98 \, g}$ = 0.135 mol
Moles of Na$_2$CO$_3$ = 12.0 g x $\frac{1 \, mol}{105.99 \, g}$ = 0.113 mol → limiting
Mass of CaCO$_3$ produced = 0.113 mol x $\frac{100.09 \, g}{1 \, mol}$ = 11.33 g = Theoretical yield.
% yield = $\frac{10.5 \, g}{11.33 \, g}$ x 100 = 92.7 %

Topic _1
Atomic structure & Properties

Exam Weighting : 7-9%

Topic 1 Key Point Review

Isotope
- Atoms of the same element with different numbers of neutrons, resulting in different atomic masses but identical chemical properties.
- C-12 and C-14

Mass spectrum
- A graph that shows the relative abundance of isotopes based on their mass-to-charge ratio (x-axis).
- Peaks (y axis) represent the different isotopes and their relative abundance.
- The average atomic mass can be calculated from the mass spectrum by multiplying the mass of each isotope by its relative abundance and summing the results.

Electron configuration
- Shell = The principal energy level (n) where electrons are located, such as n = 1, 2, 3, etc.
- Subshell = The division of shells into orbitals (s, p, d, f) that describe the shape of the orbital where electrons are found.
- Electron Filling Order
    - Electrons fill orbitals in increasing energy order, typically following the Aufbau principle: 1s < 2s < 2p < 3s < 3p < 4s < 3d < 4p, etc.
- Electron Removal Order (Cation formation)
    - When forming cations, electrons are removed first from the outermost shell(highest principal energy level). For example, for transition metals, electrons from the 4s orbital are removed before the 3d orbital.
- It determines the chemical reactivity and properties of an element by influencing how it interacts with other atoms, particularly in bonding.

Periodic trend
- Atomic radius : The distance from the nucleus to the outermost electron
- Ionization energy : The energy required to remove an electron from an atom in its gaseous state
- Electron affinity : The energy change that occurs when an electron is added to a neutral atom
- Electronegativity : A measure of an atom's ability to attract and hold onto electrons in a chemical bond
- Metals: Found on the left side of the periodic table, they tend to form cations (positive ions).
    - When a metal forms a cation, its atomic size decreases because it loses electrons, reducing electron-electron repulsion and the number of occupied electron shells also decreases.
- Nonmetals: Found on the right side of the periodic table, they tend to form anions (negative ions).
    - When a nonmetal forms an anion, its atomic size increases due to the addition of electrons, which increases electron-electron repulsion and may slightly expand the electron cloud.

Analysis of periodic trend
- From right to left : Relatively similar shell size / compare effective nuclear charge
    - The shell size remains relatively similar, but the effective nuclear charge increases as more protons are added, pulling electrons closer and reducing atomic radius.
    - Atomic radius decrease
    - Ionization energy increases
    - Electronegativity increases
- From top to bottom : Comparable effective nuclear charge / compare shell size
    - The effective nuclear charge remains relatively comparable, but the shell size increases as additional electron shells are added, resulting in a larger atomic radius and lower ionization energy.
    - Atomic radius increases
    - Ionization energy decreases
    - Electronegativity decreases

Photoelectron spectrum
- A graph displaying the energy required to remove electrons from different orbitals in an atom, helping to determine the binding energies and arrangement of electrons within the atom.
- X-axis: Represents the binding energy of electrons, which corresponds to the energy required to remove electrons from specific orbitals.
    - $E = h\nu$
    - $C = \lambda \nu$
    - $E = hc / \lambda$
    - h = Planck's constant = 6.626×10^{-34} Js
    - c = speed of light = 2.998×10^{8} m/s
    - Avogadro's number = 6.022×10^{23} mol^{-1}
- Y-axis: Represents the relative number of electrons ejected from each orbital, showing the intensity of each peak.

True/False Questions

Read the following statements carefully and determine whether each one is true or false. Place a tick (✔) in the appropriate box. If the statement is false, correct the incorrect part of the statement.

	Statement	True	False
Q1	The first ionization energy of aluminum is lower than that of magnesium because aluminum has an electron in the 3p orbital, which is higher in energy than the 3s orbital of magnesium.		
Q2	The effective nuclear charge experienced by an electron in the 3p orbital of chlorine is greater than that experienced by an electron in the 3p orbital of sulfur because chlorine has more protons in its nucleus, resulting in a stronger attraction for its 3p electrons.		
Q3	The electron affinity of oxygen is higher than that of fluorine because oxygen is more electronegative and more effectively attracts an additional electron.		
Q4	The first ionization energy of boron (B) is lower than that of beryllium (Be) because the electron removed from boron comes from a higher energy 2p orbital, while the electron removed from beryllium comes from a more stable, fully filled 2s orbital.		
Q5	The energy required to remove the first electron from a neutral atom is always greater than the energy required to remove the second electron because after removing the first electron, the atom becomes positively charged, making it easier to remove another electron.		
Q6	The first ionization energy of nitrogen (N) is higher than that of oxygen (O) because the electron removed from nitrogen comes from a half-filled 2p orbital, which is more stable compared to the 2p orbital in oxygen where electron-electron repulsion is greater due to paired electrons.		
Q7	The ionization energy of an element generally increases across a period because the additional protons increase the nuclear attraction for the electrons, without significantly increasing shielding.		
Q8	Isoelectronic species always have identical sizes because they have the same number of electrons.		
Q9	In the photoelectron spectrum of nitrogen, the peak corresponding to the 2s orbital will appear at a higher binding energy than the peak corresponding to the 2p orbital because the 2s orbital is more tightly bound to the nucleus and thus has a higher binding energy compared to the 2p orbital.		
Q10	The reactivity of alkali metals decreases as you move down the group due to decreasing ionization energies and increasing atomic radii.		

Concept Check Questions

When solving Free-Response Questions (FRQs), it is essential to clearly and accurately explain your reasoning. Make sure to outline the steps in your solution process thoroughly, showing all calculations with appropriate numbers and units. This demonstrates a full understanding of the problem and ensures that your answer is both correct and complete.

Q11
Arrange the following elements in order of increasing atomic radius: Mg, Al, Si, Na.
Explain the reasoning behind your arrangement based on atomic structure.

Q12
Compare the ionic radius of Cu^+ and Cu^{2+}. Which ion has a smaller radius, and why?

Q13
Compare the sizes of a cation, its neutral atom, and its anion. Explain the trend in size.

Q14
Compare the first ionization energies of Aluminum and Silicon.
Arrange them in order of increasing first ionization energy and explain the trend.

Q15
Compare the first ionization energies of Phosphorus and Arsenic.
Arrange them in order of increasing first ionization energy and explain the trend.

Q16
Explain why the first ionization energy of sulfur is lower than that of phosphorus, even though sulfur is to the right of phosphorus in the periodic table.

Q17
Explain why the second ionization energy of sodium is significantly higher than its first ionization energy.

Q18
Explain why the third ionization energy of magnesium is significantly higher than its first and second ionization energies.

Q19
Explain how metallic character changes as you move across a period from left to right and down a group in the periodic table. Which element between Na and Mg would exhibit a higher metallic character, and why?

Q20
Compare the electronegativity of F and Ar.
Which element has higher electronegativity and why?

Multiple Choice Questions

The following questions are multiple-choice.
Choose the correct answer and explain why the other options are incorrect.

Q21
Which of the following elements would require the most energy to remove one electron, given their ground state electron configurations?

A) $1s^2\ 2s^2\ 2p^6\ 3s^1$
B) $1s^2\ 2s^2\ 2p^6\ 3s^2\ 3p^1$
C) $1s^2\ 2s^2\ 2p^6\ 3s^2\ 3p^3$
D) $1s^2\ 2s^2\ 2p^6\ 3s^2\ 3p^5$

Q22
Which of the following would have the largest jump in ionization energy between the second and third ionizations?

A) Sodium (Na)
B) Magnesium (Mg)
C) Aluminum (Al)
D) Silicon (Si)

Q23
Consider the isoelectronic species: O^{2-}, F^-, Na^+, and Mg^{2+}.
Which of the following has the largest ionic radius?

A) O^{2-}
B) F^-
C) Na^+
D) Mg^{2+}

Q24
Which of the following statements is incorrect?

A) The atomic radius of Na is smaller than that of K because Na is above K in the same group, and has fewer electron shells, resulting in a smaller atomic size.
B) The first ionization energy of Cl is higher than that of S because Cl has a smaller atomic radius, which increases the Coulombic attraction between the nucleus and the outermost electron, making it harder to remove.
C) Atomic radius decreases across a period from left to right because the effective nuclear charge increases as more protons are added, pulling the electrons closer to the nucleus.
D) The first ionization energy of K is higher than that of Na because K has a greater number of protons, leading to a stronger nuclear attraction for its valence electron.

Q25
Which of the following statements about the photoelectron spectrum (PES) of nitrogen (N) is incorrect?

A) In the PES of nitrogen, the x-axis represents the binding energy of electrons, with peaks corresponding to electrons in different orbitals.
B) In the PES of nitrogen, the y-axis represents the relative number of electrons ejected at each binding energy, indicating the relative abundance of electrons in each orbital.
C) In the PES of nitrogen, the peak with the highest binding energy corresponds to the electrons in the 1s orbital, due to the strong Coulombic attraction to the nucleus.
D) In the PES of nitrogen, the peak corresponding to the 2p electrons has a higher binding energy than the peak corresponding to the 2s electrons, reflecting the greater effective nuclear charge experienced by the 2p electrons.

Q26
Consider the photoelectron spectra (PES) of carbon and oxygen.
Which of the following statements is incorrect?

A) In the PES of oxygen, the peaks corresponding to the 1s electrons appear at a higher binding energy on the x-axis compared to carbon, due to the higher effective nuclear charge in oxygen.
B) In the PES of carbon, the 2p peak appears at a lower binding energy than the 2s peak on the x-axis, reflecting the relative energies of these orbitals.
C) In the PES of oxygen, the y-axis peak heights corresponding to the 2p electrons are taller than those of carbon because oxygen has more 2p electrons than carbon.
D) In the PES of carbon and oxygen, the 2p peaks appear at similar binding energies on the x-axis because both elements experience nearly the same effective nuclear charge on their 2p electrons.

Q27
Which of the following statements about alkali metals is incorrect?

A) All alkali metals react with water to produce hydrogen gas and a corresponding hydroxide, with the reactivity increasing as you move down the group.
B) The reaction of alkali metals with water becomes more vigorous as you move down the group due to the decreasing ionization energy, which makes it easier for the metal to lose its outer electron.
C) All alkali metals, from lithium to cesium, have similar effective nuclear charges, which explains why their reactivity with water is nearly identical across the group.
D) When lithium reacts with water, it produces hydrogen gas less rapidly than sodium due to lithium's smaller atomic radius and higher effective nuclear charge.

Q28
Which of the following statements about interpreting a mass spectrum is incorrect?

A) In a mass spectrum, different peaks correspond to different isotopes of an element, with each peak's position on the x-axis reflecting the mass-to-charge ratio (m/z) of that isotope.
B) The x-axis of a mass spectrum represents the mass-to-charge ratio (m/z), while the y-axis represents the relative abundance or intensity of each isotope detected.
C) In a mass spectrum, each peak represents a different oxidation state of the element, with peaks at higher m/z values corresponding to higher oxidation states.
D) The average atomic mass of an element can be calculated by taking a weighted average of the m/z values of the peaks, using the relative abundances as weights.

Q29
An element X has two naturally occurring isotopes: 63X and 65X. The relative abundance of 63X is 75.0%, and the relative abundance of 65X is 25.0%.
The atomic masses of these isotopes are 62.93 amu and 64.93 amu, respectively.
What is the average atomic mass of element X?

A) 63.43 amu
B) 63.93 amu
C) 64.43 amu
D) 64.93 amu

Q30
An element Z has two naturally occurring isotopes: ^{10}Z and ^{11}Z. In a sample of 10 atoms, 7 atoms are ^{10}Z, and 3 atoms are ^{11}Z. The atomic masses of these isotopes are 10.012 amu and 11.009 amu, respectively. Based on this information, calculate the average atomic mass of element Z and identify the element.

A) Neon
B) Boron
C) Nitrogen
D) Carbon

Worked solution with answer for Topic 1

		Statement	True	False
	Q1	The first ionization energy of aluminum is lower than that of magnesium because aluminum has an electron in the 3p orbital, which is higher in energy than the 3s orbital of magnesium.	v	
	Q2	The effective nuclear charge experienced by an electron in the 3p orbital of chlorine is greater than that experienced by an electron in the 3p orbital of sulfur because chlorine has more protons in its nucleus, resulting in a stronger attraction for its 3p electrons.	v	
	Q3	The electron affinity of oxygen is ~~higher~~ lower than that of fluorine because oxygen is ~~more~~ less electronegative and ~~more~~ less effectively attracts an additional electron.		v
	Q4	The first ionization energy of boron (B) is lower than that of beryllium (Be) because the electron removed from boron comes from a higher energy 2p orbital, while the electron removed from beryllium comes from a more stable, fully filled 2s orbital.	v	
	Q5	The energy required to remove the first electron from a neutral atom is always ~~greater~~ less than the energy required to remove the second electron because after removing the first electron, the atom becomes positively charged, making it ~~easier~~ difficult to remove another electron.		v
	Q6	The first ionization energy of nitrogen (N) is higher than that of oxygen (O) because the electron removed from nitrogen comes from a half-filled 2p orbital, which is more stable compared to the 2p orbital in oxygen where electron-electron repulsion is greater due to paired electrons.	v	
	Q7	The ionization energy of an element generally increases across a period because the additional protons increase the nuclear attraction for the electrons, without significantly increasing shielding.	v	
	Q8	Isoelectronic species ~~always~~ have ~~identical~~ different sizes because they have the same number of electrons but have the different number of protons.		v
	Q9	In the photoelectron spectrum of nitrogen, the peak corresponding to the 2s orbital will appear at a higher binding energy than the peak corresponding to the 2p orbital because the 2s orbital is more tightly bound to the nucleus and thus has a higher binding energy compared to the 2p orbital.	v	
	Q10	The reactivity of alkali metals ~~decreases~~ increases as you move down the group due to decreasing ionization energies and increasing atomic radii.		v

A11

As you move across a period from left to right (in this case, from Na to Si), the number of protons in the nucleus increases. This increase in positive charge (effective nuclear charge) results in a stronger Coulombic attraction between the nucleus and the electrons. This stronger attraction pulls the electrons closer to the nucleus, leading to a smaller atomic radius. Therefore, silicon has the smallest atomic radius, followed by aluminum and magnesium, with sodium having the largest radius because Coulombic attraction increases across a period.

A12

Cu^+: Electron configuration is $[Ar] 3d^{10}$
Cu^{2+}: Electron configuration is $[Ar] 3d^9$
As Cu loses electrons to form Cu^+ and Cu^{2+}, the effective nuclear charge per electron increases. In Cu^{2+}, with fewer electrons, the Coulombic force between the nucleus and the remaining electrons is stronger, pulling the electrons closer to the nucleus, resulting in a smaller ionic radius for Cu^{2+}.

A13

The cation is smaller than the neutral atom, which in turn is smaller than the anion. When an atom becomes a cation, it loses electrons, often resulting in a reduction of the electron shell size and an increase in the effective nuclear charge, which pulls the remaining electrons closer to the nucleus. In contrast, when an atom gains electrons to become an anion, the added electrons increase electron-electron repulsion, causing the electron cloud to expand and resulting in a larger radius compared to the neutral atom.

A14

Silicon has a higher first ionization energy than Aluminum because Si has a greater effective nuclear charge, resulting in a stronger Coulombic attraction between the nucleus and the outermost electron without a significant increase in shielding. This makes it more difficult to remove an electron from Si compared to Al, following the general trend across a period where ionization energy increases from left to right.

A15

Phosphorus has a higher first ionization energy than Arsenic. Both elements are in the same group, meaning they have a comparable effective nuclear charge because the number of protons increases proportionally with the increase in electron shielding. However, as you move down the group, the principal quantum number (n) increases, which means the outermost electrons in arsenic are located in a higher energy level further from the nucleus. This greater distance reduces the Coulombic force of attraction between the nucleus and the outermost electrons, making them easier to remove. As a result, arsenic, which is below phosphorus in the periodic table, has a lower first ionization energy.

A16

Although sulfur is to the right of phosphorus, the first ionization energy of sulfur is lower due to electron-electron repulsion. Sulfur has one more electron than phosphorus, which leads to a pairing of electrons in one of the 3p orbitals. This pairing causes increased repulsion between the paired electrons, making it easier to remove one of them compared to removing an unpaired electron in phosphorus, where all 3p electrons are unpaired and experience less repulsion.

A17

The first ionization energy of sodium involves removing the single electron from its 3s orbital, resulting in a stable noble gas configuration. After this electron is removed, the sodium atom becomes a positively charged ion. The second ionization energy is much higher because it involves removing an electron from this positively charged ion, which is more difficult than removing an electron from a neutral atom. The remaining electrons are more strongly attracted to the nucleus due to the increased Coulombic force in the positively charged ion, making it significantly harder to remove another electron. Additionally, the electron to be removed is from a more stable, inner shell, which further increases the energy required.

A18

The first and second ionization energies of magnesium involve removing the two 3s electrons, resulting in a stable noble gas configuration (Ne). The third ionization energy, however, involves removing an electron from the 2p orbital, which is closer to the nucleus and more strongly attracted due to the effective nuclear charge. Removing this electron disrupts the stable, fully-filled 2p orbital, requiring significantly more energy, thus the third ionization energy is much higher.

A19

Across a Period: As you move from left to right across a period, metallic character decreases. This is because elements become less likely to lose electrons as they increase their effective nuclear charge, making it harder to remove electrons.

Down a Group: As you move down a group, metallic character increases. The atoms have more electron shells, increasing the atomic radius and reducing the effective nuclear charge felt by the valence electrons, making them easier to lose.

Na exhibits a higher metallic character than Mg because it is to the left of Mg in the same period, meaning it has a lower ionization energy and more readily loses its valence electron, which is a key characteristic of metals.

A20

Fluorine has a higher electronegativity than argon. Fluorine is the most electronegative element on the periodic table, with a strong tendency to attract electrons due to its small atomic size and high effective nuclear charge. Argon, on the other hand, is a noble gas with a full valence electron shell and does not tend to attract additional electrons, as it is already stable. In fact, argon is typically not assigned an electronegativity value because it does not readily form bonds.

A21 (D)

A22 (B)

Magnesium has two valence electrons, and after removing these two, the third electron comes from an inner shell (closer to the nucleus). This electron experiences a greater nuclear charge and stronger Coulombic force, making it much more difficult to remove. Therefore, there is a large jump in ionization energy between the second and third ionizations.

A23 (A)

Isoelectronic species have the same number of electrons but differ in their nuclear charge. The species with the smallest nuclear charge (fewest protons) will have the largest ionic radius because the electrons are less strongly attracted to the nucleus. Among the given species, O^{2-} has the fewest protons (8), resulting in the largest ionic radius.

A24 (D)
The first ionization energy of K is actually lower than that of Na. Although K has more protons, it also has an additional electron shell compared to Na, increasing the distance between the nucleus and the valence electron, which reduces the effective nuclear attraction and makes it easier to remove the valence electron.

A25 (D)
The 2s electrons in nitrogen experience a greater effective nuclear charge compared to the 2p electrons because they are closer to the nucleus and experience less shielding. Therefore, the 2s electrons have a higher binding energy than the 2p electrons. The statement is incorrect because it incorrectly suggests that 2p electrons have a higher binding energy than 2s electrons.

A26 (D)
The effective nuclear charge experienced by the 2p electrons in oxygen is greater than in carbon because oxygen has more protons in the nucleus. This results in the 2p electrons in oxygen having a higher binding energy compared to carbon. Therefore, the 2p peaks do not appear at similar binding energies.

A27 (C)
The effective nuclear charge experienced by the outermost electron decreases as you move down the group from lithium to cesium, due to increased shielding and distance from the nucleus. This leads to an increase in reactivity down the group, not identical reactivity. Therefore, the statement is incorrect.

A28 (C)
In a mass spectrum, peaks represent different isotopes of an element, not oxidation states. The x-axis represents the mass-to-charge ratio (m/z), and the y-axis represents the relative abundance of each isotope. Therefore, the statement is incorrect.

A29 (A)
Average atomic mass = $(0.750)(62.93 \text{ amu}) + (0.250)(64.93 \text{ amu}) = 63.43$ amu

A30 (B)
Average atomic mass = $\frac{(7 \times 10.012) + (3 \times 11.009)}{10} = 10.31$

Topic _2
Compounds Sturcture & Properties

Exam Weighting : 7-9%

Topic 2 Key Point Review

Ionic bond
- Bond Formation Process
  - Formed between metals and nonmetals through the transfer of electrons. Metals lose electrons to form cations, while nonmetals gain electrons to form anions. The electrostatic attraction between oppositely charged ions creates the bond.
- Physical Properties
  - Melting/Boiling Point: High due to strong electrostatic forces between ions.
  - Vapor Pressure: Low, because ionic compounds typically do not vaporize easily.
  - Conductivity:
    - Solid: Non-conductive (ions are locked in place).
    - Liquid: Conductive (ions are free to move).
    - Aqueous: Conductive (dissolved ions move freely in water).
      - Precipitate (ppt) = not ionize in water → low conductivity

Metallic bond
- Bond Formation Process:
  - Formed between metal atoms through the delocalization of valence electrons. These electrons form a "sea of electrons" that move freely around positively charged metal cations, resulting in a strong attraction between them.
- Physical Properties:
  - Melting/Boiling Point: Generally high due to strong metallic bonding.
  - Vapor Pressure: Typically low for solid metals, but can vary with different metals.
  - Conductivity:
    - Solid: Conductive (mobile electrons).
    - Liquid: Conductive (electrons remain delocalized).
    - Aqueous: Not applicable, as metals don't dissolve to form solutions.

Covalent network bond
- Bond Formation Process:
  - Formed by the sharing of electrons between nonmetal atoms, resulting in an extended network of covalent bonds throughout a solid (e.g., diamond, quartz). Each atom is covalently bonded to multiple others, creating a large, stable structure.
- Physical Properties:
  - Melting/Boiling Point: Extremely high due to the strength of the covalent bonds throughout the entire structure.
  - Vapor Pressure: Very low, as these substances do not vaporize easily.
  - Conductivity:
    - Solid: Generally non-conductive (no free electrons or ions), except for materials like graphite.
    - Liquid: Usually non-conductive (many network solids do not melt easily).
    - Aqueous: Non-conductive (does not dissolve in water).

Covalent bond (molecule)
- Bond Formation Process:
    - Formed by the sharing of electrons between nonmetal atoms to create discrete molecules. The covalent bond involves the sharing of electron pairs between atoms.
- Physical Properties:
    - Melting/Boiling Point: Generally low to moderate, depending on the strength of intermolecular forces (e.g., London dispersion, dipole-dipole, hydrogen bonding).
    - Vapor Pressure: Can be high for substances with weak intermolecular forces, meaning they evaporate easily (e.g., volatile liquids).
    - Conductivity:
        - Solid: Non-conductive (molecules do not have free-moving charges).
        - Liquid: Non-conductive (molecules remain neutral).
        - Aqueous: Non-conductive, unless the molecule ionizes in water
            - Strong acid = 100% ionize in water → conductive

Lewis structure
- Octet Rule
    - Atoms tend to bond in such a way that they have 8 electrons in their valence shell.
    - Achieving an octet results in a stable electronic configuration similar to noble gases.
    - Nonmetals in the second period (C, N, O, F) follow the octet rule strictly.
- Incomplete Octet
    - Some elements are stable with fewer than 8 electrons in their valence shell.
    - Common examples
        - Hydrogen (H): stable with 2 electrons.
        - Boron (B) and Beryllium (Be): stable with 6 and 4 electrons, respectively.
- Expansion of Octet
    - Elements in the third period and beyond can hold more than 8 electrons due to available d-orbitals.
    - Common in elements like P (Phosphorus), S (Sulfur), Xe (Xenon)
- Formal Charge
    - Used to determine the most stable Lewis structure when multiple possibilities exist.
    - Formula of formal Charge = (Valence Electrons)−(Occupied electrons)
    - The structure with the least formal charges and negative charges on more electronegative atoms is favored.
- Resonance structure
    - Resonance occurs when two or more valid Lewis structures can be drawn for a molecule or ion, differing only in the positions of electrons (not atoms).
    - Resonance structures represent the delocalization of electrons across multiple atoms, stabilizing the molecule.
    - The true structure of the molecule is a hybrid (blend) of all resonance structures, called the resonance hybrid.

VSEPR

To predict the 3D shape (geometry) of molecules based on the repulsion between electron pairs in the valence shell of the central atom.

Domain	Bonding pair + Lone pair	Molecular geometry	Bond angle (°)	Orbital hybridization
2	2 + 0	Linear	180	sp
3	3 + 0	Trigonal planar	120	sp^2
	2 + 1	Bent	Less than 120	
4	4 + 0	Tetrahedral	109.5	sp^3
	3 + 1	Trigonal pyramidal	107 (less than 109.5)	
	2 + 2	Bent	104.5 (less than 109.5)	
5	5 + 0	Trigonal bipyramidal	120 / 90	sp^3d
	4 + 1	Seesaw	Not necessary to remember	
	3 + 2	T-shaped	Not necessary to remember	
	2 + 3	Linear	Not necessary to remember	
6	6 + 0	Octahedral	90 / 90	sp^3d^2
	5 + 1	Square pyramidal	Not necessary to remember	
	4 + 2	Square planar	Not necessary to remember	

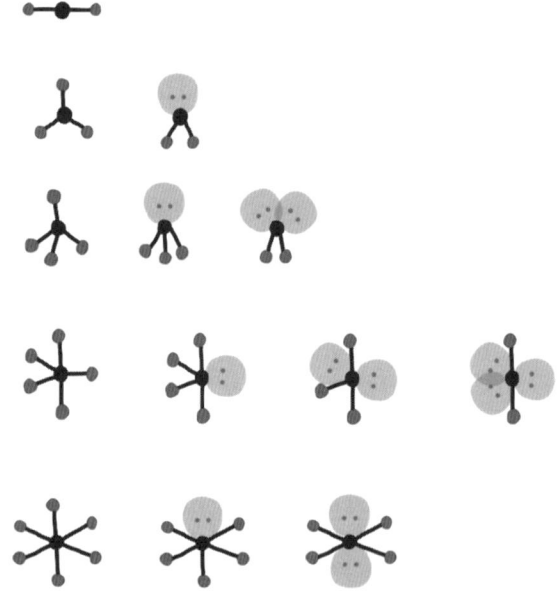

True/False Questions

Read the following statements carefully and determine whether each one is true or false. Place a tick (✓) in the appropriate box. If the statement is false, correct the incorrect part of the statement.

	Statement	True	False
Q31	Ionic bonds typically form between metals and non-metals because the large difference in electronegativity allows the metal to donate electrons to the non-metal, forming a stable ionic compound.		
Q32	Covalent network solids, like diamond, have low melting points because the individual covalent bonds are weak and easy to break.		
Q33	In metallic bonding, the electrons are localized between specific metal atoms, leading to strong directional bonds because the metal atoms share electrons exclusively with their nearest neighbors.		
Q34	A covalent bond involves the sharing of electron pairs between atoms, typically between non-metals, because non-metals have similar electronegativities, making it energetically favorable to share electrons rather than transfer them.		
Q35	Ionic compounds generally have low electrical conductivity in their solid state but become conductive when dissolved in water or melted because the ions are free to move in the liquid or aqueous state, allowing them to carry an electric current.		
Q36	The strength of metallic bonds decreases with an increasing number of delocalized electrons because more electrons create greater repulsion between atoms, weakening the overall bond.		
Q37	Covalent network solids are generally poor conductors of electricity because there are no free-moving charged particles within the structure, making it difficult for electrical current to pass through.		
Q38	Ionic compounds tend to have low melting and boiling points because the electrostatic forces between oppositely charged ions are weak, allowing the ions to separate easily.		
Q39	In a metallic bond, the bond strength is largely dependent on the size of the metal atoms, with smaller atoms generally forming stronger bonds because the nucleus of smaller atoms can attract delocalized electrons more effectively.		
Q40	Covalent compounds are always soluble in water because water is a polar solvent, and covalent compounds always have polar molecules.		

Concept Check Questions

When solving Free-Response Questions (FRQs), it is essential to clearly and accurately explain your reasoning. Make sure to outline the steps in your solution process thoroughly, showing all calculations with appropriate numbers and units. This demonstrates a full understanding of the problem and ensures that your answer is both correct and complete.

Q41
Explain the structure of an ionic solid using sodium chloride (NaCl) as an example. In your explanation, include the following:
- The type of particles involved in the bonding.
- The arrangement of these particles in the solid state.
- How the electrostatic forces between ions contribute to the overall stability of the ionic compound.

Q42
Describe the conditions under which an ionic compound, such as magnesium chloride, will conduct electricity. In your response, explain why ionic compounds conduct electricity in some states but not in others, and provide an example for each state.

Q43
Compare the melting points of two ionic compounds: sodium chloride and magnesium oxide. In your response, consider the Coulombic forces acting between the ions and explain why one compound has a higher melting point than the other.

Q44
Lithium fluoride and potassium bromide are both ionic compounds. Predict which compound has the higher lattice energy and explain your reasoning using the concept of Coulomb's Law. Consider both the charges on the ions and the ionic radii in your explanation.

Q45
Explain the structure of a covalent molecule using methane (CH_4) as an example. In your explanation, include the following:
- The type of bonding involved.
- The geometric arrangement of atoms around the central atom.

Q46
Describe why most covalent compounds do not conduct electricity in their solid or liquid states. In your response, explain the difference between covalent compounds and ionic compounds in terms of electrical conductivity.

Q47
Compare and contrast polar covalent bonds and nonpolar covalent bonds. In your response, explain the role of electronegativity differences and provide an example of each type of bond.

Q48
Explain the structure and properties of a covalent network solid using diamond as an example. In your explanation, discuss how the bonding within the network affects its physical properties.

Q49
Describe the nature of metallic bonding and how it leads to the characteristic properties of metals, such as electrical conductivity and malleability. Include in your explanation the concept of the "sea of electrons."

Q50
You are given an unknown white crystalline solid and asked to determine the type of bonding present in the solid (ionic, covalent network, or metallic). Design an experiment to identify the bonding type. In your response, describe the tests you would perform, the expected results for each bonding type, and explain how these results would help you identify the bonding type in the solid.

Multiple Choice Questions

The following questions are multiple-choice.
Choose the correct answer and explain why the other options are incorrect.

Q51
Which of the following compounds has the highest lattice energy, and why?

A) NaCl, because both Na^+ and Cl^- have smaller radii compared to other options, leading to stronger electrostatic forces.
B) MgO, because the charges on the ions (Mg^{2+} and O^{2-}) are higher than those in the other compounds, resulting in stronger electrostatic attractions and thus a higher lattice energy.
C) KBr, because K^+ and Br^- ions have a good balance of size and charge, leading to moderate but efficient packing in the lattice structure.
D) BaS, because Ba^{2+} and S^{2-} are large ions, which might allow the lattice to form with less repulsion between like charges.

Q52
Which molecule has a trigonal planar geometry, and why?

A) NH_3, because nitrogen forms three bonds and one lone pair.
B) BF_3, because boron forms three bonds and has no lone pairs.
C) H_2O, because oxygen forms two bonds and has two lone pairs.
D) CO_2, because the molecule is linear with two double bonds.

Q53
Which of the following molecules exhibits a dipole moment, and why?

A) CCl₄, because it has polar C-Cl bonds, although the molecule's tetrahedral geometry makes the overall molecule polar molecule due to symmetric charge distribution.
B) CO₂, because it has polar C=O bonds, but the linear shape of the molecule means the dipoles cancel out, resulting in net dipole moment.
C) CH₄, because it has polar C-H bonds, yet the tetrahedral shape ensures that the molecule has net dipole moment due to symmetric charge distribution.
D) H₂O, because it has polar O-H bonds, and the bent shape of the molecule prevents the dipoles from canceling out, resulting in a net dipole moment.

Q54
Which property of metals is best explained by the "sea of electrons" model, and why?

A) High melting point, because the localized electrons form a strong bond with metal cations, requiring a large amount of energy to break.
B) Brittleness, because the rigid structure of the metal cations and their interactions with delocalized electrons prevent the metal from deforming under stress.
C) Malleability, because the non-directional nature of metallic bonds allows metal atoms to slide past each other without breaking the metallic bonds, unlike in ionic or covalent network solids.
D) Low density, because the "sea of electrons" provides an efficient packing of metal cations, reducing the overall mass per unit volume.

Q55
Which of the following solids is an example of a covalent network solid, and what is its characteristic property?

A) NaCl, because it forms a crystalline lattice where each ion is surrounded by oppositely charged ions, but it is not a covalent network solid due to ionic bonding.
B) SiO_2, because it forms an extensive 3D network of covalent bonds between silicon and oxygen atoms, resulting in very high melting and boiling points, characteristic of covalent network solids.
C) C(graphite), because it consists of atoms held together by metallic bonds, which are delocalized electrons around a lattice of metal cations, not by covalent bonds.
D) CO_2, because it forms a simple molecular structure with covalent bonds within each molecule, but it exists as discrete molecules rather than a covalent network.

Q56
You are testing the conductivity of four different substances in both solid and molten states. Which substance is most likely an ionic compound based on the following observations, and why?

A) Substance A conducts electricity well in both solid and molten states, suggesting it has a "sea of electrons," typical of metallic bonds.
B) Substance B does not conduct electricity in either the solid or molten state, which indicates it may have a covalent network structure with no free ions or electrons.
C) Substance C does not conduct electricity in the solid state but conducts well when molten, implying the presence of free-moving ions in the molten state, characteristic of an ionic compound.
D) Substance D conducts electricity poorly in the solid state and slightly better in the molten state, but not as well as expected, suggesting it might be a polar covalent compound with some degree of ionization when molten.

Q57
Which of the following molecules contains only covalent bonds but is nonpolar overall, and why?

A) HCl, because it contains a polar covalent bond, but the molecule is polar due to the difference in electronegativity between hydrogen and chlorine.
B) NH_3, because it contains polar covalent bonds, but the molecule is polar due to its trigonal pyramidal shape, which does not cancel out the dipoles.
C) CF_4, because it contains polar C-F bonds, but due to its tetrahedral shape, the dipoles cancel out, resulting in a nonpolar molecule.
D) CO, because it contains a polar covalent bond between carbon and oxygen, leading to an overall polar molecule.

Q58
Which of the following statements best explains the concept of resonance as it applies to molecules like ozone (O), and why?

A) Resonance occurs when a molecule can exist in two or more forms with different numbers of bonds between atoms, such as in ozone, where one structure has a double bond and the other has a single bond, leading to different physical properties.
B) Resonance structures are different isomers of a molecule, like in O, where one oxygen is double-bonded to the central oxygen in one structure, and the other oxygen is double-bonded in another structure, resulting in two distinct molecules.
C) Resonance structures depict the delocalization of electrons across multiple atoms in a molecule, as in O, where the actual structure is a hybrid of two equivalent forms with delocalized electrons, resulting in bond lengths that are intermediate between single and double bonds.
D) Resonance explains why some molecules, like O, have a single, stable structure that switches rapidly between two forms, with bonds fluctuating between single and double bonds, giving rise to an average bond length.

Q59
Which of the following Lewis structures is incorrect based on formal charge calculations?

A) In CO_2, the structure where each oxygen is double-bonded to the carbon atom, resulting in a formal charge of 0 on all atoms.
B) In H_2O, the structure where the oxygen atom has two single bonds to hydrogen atoms and two lone pairs, resulting in a formal charge of 0 on all atoms.
C) In NH_4^+, the structure where nitrogen is single-bonded to four hydrogen atoms, with no lone pairs on nitrogen, resulting in a formal charge of +1 on the nitrogen atom and 0 on the hydrogen atoms
D) In NO_3^-, the structure where nitrogen is double-bonded to one oxygen and singly bonded to the other two, with a formal charge of 0 on all atoms.

Q60
Which of the following statements about graphite, SiO_2, and diamond is incorrect?

A) Diamond has a three-dimensional covalent network structure where each carbon atom is tetrahedrally bonded to four other carbon atoms, resulting in a very hard material with a high melting point.
B) Graphite consists of layers of carbon atoms arranged in a hexagonal lattice, where each carbon atom is bonded to three others within the layer, allowing the layers to slide over each other, making graphite a good lubricant.
C) SiO_2 (quartz) has a three-dimensional covalent network structure similar to diamond, where each silicon atom is bonded to four oxygen atoms, making it hard and having a high melting point.
D) Graphite, like diamond, is an excellent conductor of electricity because both have strong covalent bonds between carbon atoms that allow for free electron movement throughout the entire structure.

Worked solution with answer for Topic 2

	Statement	True	False
A31	Ionic bonds typically form between metals and non-metals because the large difference in electronegativity allows the metal to donate electrons to the non-metal, forming a stable ionic compound.	v	
A32	Covalent network solids, like diamond, have ~~low~~ high melting points because the individual covalent bonds are ~~weak~~ strong and extended throughout the entire structure so they are ~~easy~~ difficult to break.		v
A33	In metallic bonding, the electrons are ~~localized~~ delocalized between specific metal atoms, ~~leading to strong directional bonds because the metal atoms share electrons exclusively with their nearest neighbors.~~ and free to move throughout the entire metal structure, leading to a 'sea of electrons' rather than directional bonds.		v
A34	A covalent bond involves the sharing of electron pairs between atoms, typically between non-metals, because non-metals have similar electronegativities, making it energetically favorable to share electrons rather than transfer them.	v	
A35	Ionic compounds generally have low electrical conductivity in their solid state but become conductive when dissolved in water or melted because the ions are free to move in the liquid or aqueous state, allowing them to carry an electric current.	v	
A36	The strength of metallic bonds ~~decreases~~ increases with an increasing number of delocalized electrons because ~~more electrons create greater repulsion between atoms, weakening the overall bond.~~ this enhances the attractive force between the positively charged metal cations and the delocalized electrons.		v
A37	Covalent network solids are generally poor conductors of electricity because there are no free-moving charged particles within the structure, making it difficult for electrical current to pass through.	v	
A38	Ionic compounds tend to have ~~low~~ high melting and boiling points because the electrostatic forces between oppositely charged ions are ~~weak~~ strong, ~~allowing the ions to separate easily.~~ requiring a lot of energy to overcome.		v
A39	In a metallic bond, the bond strength is largely dependent on the size of the metal atoms, with smaller atoms generally forming stronger bonds because the nucleus of smaller atoms can attract delocalized electrons more effectively.	v	
A40	Covalent compounds are ~~always~~ sometimes soluble in water because water is a polar solvent, and covalent compounds ~~always~~ sometimes have polar molecules. However, non-polar covalent compounds do not dissolve well in polar solvents like water.		v

A41

Type of particles: In NaCl, the particles involved in bonding are positively charged sodium ions and negatively charged chloride ions.
Arrangement: NaCl forms a crystalline lattice structure where each Na$^+$ ion is surrounded by Cl$^-$ ions and vice versa. This arrangement maximizes the attraction between oppositely charged ions and minimizes repulsion between like charges.
Electrostatic forces: The strong electrostatic attraction between the oppositely charged ions creates a stable, solid ionic structure, contributing to the high melting point and hardness of the compound.

A42

Solid state: Ionic compounds like magnesium chloride do not conduct electricity in the solid state because the ions are locked in place within the crystal lattice and cannot move freely.
Molten state or aqueous solution: Ionic compounds conduct electricity when melted or dissolved in water because the ions are free to move. In the molten state, the crystal lattice breaks down, allowing Mg^{2+} and Cl$^-$ ions to move freely and carry an electrical current.
Example: In solid magnesium chloride, the ions are fixed in position and cannot move. When magnesium chloride is dissolved in water or melted, the ions are free to move and can conduct electricity.

A43

NaCl is composed of Na$^+$ and Cl$^-$ ions, while MgO consists of Mg^{2+} and O^{2-} ions. According to Coulomb's Law, the strength of the electrostatic force between ions is directly proportional to the product of the charges of the ions and inversely proportional to the square of the distance between them.
MgO has a higher melting point than NaCl because the charges on the ions in MgO (Mg^{2+} and O^{2-}) are larger than those in NaCl (Na$^+$ and Cl$^-$). This results in stronger electrostatic forces in MgO, requiring more energy to break the bonds, leading to a higher melting point. Additionally, Mg^{2+} and O^{2-} are smaller ions than Na$^+$ and Cl$^-$, so the distance between the ions is smaller, further increasing the electrostatic force. The stronger Coulombic forces in MgO give it a higher melting point than NaCl.

A44

LiF is composed of Li$^+$ and F$^-$ ions, while KBr consists of K$^+$ and Br$^-$ ions. Lattice energy depends on the product of the charges of the ions and the distance between them (ionic radius). Both compounds have ions with the same charges. The ionic radius of Li$^+$ is smaller than that of K$^+$, and the ionic radius of F$^-$ is smaller than that of Br$^-$. Since LiF has smaller ions, the distance between the Li$^+$ and F$^-$ ions is smaller than that between K$^+$ and Br$^-$ in KBr, resulting in stronger electrostatic attractions in LiF. LiF has a higher lattice energy than KBr because the smaller ionic radii of Li$^+$ and F$^-$ lead to stronger Coulombic forces between the ions.

A45

Methane (CH$_4$) is held together by covalent bonds, where each hydrogen atom shares one electron with the central carbon atom, resulting in four C-H bonds. The carbon atom in CH$_4$ is sp^3 hybridized, leading to a tetrahedral arrangement of the four hydrogen atoms around the carbon. This geometry minimizes electron pair repulsion according to VSEPR (Valence Shell Electron Pair Repulsion) theory.

A46

Covalent compounds do not conduct electricity because they do not have free-moving charged particles (ions or electrons) in either their solid or liquid states. Unlike ionic compounds, which conduct electricity when melted or dissolved in water due to the presence of free ions, covalent compounds consist of molecules where electrons are shared between atoms in fixed bonds, leaving no free charges to carry an electric current.

A47

Polar covalent bonds occur when there is a significant difference in electronegativity between the two atoms involved in the bond, leading to an unequal sharing of electrons. Nonpolar covalent bonds occur when the electronegativity difference is minimal or zero, resulting in equal sharing of electrons. In a water molecule (H_2O), the oxygen atom is more electronegative than the hydrogen atoms, causing the shared electrons to be pulled closer to the oxygen, making the O-H bonds polar. In a molecule of oxygen (O_2), both oxygen atoms have the same electronegativity, leading to equal sharing of electrons and a nonpolar covalent bond.

A48

Diamond is a covalent network solid where each carbon atom is covalently bonded to four other carbon atoms in a tetrahedral structure, forming an extensive 3D network. The strong covalent bonds throughout the network give diamond its remarkable hardness and high melting point. Because of the strong covalent bonds in all directions, diamond is extremely hard, has a very high melting point, and is a poor conductor of electricity because it lacks free-moving electrons or ions.

A49

Metallic bonding involves the attraction between positively charged metal cations and a "sea of delocalized electrons" that move freely throughout the metal lattice. The free-moving electrons in the "sea" allow metals to conduct electricity efficiently, as these electrons can carry electrical current through the material. The non-directional nature of metallic bonds allows metal atoms to slide past each other without breaking the bond, making metals malleable and ductile.

A50

Measure the electrical conductivity of the solid in its solid state and then in a molten state or when dissolved in water (if it dissolves).
Ionic bond: Poor conductivity in the solid state, but good conductivity when melted or dissolved in water due to the presence of free-moving ions.
Covalent network: Poor conductivity in both solid and molten states because there are no free-moving charged particles.
Metallic bond: Good conductivity in the solid state due to the presence of delocalized electrons.

A51 (B)

Lattice energy is the energy required to separate one mole of an ionic compound into its gaseous ions, and it's directly related to the Coulombic force between the ions. The Coulombic force depends on two main factors:
Ionic Charge: Higher charges result in stronger electrostatic forces between the ions, leading to higher lattice energy.
Ionic Radius: Smaller ions have a shorter distance between their centers, which increases the strength of the electrostatic attraction.

When evaluating lattice energy, ionic charge should be considered first because it has the greatest impact. After that, the ionic radius should be considered, as smaller ions will also result in a higher lattice energy.

A52 (B)

Boron trifluoride (BF_3) has a central boron atom bonded to three fluorine atoms. Boron does not have any lone pairs, and the three bonding pairs of electrons arrange themselves as far apart as possible, resulting in a trigonal planar geometry with bond angles of 120°..
Ammonia (NH_3) has a nitrogen atom bonded to three hydrogen atoms, but nitrogen also has one lone pair of electrons. The lone pair repels the bonding pairs, resulting in a trigonal pyramidal geometry, not trigonal planar.
Water (H_2O) has an oxygen atom bonded to two hydrogen atoms and two lone pairs of electrons. The repulsion between the lone pairs and bonding pairs leads to a bent geometry with bond angles around 104.5°, not trigonal planar.
Carbon dioxide (CO_2) has a linear geometry because the carbon atom forms double bonds with two oxygen atoms, with no lone pairs on the carbon. This gives CO_2 a bond angle of 180°, not trigonal planar.

A53 (D)

A polar bond occurs when there is a significant difference in electronegativity between the two atoms, causing an unequal sharing of electrons. This creates a dipole, with one end of the bond being partially negative and the other partially positive.
A nonpolar bond occurs when the atoms involved have similar or identical electronegativities, leading to equal sharing of electrons and no dipole formation.
A polar molecule has a net dipole moment because the dipoles from polar bonds do not cancel out due to the molecule's shape (asymmetry).
A nonpolar molecule has no net dipole moment because either the molecule contains only nonpolar bonds, or the polar bonds are arranged symmetrically so that the dipoles cancel out.
- CCl_4: Although each C-Cl bond is polar, the molecule is tetrahedral and symmetrical. The dipoles cancel out, making CCl_4 a nonpolar molecule.
- CO_2: Each C=O bond is polar, but the molecule is linear, so the dipoles are directly opposite and cancel out, making CO_2 a nonpolar molecule.
- CH_4: The C-H bonds are considered nonpolar due to the small difference in electronegativity, and the molecule is symmetric, making CH_4 nonpolar.
- H_2O: The O-H bonds are polar, and because H_2O has a bent shape, the dipoles do not cancel out. This results in a net dipole moment, making H_2O a polar molecule.

A54 (C)

Malleability, because the non-directional metallic bonds allow metal atoms to slide past each other without breaking.

A55 (B)

SiO_2, because it forms a 3D network of covalent bonds, resulting in high melting and boiling points.

A56 (C)

Ionic Compounds
- **Solid State:** Ionic compounds do not conduct electricity in the solid state because the ions are fixed in place within the crystal lattice and cannot move freely.
- **Molten State:** When melted, the crystal lattice breaks down, allowing the ions to move freely. This mobility of ions in the molten state allows ionic compounds to conduct electricity.

Metallic Compounds
- **Solid and Molten State:** Metallic compounds conduct electricity in both solid and molten states due to the presence of delocalized electrons. These free-moving electrons allow for the conduction of electricity throughout the metal.

Covalent Network Solids
- **Solid and Molten State:** Covalent network solids do not conduct electricity in either state. The atoms are bonded in a continuous network, and there are no free-moving charged particles to carry an electrical current.

Covalent Compounds
- **Solid and Molten State:** Covalent compounds generally do not conduct electricity well. In some cases, they may conduct electricity slightly when molten due to partial ionization (such as strong acid, weak acid), but they are not as conductive as ionic or metallic compounds.

A57 (C)

HCl has a polar covalent bond due to the difference in electronegativity between hydrogen and chlorine. Since it's a linear molecule with only one bond, HCl is polar.

NH_3 (ammonia) has polar N-H bonds. Due to its trigonal pyramidal shape, the dipoles do not cancel out, making the molecule polar.

CF_4 (carbon tetrafluoride) has polar C-F bonds, but it has a tetrahedral shape. In this shape, the dipoles from the four C-F bonds are symmetrically arranged, canceling each other out, resulting in a nonpolar molecule.

CO has a polar covalent bond due to the difference in electronegativity between carbon and oxygen. This makes CO a polar molecule.

A58 (C)

Resonance occurs when a molecule can be represented by two or more valid Lewis structures that differ only in the placement of electrons (not atoms). These structures are called resonance structures.

In reality, the molecule does not oscillate between these forms; instead, the true structure is a resonance hybrid, which is a blend of all possible resonance structures.

In the case of ozone (O_3), the molecule can be drawn with one double bond and one single bond in two different ways. However, the actual structure has bond lengths that are intermediate between a single and a double bond, indicating that the electrons are delocalized across the molecule.

Delocalization of electrons means that the electrons are spread out over several atoms, rather than being localized between two specific atoms. This delocalization adds stability to the molecule.

A59 (D)

Formal Charge Calculation Formula:

Formal Charge (FC)
= (Valence Electrons) - (Nonbonding Electrons + 1/2 * Bonding Electrons)
= (Valence Electrons) – (occupied electrons)

A) Carbon (4 - 4 = 0), Oxygen (6 – 6 = 0)
B) Oxygen (6 - 6 = 0), Hydrogen (1 - 1 = 0)
C) Nitrogen (5 - 4 = +1), Hydrogen (1 - 1 = 0)
D) Nitrogen (5 - 4 = +1), Oxygen in double bond (6 – 6 = 0), Oxygen in single bond (each) (6 - 7 = -1)

A60 (D)

In graphite, carbon atoms are bonded in layers with each carbon atom forming three sigma bonds with other carbons, creating a hexagonal pattern within each layer. The fourth valence electron of each carbon is not involved in bonding within the layer and is instead delocalized across the layer. These delocalized electrons are free to move within the layers, allowing graphite to conduct electricity only within the layers.

In contrast, diamond is a poor conductor of electricity. In diamond, each carbon atom forms four covalent bonds with other carbon atoms in a tetrahedral structure, creating a very strong and rigid three-dimensional network. All electrons in diamond are involved in bonding, leaving no free electrons available to conduct electricity. Thus, diamond is an excellent insulator.

Topic _3
Properties of Substances & Mixtures

Exam Weighting : 18-22%

Topic 3 Key Point Review

Polar molecule & Nonpolar molecule
- Polar Molecule: Molecule with an uneven distribution of charge, resulting in a dipole moment
  - Polar covalent bond + Asymmetric geometry
- Nonpolar Molecule: Molecule with an even distribution of charge, no dipole moment
  - Nonpolar covalent bond + Symmetric geometry
  - Polar covalent bond + Symmetric geometry

London dispersion force
- Weak, temporary attractive force due to instantaneous dipoles created by polarization of electrons.
- Present in all molecules, but dominant in nonpolar molecules.
- The greater the size of the electron cloud, the stronger the LDF (larger atoms/molecules have stronger LDFs).
- The greater the surface area, the stronger the LDF (molecules with larger surface areas experience stronger forces).

Dipole-induced dipole force
- Occurs when a polar molecule induces a dipole in a nonpolar molecule.
- Strength depends on the polarizability of the nonpolar molecule.

Dipole-dipole force
- Dipole moments arise when there is a significant difference in electronegativity between atoms in a bond, creating partial positive and partial negative charges.
- Attractive force between polar molecules due to the interaction of their dipole moments.
- More pronounced in molecules with larger dipole moments, meaning the greater the difference in electronegativity between bonded atoms, the stronger the dipole-dipole interaction.
- Stronger than London dispersion forces but weaker than ion-dipole and hydrogen bonds.

Ion-dipole force
- Attractive force between an ion and a polar molecule.
- Important in solutions where ionic compounds dissolve in polar solvents (e.g., Na^+ in water).
- Strength of ion-dipole force determined by comlombic's force
- Strength of ion-dipole force depends on:
  - Charge of the ion: Higher charge on the ion results in a stronger ion-dipole force.
  - Magnitude of the dipole: Molecules with stronger dipoles (greater electronegativity differences) will interact more strongly with ions.
  - Distance between the ion and the dipole: The closer the ion and dipole, the stronger the interaction.

Hydrogen bond
- Strong type of dipole-dipole interaction involving hydrogen bonded to N, O, or F.
- Responsible for the unique properties of water (e.g., high boiling point).

Real gas vs. ideal gas

	Ideal gas	Real gas
Volume	Assumed to be negligible (particles are treated as point masses with no volume).	Gas particles have finite volume, especially at high pressures where the actual volume of the particles becomes significant relative to the space between them. As pressure increases, the volume occupied by gas particles affects the overall behavior, deviating from ideal gas predictions.
Pressure	Assumes perfect elastic collisions and no loss of energy; no attractive or repulsive forces between particles, so the measured pressure is ideal.	Due to intermolecular attractions, the actual pressure exerted by a real gas is lower than predicted by the ideal gas law because particles attract each other, reducing the force of collisions with container walls.
Intermolecular forces	No intermolecular forces between particles; gas particles are free to move without any attraction or repulsion.	**Intermolecular Forces:** Intermolecular attractions are present, especially at low temperatures, leading to deviations from ideal behavior.
Equation	$PV = nRT$	Deviates from ideal behavior at high pressures and low temperatures. To account for these deviations, the van der Waals equation is used: $(P + \frac{a}{V^2})(V - b) = nRT$

Dilution for making solution
- $M_1V_1 = M_2V_2$

Dilution with solid solute	Dilution from stock solution
1) Use a balance to accurately measure the mass of the solid solute required for the desired concentration. 2) Transfer the solute into a volumetric flask. 3) Add a small amount of solvent (usually distilled water) to dissolve the solute completely, swirling to assist dissolution. 4) After the solute is dissolved, slowly add more solvent until the solution reaches the calibration mark.	1) Use a buret or pipette to accurately measure the required volume of the stock solution (high-concentration solution). 2) Transfer the measured stock solution into a clean volumetric flask. 3) Add a small amount of solvent (usually distilled water) to the flask, swirling gently to start diluting the stock solution. 4) Carefully add solvent until the solution reaches the calibration mark.

Beer's law
- Formula : A = ε bc
    - A = absorbance (no units)
    - ε = molar absorptivity = a constant that depends on the substance and wavelength of light
    - c = molar concentration (mol/L)
    - b = path length (cm)
- Absorbance is directly proportional to both the concentration of the solute and the path length.
- Molar absorptivity (ε) is a measure of how strongly a substance absorbs light at a particular wavelength.
- Used to determine the concentration of an unknown solution by measuring its absorbance.

Chromatography
- A technique used to separate the components of a mixture based on their different interactions with a stationary phase and a mobile phase.
- Stationary phase
    - The phase that does not move and interacts with the sample components.
    - Paper (cellulose – polar), silica (polar)
    - The nature of the stationary phase (polar or nonpolar) affects how different components of the mixture are retained.
- Mobile phase
    - The phase that moves through the stationary phase, carrying the sample components with it.
    - The interaction between the mobile phase and the components determines how quickly they travel through the stationary phase.
- Polar sample
    - If the stationary phase is polar, polar components will have stronger interactions with the stationary phase and move slower through the system.
    - If the mobile phase is nonpolar, polar components will interact less with it and travel slower compared to nonpolar components.
- Nonpolar sample
    - If the stationary phase is polar, nonpolar components will have weaker interactions with it and move faster.
    - If the mobile phase is nonpolar, nonpolar components will interact more with the mobile phase and move faster.

True/False Questions

Read the following statements carefully and determine whether each one is true or false. Place a tick (✔) in the appropriate box. If the statement is false, correct the incorrect part of the statement.

		Statement	True	False
Q61		London dispersion forces are the strongest type of intermolecular force because they occur in all molecules, regardless of whether they are polar or nonpolar. Also, London dispersion forces increase with the size of the molecule because larger molecules have more electrons, which increases the likelihood of temporary dipoles forming.		
Q62		Hydrogen bonds are a special type of dipole-dipole interaction that occur when hydrogen is bonded to a highly electronegative atom like nitrogen, oxygen, or fluorine, because these atoms create a significant positive charge on the hydrogen atom.		
Q63		Dipole-dipole forces are stronger than London dispersion forces because dipole-dipole interactions result from permanent dipoles in polar molecules, while London dispersion forces are temporary.		
Q64		Ion-dipole forces are weaker than dipole-dipole forces because ions are always smaller than dipole molecules, leading to less effective interactions. It is crucial in the process of dissolving ionic compounds in water because the ions interact with the dipole of water molecules, allowing them to dissociate and spread throughout the solution.		
Q65		Dipole-induced dipole interactions occur when a nonpolar molecule induces a dipole in a polar molecule, resulting in an attraction between them because the nonpolar molecule temporarily disturbs the electron cloud of the polar molecule.		
Q66		The strength of hydrogen bonds is generally comparable to covalent bonds because both involve the sharing of electrons between atoms, which creates a strong attraction.		
Q67		According to Beer's Law, absorbance is directly proportional to the concentration of a solution because the law states that absorbance equals the product of the molar absorptivity, path length, and concentration.		
Q68		In paper chromatography, the stationary phase is the paper, and the mobile phase is the solvent. The sample interacts differently with the stationary phase (paper) and the mobile phase (solvent), causing it to separate as it travels up the paper.		
Q69		The ideal gas law, PV=nRT, assumes that gas particles have no volume and experience no intermolecular forces because these assumptions simplify the behavior of real gases to approximate ideal gas behavior.		

Q70	At high pressures, real gases exert less pressure than predicted by the ideal gas law because intermolecular attractions become significant, reducing the impact of collisions with the container walls.		
Q71	Molarity is defined as the number of moles of solute per kilogram of solvent because it measures the concentration of a solute in a given amount of solvent.		
Q72	To prepare a dilute solution from a solid solute, you should first dissolve the solute completely in a small volume of solvent within a volumetric flask. After the solute is fully dissolved, you add more solvent until the solution reaches the calibration mark on the flask.		
Q73	To prepare a dilute solution from a concentrated stock solution using a volumetric flask, you should add the required amount of stock solution to the flask using buret and then fill the flask with solvent up to the calibration mark because this ensures that the final volume is accurate, and the solution concentration is correct.		
Q74	The strength of London dispersion forces increases with larger electron cloud size and greater surface area because both factors lead to more significant temporary dipoles and stronger intermolecular attractions.		
Q75	Cl_2 exhibits stronger London dispersion forces than I_2 because chlorine molecules have a larger electron cloud and greater polarizability, leading to stronger temporary dipoles and, consequently, stronger intermolecular attractions compared to iodine.		

Concept Check Questions

When solving Free-Response Questions (FRQs), it is essential to clearly and accurately explain your reasoning. Make sure to outline the steps in your solution process thoroughly, showing all calculations with appropriate numbers and units. This demonstrates a full understanding of the problem and ensures that your answer is both correct and complete.

Q76
Compare the London Dispersion Forces in two alkanes: pentane (C_5H_{12}) and octane (C_8H_{18}). Explain how the differences in their molecular sizes and shapes influence their boiling points and vapor pressure.

Q77
Compare the dipole-dipole interactions in hydrogen chloride (HCl) and hydrogen iodide (HI). Explain how the difference in electronegativity and molecular size affects their boiling points and other physical properties.

Q78
Compare the intermolecular forces between water (H_2O) molecules and hydrogen sulfide (H_2S) molecules. Explain how these forces influence the boiling points and vapor pressures of the two substances.

Q79
Compare the ion-dipole interactions between sodium chloride (NaCl) in water and magnesium sulfide (MgS) in water. Draw a model representing these interactions and explain how the differences in ionic charges and sizes affect solubility.

Q80
Explain the dipole-induced dipole interactions that occur between water (H$_2$O) and benzene (C$_6$H$_6$). Discuss how these interactions influence the solubility of benzene in water and the overall behavior of the mixture.

Q81
In a chromatography experiment, compare the relative strengths of interactions between the solvent (mobile phase), the paper (stationary phase), and the sample components. Explain how these differences in interaction strength affect the movement of the sample components during the experiment.
(solvent = nonpolar, sample = polar + nonpolar)

Q82

You are tasked with preparing a 250 mL diluted solution of hydrochloric acid (HCl) from a 6.00 M stock solution to a final concentration of 0.50 M. You have the following equipment available:
- 250 mL volumetric flask
- 100 mL graduated cylinder
- 50 mL burette
- 10 mL pipette
- Beakers of various sizes
- Distilled water

(a)
Identify the specific equipment you would use.

(b)
Describe the step-by-step procedure you would use to prepare the diluted solution.

Step 1	
Step 2	
Step 3	
Step 4	
Step 5	

Q83

Methane (CH₄) is a molecular gas under standard conditions and exhibits properties typical of nonpolar molecules.
A sample of $CH_4(g)$ is stored in a rigid 8.00 L container at 5.20 atm and 310 K.

(a)
Calculate the number of moles of $CH_4(g)$ in the container.

(b)
The rigid 8.00 L container of $CH_4(g)$ is cooled to a temperature of 280 K.
Calculate the new pressure, in atm, of the $CH_4(g)$.

Q84
Answer the following questions about the compounds PH_3 and PF_3.

(a)
PH_3 is slightly soluble in water, whereas PF_3 is highly soluble in water. Explain this observation in terms of the types and relative strengths of the intermolecular forces between each of the solutes and water.

(b)
Compare the boiling points of PH_3 and PF_3, providing an explanation based on the molecular structures and the types of intermolecular forces present.

Q85

A student is preparing a calibration curve using solutions of CuSO₄(aq) with known concentrations. Below is a list of procedural steps, but some key steps are missing. Complete the procedure by filling in the missing step.

Step 1	Prepare several standard solutions by diluting a CuSO₄(aq) stock solution with distilled water.
Step 2	Rinse the cuvette with distilled water.
Step 3	
Step 4	Measure the absorbance of the standard solution using a spectrophotometer.
Step 5	Repeats steps 2-4 for each of the standard solution.

Q86

A student is conducting an experiment with $N_2(g)$. Initially, a sample of the gas is in a rigid container at 310 K and 0.90 atm. The student then increases the temperature of the $N_2(g)$ in the container to 450 K.

(a)
Describe the effect of increasing the temperature on the motion of the $N_2(g)$ molecules.

(b)
Calculate the pressure of the $N_2(g)$ in the container at 450 K.

(c)
Using kinetic molecular theory, briefly explain why the pressure of the $N_2(g)$ in the container changes as it is heated to 450 K.

(d)
The student measures the actual pressure of the $N_2(g)$ in the container at 200 K and finds it to be slightly lower than the pressure predicted by the ideal gas law. Provide a possible explanation for this observation.

Q87

A student investigates the polarity of three different dyes, labeled Dyes X, Y, and Z, and an unknown sample containing one of these dyes, using paper chromatography. The student places a drop of each dye on a piece of chromatography paper (which is polar) and develops the chromatogram using a nonpolar solvent. After development, the following observations are made:
- Dye X travels the farthest distance up the paper.
- Dye Y travels a moderate distance, but not as far as Dye X.
- Dye Z barely moves from the origin.
- The unknown sample travels the same distance as Dye Y.

(a)
Based on these observations, which dye (X, Y, or Z) is the least polar? Justify your answer in terms of the interactions between the dyes and the solvent, as well as between the dyes and the paper.

(b)
Which dye is present in the unknown sample? Justify your answer using the information from the observations.

Q88

A student performs a column chromatography experiment to separate a mixture of three compounds, labeled A, B, and C, using a silica (SiO_2) column as the stationary phase and a nonpolar solvent as the mobile phase. The student observes the following:
- Compound A elutes first from the column.
- Compound B elutes after Compound A, but before Compound C.
- Compound C remains in the column for a significantly longer time before eluting.

(a)
Based on these observations, which compound (A, B, or C) is the most polar? Justify your answer in terms of the interactions between the compounds and the silica (SiO_2) stationary phase.

(b)
Explain why the order of elution (A, B, then C) occurs when using a nonpolar solvent as the mobile phase. Consider the polarity of the compounds and the nature of the interactions with the stationary phase.

Q89

A student investigates the behavior of a gas using a rigid cylinder with a movable piston of negligible mass, as shown in the diagram below. The cylinder contains 0.400 mol of N_2 (g).

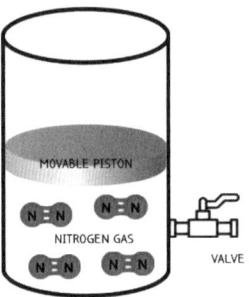

(a)
The cylinder has a volume of 10.0 L at 25°C and 1.20 atm.
Calculate the density of the N_2(g), in g/L, under these conditions.

(b)
To change the density of the N_2 (g), the student opens the valve on the side of the cylinder, pushes down on the piston to release some of the gas, and then closes the valve. The temperature of the gas remains constant at 25°C.
Will this action change the density of the gas remaining in the cylinder?
Justify your answer.

(c)
The student tries to change the density of the N_2 (g) by cooling the cylinder to −60°C, which causes the volume of the gas to decrease. Using principles of kinetic molecular theory, explain why the volume of the N_2 (g) decreases when the temperature decreases to −60°C.

Q90
A chemical reaction between citric acid ($C_6H_8O_7$) and sodium carbonate (Na_2CO_3) occurs in the presence of water to produce carbon dioxide, water, and sodium citrate ($Na_3C_6H_5O_7$), as represented by the following equation:

$$C_6H_8O_7 \text{ (aq)} + Na_2CO_3 \text{ (aq)} \rightarrow CO_2\text{(g)} + H_2O\text{(l)} + Na_3C_6H_5O_7\text{(aq)}$$

A student combines equal masses of $C_6H_8O_7$ (s) and Na_2CO_3(s) in a reaction vessel with sufficient water at 25.0 °C. The student determines that 0.0150 mol of CO_2(g) is produced after the reaction goes to completion.

(a)
Calculate the number of grams of CO_2(g) produced.

(b)
The CO_2(g) produced from the reaction at 25.0°C was collected and found to have a pressure of 1.10 atm. Calculate the volume of CO_2(g), in liters.

Multiple Choice Questions

The following questions are multiple-choice.
Choose the correct answer and explain why the other options are incorrect.

Q91
A student performs a titration experiment to determine the concentration of an 15.0 mL of unknown concentration H_2SO_4 solution using 0.100 M $Ba(OH)_2$ as the titrant. The student adds phenolphthalein as an indicator, which turns pink in basic solutions. During the experiment, the student notices that the solution turns light pink after adding 30.00 mL of $Ba(OH)_2$. What is the concentration of the unknown H_2SO_4 solution?

A) 0.150 M
B) 0.200 M
C) 0.300 M
D) 0.600 M

Q92
A student is tasked with preparing 250.0 mL of a 0.500 M KNO_3 solution. After dissolving the calculated amount of KNO_3 in a beaker with some distilled water, the student transfers the solution to a 250.0 mL volumetric flask and adds distilled water up to the calibration mark. However, the student accidentally adds water slightly above the calibration mark. Which of the following statements is correct?

A) The concentration of the solution is slightly higher than 0.500 M.
B) The concentration of the solution is exactly 0.500 M.
C) The concentration of the solution is slightly lower than 0.500 M.
D) The concentration of the solution cannot be determined without more data.

Q93
A student performs a gas collection experiment by reacting an excess of zinc (Zn) with hydrochloric acid (HCl) to produce hydrogen gas (H_2). The student collects 0.500 L of $H_2(g)$ over water at 25.0°C and 0.97 atm. The vapor pressure of water at 25.0°C is 23.8 mmHg. What is the partial pressure of the H_2 (g)collected, in atm?

A) 0.94 atm
B) 0.98 atm
C) 1.0 atm
D) 1.3 atm

Q94
A student is performing paper chromatography to separate a mixture of dyes. The student uses water as the solvent and notices that one of the dyes (Dye A) does not travel far from the origin, while another dye (Dye B) travels almost to the top of the paper. What can be inferred about the relative polarity of the dyes?

A) Dye A is more polar than Dye B.
B) Dye A is less polar than Dye B.
C) Both dyes have the same polarity.
D) The polarity of the dyes cannot be determined from this information.

Q95

A student performs a water displacement experiment to collect an unknown gas produced by the decomposition of metal chlorate. The mass of the gas collected at 25.0°C and a total pressure of 755.0 mmHg is 0.314 g. The vapor pressure of water at 25.0°C is 23.8 mmHg. The student collects 250.0 mL of gas. What is identity of the unknown gas collected?

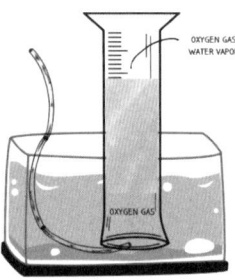

A) oxygen gas
B) nitrogen gas
C) carbon dioxide gas
D) carbon monoxide gas

Q96

A student is investigating the vapor pressure of three different liquids: ethanol (C_2H_5OH), hexane (C_6H_{14}), and water (H_2O). The student observes the following boiling points:
- Ethanol: 0.07 bars
- Hexane: 0.16 bars
- Water: 0.032 bars

Based on this data, which of the following correctly explains the boiling points of the liquids?

A) Hexane has the lowest boiling point due to strong hydrogen bonding between its molecules.
B) Water has the highest boiling point due to its ability to form strong hydrogen bonds, which require more energy to break.
C) Ethanol has a lower boiling point than water because it is a larger molecule with more London dispersion forces.
D) Hexane has a higher boiling point than ethanol due to dipole-dipole interactions.

Q97
A student dissolves iodine (I_2) in two different solvents: carbon tetrachloride (CCl_4) and water (H_2O). The student observes that iodine dissolves well in CCl_4 but not in water. Which of the following statements best explains this observation?

A) Iodine dissolves well in hexane because water's strong hydrogen bonds make it difficult for iodine to dissolve. Additionally, London dispersion forces between hexane and iodine allow for strong interactions, making iodine more soluble in hexane.
B) Iodine dissolves well in hexane because the hydrogen bonding between iodine and hexane is stronger than that between iodine and water.
C) Iodine dissolves well in hexane because hexane's strong dipole-dipole interactions enable it to easily interact with iodine.
D) Iodine does not dissolve well in hexane because London dispersion forces between hexane and iodine are weak, whereas water's hydrogen bonds better accommodate iodine molecules.

Q98
A student is comparing the solubility of sodium chloride (NaCl) and glucose ($C_6H_{12}O_6$) in water at room temperature. The student observes that both compounds dissolve well in water, but for different reasons. Which of the following best explains the solubility behavior of these two substances?

A) Sodium chloride dissolves in water primarily due to London dispersion forces between NaCl and H_2O.
B) Glucose dissolves in water due to ionic interactions between glucose and water molecules.
C) Sodium chloride dissolves in water due to ion-dipole interactions, while glucose dissolves due to hydrogen bonding with water.
D) Both sodium chloride and glucose dissolve in water due to the formation of covalent bonds with water molecules.

Q99
A student is investigating the vapor pressures of three different liquids at 25°C: ethanol (C_2H_5OH), acetone (C_3H_6O), and water (H_2O). The student measures the vapor pressures and observes the following:
- Ethanol: 59.3 mmHg
- Acetone: 231 mmHg
- Water: 23.8 mmHg

Based on this data, which of the following correctly predicts the relative strength of intermolecular forces in these liquids?

A) Acetone has the strongest intermolecular forces because it has the highest vapor pressure.
B) Water has the weakest intermolecular forces because it has the lowest vapor pressure.
C) Water has the strongest intermolecular forces due to extensive hydrogen bonding, resulting in the lowest vapor pressure.
D) Ethanol has the weakest intermolecular forces because its vapor pressure is between that of water and acetone.

Q100
A student is comparing the boiling points of two compounds: chloroform ($CHCl_3$) and carbon tetrachloride (CCl_4). The boiling point of $CHCl_3$ is 334 K, while the boiling point of CCl_4 is 350 K. Which of the following statements best explains why CCl_4 has a higher boiling point than $CHCl_3$?

A) CCl_4 has a higher boiling point because it exhibits stronger hydrogen bonding than $CHCl_3$, leading to increased intermolecular forces.
B) $CHCl_3$ has a lower boiling point than CCl_4 because it has weaker London dispersion forces, despite its dipole-dipole interactions.
C) $CHCl_3$ has a lower boiling point than CCl_4 because $CHCl_3$ has a smaller molecular size and less complex molecular structure, resulting in weaker intermolecular forces.
D) CCl_4 has a higher boiling point because the combined dipole-dipole and London dispersion forces in $CHCl_3$ are weaker than the stronger London dispersion forces in CCl_4, due to CCl_4's larger electron cloud and greater polarizability.

Worked solution with answer for Topic 3

	Statement	True	False
A61	~~London dispersion forces are the not strongest type of intermolecular force because they occur in all molecules, regardless of whether they are polar or nonpolar.~~ London dispersion forces are not the strongest type of intermolecular force; they are actually the weakest compared to dipole-dipole interactions and hydrogen bonds especially in molecules of similar molar mass. , although they do occur in all molecules. Also, London dispersion forces increase with the size of the molecule because larger molecules have more electrons, which increases the likelihood of temporary dipoles forming.		v
A62	Hydrogen bonds are a special type of dipole-dipole interaction that occur when hydrogen is bonded to a highly electronegative atom like nitrogen, oxygen, or fluorine, because these atoms create a significant positive charge on the hydrogen atom.	v	
A63	Dipole-dipole forces are stronger than London dispersion forces because dipole-dipole interactions result from permanent dipoles in polar molecules, while London dispersion forces are temporary.	v	
A64	Ion-dipole forces are ~~weaker~~ stronger than dipole-dipole forces because ~~ions are always smaller than dipole molecules, leading to less effective interactions.~~ the full charge of the ion interacts more strongly with the dipole. It is crucial in the process of dissolving ionic compounds in water because the ions interact with the dipole of water molecules, allowing them to dissociate and spread throughout the solution.		v
A65	Dipole-induced dipole interactions occur when a ~~nonpolar~~ polar molecule induces a dipole in a ~~polar~~ nonpolar molecule, resulting in an attraction between them because the ~~nonpolar~~ polar molecule temporarily disturbs the electron cloud of the ~~polar~~ nonpolar molecule.		v
A66	The strength of hydrogen bonds is generally ~~not~~ comparable to covalent bonds ~~because both involve the sharing of electrons between atoms, which creates a strong attraction~~ because covalent bonds are much stronger than hydrogen bonds, even though hydrogen bonds are stronger than other types of intermolecular forces.		v
A67	According to Beer's Law, absorbance is directly proportional to the concentration of a solution because the law states that absorbance equals the product of the molar absorptivity, path length, and concentration.	v	
A68	In paper chromatography, the stationary phase is the paper, and the mobile phase is the solvent. The sample interacts differently with the stationary phase (paper) and the mobile phase (solvent), causing it to separate as it travels up the paper.	v	
A69	The ideal gas law, PV=nRT, assumes that gas particles have no volume and experience no intermolecular forces because these assumptions simplify the behavior of real gases to approximate ideal gas behavior.	v	
A70	At high pressures, real gases exert less pressure than predicted by the ideal gas law because intermolecular attractions become significant, reducing the impact of collisions with the container walls.	v	

A71	Molarity is defined as the number of moles of solute per ~~kilogram~~ liter of solvent because it measures the concentration of a solute in a given amount of solvent.		v
A72	To prepare a dilute solution from a solid solute, you should first dissolve the solute completely in a small volume of solvent within a volumetric flask. After the solute is fully dissolved, you add more solvent until the solution reaches the calibration mark on the flask.	v	
A73	To prepare a dilute solution from a concentrated stock solution using a volumetric flask, you should add the required amount of stock solution to the flask using buret and then fill the flask with solvent up to the calibration mark because this ensures that the final volume is accurate, and the solution concentration is correct.	v	
A74	The strength of London dispersion forces increases with larger electron cloud size and greater surface area because both factors lead to more significant temporary dipoles and stronger intermolecular attractions.	v	
A75	Cl_2 exhibits ~~stronger~~ weaker London dispersion forces than I_2 because ~~chlorine~~ iodine molecules have a larger electron cloud and greater polarizability, leading to stronger temporary dipoles and, consequently, stronger intermolecular attractions compared to ~~iodine~~ chlorine.		v

A76

London Dispersion Forces: Octane (C_8H_{18}) has stronger London dispersion forces than pentane (C_5H_{12}) due to its larger molecular size and greater surface area.
Boiling Points: Octane's larger size leads to more significant temporary dipoles, increasing its boiling point compared to pentane.
Vapor Pressure: Pentane has a higher vapor pressure than octane because it has weaker intermolecular forces, making it more volatile.

A77

Dipole-Dipole Interactions: HCl has stronger dipole-dipole interactions than HI due to the higher electronegativity difference between H and Cl compared to H and I.
Boiling Points: HCl has a higher boiling point than HI because of the stronger dipole-dipole interactions despite HI's larger molecular size, which increases London dispersion forces.
Physical Properties: The higher electronegativity of Cl also results in a more polar molecule, affecting properties like solubility and reactivity.

A78

Intermolecular Forces: Water (H_2O) molecules exhibit strong hydrogen bonding due to the highly electronegative oxygen, while H_2S molecules mainly have dipole-dipole interactions and no hydrogen bonds due to sulfur's lower electronegativity.
Water – Hydrogen bonding + Dipole dipole interaction + London dispersion force
H_2S - Dipole dipole interaction + London dispersion force
Boiling Points: Water has a much higher boiling point than H_2S because hydrogen bonds in water molecules are significantly stronger than the dipole-dipole interactions in H_2S.
Vapor Pressure: H_2S has a higher vapor pressure than water because weaker intermolecular forces in H_2S allow it to evaporate more easily.

A79

Ion dipole force is directly related to the electrostatic attraction.
The greater the charge, the greater the interaction.
The smaller the size of ion, the greater the interaction.
NaCl dissociates into Na⁺ and Cl⁻, which interact with water's dipoles. MgS dissociates into Mg^{2+} and S^{2-}.
Charge : $Na^+ < Mg^{2+}$, $Cl^- > S^{2-}$
Size of ions : $Na^+ > Mg^{2+}$, $Cl^- < S^{2-}$
MgS has greater ion dipole force than NaCl.
Model :

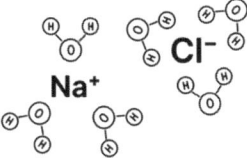

A80

Dipole-Induced Dipole Interactions: Water, being polar, induces a dipole in the nonpolar benzene molecules, but these interactions are weak compared to water's hydrogen bonding.
Solubility: Benzene has very low solubility in water because the weak dipole-induced dipole interactions are insufficient to overcome water's strong hydrogen bonds.
Behavior of the Mixture: Benzene and water form two separate layers due to the significant difference in polarity and the minimal interaction between them.

A81

Interactions: Polar components interact more strongly with the polar stationary phase (paper) and less with the nonpolar mobile phase (solvent). Nonpolar components interact more with the mobile phase.
Movement: Nonpolar components travel further up the paper, while polar components remain closer to the origin because they adhere more strongly to the stationary phase.

A82

(a)
- 250 mL volumetric flask
- 50 mL burette
- Distilled water

(b)
M1V1 = M2V2
(6.00M)(V1) = (0.50M)(250mL)
V1 = 20.83 mL
- **Step 1:** Measure 20.83 mL of the 6.00 M HCl stock solution using the burette.
- **Step 2:** Transfer the measured HCl into the 250 mL volumetric flask.
- **Step 3:** Add distilled water to the flask until the solution reaches the calibration mark.
- **Step 4:** The 0.50 M HCl solution is now ready for use.

A83

(a)
PV = nRT
(5.20 atm)(8.00 L) = n (0.08206 Latm/molK)(310 K)
n = 1.64 mol

(b)
$$\frac{P_1}{T_1} = \frac{P_2}{T_2}$$
$$\frac{5.20 \text{ atm}}{310 \text{ K}} = \frac{P_2}{280 \text{ K}}$$
$P_2 = 4.69$ atm

A84

(a)
PF_3 is more soluble in water than PH_3 because PF_3 can form stronger hydrogen bonding, dipole-dipole interactions and London dispersion forces with water due to the high electronegativity of fluorine, making it more polar than PH_3.

(b)
PF_3 has a higher boiling point than PH_3 because it has stronger dipole-dipole interactions due to the greater electronegativity difference between P and F compared to P and H in PH_3. Additionally, PF_3 is more polar than PH_3, contributing to stronger hydrogen bonding.

A85

Rinse the cuvette with the standard solution and fill the cuvette with the standard solution.

A86

(a)
As the temperature increases, the average kinetic energy of the $N_2(g)$ molecules increases, causing them to move more rapidly.

(b)
$$\frac{P_1}{T_1} = \frac{P_2}{T_2}$$
$$\frac{0.90 \text{ atm}}{310 \text{ K}} = \frac{P_2}{450 \text{ K}}$$
$P_2 = 1.31$ atm

(c)
The pressure increases because the molecules are moving faster and colliding with the walls of the container more frequently and with greater force.

(d)
The slight deviation could be due to the real gas behavior where intermolecular attractions become significant at lower temperatures, reducing the number of collisions with the container walls.

A87

(a)
Dye X is the least polar because it travels the farthest distance up the paper. Nonpolar molecules interact more with the nonpolar solvent and less with the polar stationary phase, allowing them to move further.

(b)
The unknown sample is Dye Y because it travels the same distance as Dye Y, indicating similar interactions with the stationary and mobile phases.

A88

(a)
Compound C is the most polar because it interacts more strongly with the polar silica (SiO_2) stationary phase, causing it to elute last.

(b)
In a nonpolar solvent, nonpolar compounds (like A) interact less with the stationary phase and elute first. Polar compounds (like C) have stronger interactions with the polar stationary phase and elute last.

A89

(a)
$$PV = nRT = \frac{mass}{Molar\ mass} RT$$
$$Density = \frac{mass}{V} = \frac{(P)(Molar\ mass)}{RT} = \frac{(1.20 atm)(28.02\ g/mol)}{\left(0.08206 \frac{Latm}{molK}\right)(298K)} = 1.37\ g/L$$

(b)
The density of the gas remains constant because R, T, and P remains constant and the mass and volume of nitrogen decreases proportionately.

(c)
As the gas cools, the average kinetic energy (speed) of the N_2 molecules decreases. The molecules collide with each other and the walls of the container with less energy, which reduces the frequency and force of collisions. To maintain a constant pressure (or to balance the decreased kinetic energy), the volume of the gas decreases, causing the molecules to occupy a smaller space.
As the gas cools, the average kinetic energy (speed) of the N_2 molecules decreases. The molecules rebound with less energy when they collide with each other and the walls of the container. To maintain the rate of collisions required to sustain a certain pressure, the gas must occupy a smaller volume.

A90

(a)
Mass = mol × molar mass
= (0.0150mol)(44.01g/mol)
= 0.660 g

(b)
PV = nRT
(1.10 atm)(V) = (0.0150 mol)(0.08206 Latm/molK)(298K)
V = 0.333 L

A91

Balanced equation: $H_2SO_4 + Ba(OH)_2 \rightarrow BaSO_4 + H_2O$
Moles of $Ba(OH)_2$ used: 0.100 M × 0.03000 L = 0.00300

Since the ratio of H₂SO₄ to Ba(OH)₂ is 1:1, the moles of H₂SO₄ = 0.00300 mol.
Concentration of H₂SO₄
= Moles of H₂SO₄/ Volume = 0.00300 mol / 0.01500 L = 0.200 M

A92 (C)
Adding water above the calibration mark increases the total volume, which dilutes the solution and lowers its concentration.

A93 (A)
Convert vapor pressure of water to atm: 23.8 mmHg×(1atm/760 mmHg) = 0.0313 atm
Partial pressure of H_2 = Ptotal – Pwater = 0.97 atm – 0.0313 atm = 0.94 atm

A94 (A)
In paper chromatography, the more polar compound interacts more with the polar stationary phase (paper), so it travels a shorter distance compared to less polar compounds.

A95 (A)
P_{O2} = Ptotal – Pwater = 755 mmHg – 23.8 mmHg = 731.2 mmHg
731.2 mmHg x (1 atm / 760 mmHg) = 0.9621atm
PV = nRT
n = PV/RT = (0.9621 atm)(0.2500 L) / (0.08206 Latm/molK) (298 K)
= 0.00984 mol
Mr = mass/mol = 0.314 g / (0.00984 g/mol) = 31.9 g/mol
Unknown gas is oxygen.

A96 (B)
It takes the greatest energy to break intermolecular forces between water molecules, which leads to the lowest vapor pressure and highest boiling points. Therefore, water's strong hydrogen bonds give it the highest boiling point among the three compounds.

A97 (A)
Iodine dissolves well in hexane because both are nonpolar and can interact through London dispersion forces. However, in water, the strong hydrogen bonds make it difficult for nonpolar iodine to dissolve, as it cannot participate in these hydrogen-bonding interactions.

A98 (C)
NaCl dissolves in water through ion-dipole interactions, while glucose dissolves through hydrogen bonding with water molecules.

A99 (C)
Strong intermolecular forces (like hydrogen bonding in water) result in a lower vapor pressure.

A100 (D)
CCl_4 has a larger molecular size and more electrons, leading to stronger London dispersion forces, which result in a higher boiling point.

Topic _4
Chemical Reactions

Exam Weighting : 7-9%

Topic 4 Key Point Review

Mole calculation
Relating the number of particles (atoms, molecules, ions) to moles using Avogadro's number (6.022×10^{23}).

Mass → Mole	$n = \dfrac{\text{mass}}{\text{molar mass}}$
Gas conditions → Mole	$n = \dfrac{(\text{Pressure})(\text{Volume})}{RT}$
Solution → Mole	$n = \text{Molarity} \times \text{Volume}$
Avogadro's number → Mole	$n = \dfrac{\text{number of particles}}{6.022 \times 10^{23}}$
Volume of gas at STP → Mole	$n = \dfrac{\text{Volume (L)}}{22.4 \text{ L/mol}}$

Determine limiting reactants
- The limiting reactant is the reactant that produces the fewest moles of product when compared to the stoichiometric ratio.
- Calculate the number of moles for each reactants
- Divide the moles of each reactant by its coefficient from the balanced equation
  $$= \dfrac{\text{Mole of reactant}}{\text{Coefficient in equation}}$$
- Compare the results → The reactant with the smaller value is the limiting reactant.

Percent yield
$$= \dfrac{\text{Actual yield}}{\text{Theoretical yield (=calculated from stoichiometry)}} \times 100$$

Oxidation number
A number assigned to an atom in a compound or ion that reflects its degree of oxidation (electron loss) or reduction (electron gain).
The sum of oxidation numbers in a neutral compound = 0; for polyatomic ions, it equals the ion's charge.

Free elements	Zero
Group 1 metals in compounds	+1
Group 2 metals in compounds	+2
Oxygen in compounds	-2 (mostly) Exception : OF_2 (+2 of oxygen) Exception : H_2O_2 (-1 of oxygen)
Hydrogen in compounds	+1 (mostly) Exception : NaH (-1 of hydrogen)
Fluorine	-1 (always)
Halogens	-1 (mostly)

Redox balancing
① Assign oxidation numbers to all elements.
② Identify oxidation (increase in oxidation number) and reduction (decrease in oxidation number) half-reactions.
③ Balance the atoms involved in oxidation and reduction.
④ Balance the oxygen involved in oxidation and reduction using H_2O.
⑤ Balance the hydrogen involved in oxidation and reduction using H^+.
⑥ Balance electrons lost and gained, then combine the half-reactions.
⑦ For acidic solutions, add H^+ ions; for basic solutions, add OH^- ions to balance.
⑧ Ensure the equation is balanced in both mass and charge.

Gravimetric analysis
- A method used to determine the quantity of a substance by converting it into a solid and measuring its mass.
- Precipitate the analyte (substance of interest) from a solution.
- Filter and wash the precipitate to remove impurities.
- Dry the precipitate to a constant mass (about three times).
- Weigh the precipitate and calculate the quantity of the analyte based on the stoichiometry of the reaction.
- Highly accurate for determining the mass percent of an element or compound in a sample.

Titration
- A technique used to determine the concentration of a solution by reacting it with a solution of known concentration.
- Titrant: Solution of known concentration added from a buret.
- Analyte: Solution of unknown concentration being analyzed.
- Equivalence point: The point at which moles of titrant = moles of analyte (stoichiometrically equivalent amounts).
- Indicator: A chemical that changes color near the equivalence point to signal the end of the titration.

Concept Check Questions

When solving Free-Response Questions (FRQs), it is essential to clearly and accurately explain your reasoning. Make sure to outline the steps in your solution process thoroughly, showing all calculations with appropriate numbers and units. This demonstrates a full understanding of the problem and ensures that your answer is both correct and complete.

Q101-Q104

A student is performing a titration experiment to determine the concentration of hydrogen peroxide, H_2O_2, in an aqueous solution. The student titrates a 0.100 g sample of $H_2O_2(aq)$ with a solution of potassium permanganate, $KMnO_4(aq)$, in acidic conditions. The unbalanced chemical equation for the reaction is provided below:

$$\_\_H_2O_2(aq) + \_\_MnO_4^-(aq) \rightarrow \_\_O_2(g) + \_\_Mn^{2+}(aq) \text{ (unbalanced)}$$

Q101

Balance the redox reaction that occurs between H_2O_2 and MnO_4^- in acidic conditions.

Q102

The student used a 50.00 mL buret to add the $KMnO_4(aq)$ solution to the $H_2O_2(aq)$ solution until the purple color of the permanganate disappeared, indicating the end point of the titration. The initial volume reading of the solution in the buret was 1.00 mL, and the final reading was 24.50 mL. Calculate the volume of $KMnO_4(aq)$ that was added during the titration.

Q103
Given that the concentration of KMnO$_4$(aq) was 0.0200 M, calculate the number of moles of KMnO$_4$ that completely reacted with the H$_2$O$_2$. Calculate the number of moles of H$_2$O$_2$.

Q104
The student proposes to perform another titration using a 0.100 g sample of H$_2$O$_2$, but this time using 0.0100 M KMnO$_4$(aq) in the buret. Would this titrant concentration be a reasonable choice to use if the student followed the same procedure and used the same equipment as before? Justify your response.

Q105-Q110

In the first of two experiments, a student is assigned the task of determining the number of moles of water in one mole of $CaSO_4 \cdot nH_2O$. The student collects the data shown in the following table.

Measurement	mass
Mass of empty beaker	30.455 g
Initial mass of sample and container	33.920 g
Mass of sample and container after first heating	32.138 g
Mass of sample and container after second heating	32.131 g
Mass of sample and container after third heating	32.131 g

Q105
Explain why the student can correctly conclude that the hydrate was heated a sufficient number of times in the experiment.

Q106
(a) Calculate the total number of moles of water lost when the sample was heated.

(b) Determine the formula of the hydrated compound.

Q107
A different student heats the hydrate in an uncovered beaker, and some of the solid $CaSO_4 \cdot nH_2O$ spatters out of the beaker. This spattering will have what effect on the calculated mass of the water lost by the hydrate? Justify your answer.

Q108
In the second experiment, a student is given 3.25 g of a mixture containing anhydrous $CaSO_4$ and KNO_3. To determine the percentage by mass of $CaSO_4$ in the mixture, the student uses excess $BaCl_2(aq)$ to precipitate the sulfate ion as $BaSO_4(s)$.
Write the net ionic equation for the above reaction.

Q109
Starting with the 3.25 g sample of the mixture dissolved in water, briefly describe the steps necessary to quantitatively determine the mass of the BaSO₄ precipitate

Q110
The student determines the mass of the BaSO₄ precipitate to be 4.68 g. On the basis of this information, calculate each of the following.
(a)
The number of moles of CaSO₄ in the original mixture,

(b)
The percent by mass of CaSO₄ in the original mixture.

Q111-Q114

A student is given 50.0 mL of a solution of K_2SO_4 of unknown concentration. To determine the concentration of the solution, the student mixes the solution with excess 1.0 M $BaCl_2$(aq), causing a precipitate to form. The balanced equation for the reaction is shown below.

$$K_2SO_4 \text{ (aq)} + BaCl_2 \text{ (aq)} \rightarrow 2\ KCl(aq) + BaSO_4 \text{ (s)}$$

Q111
Write the net ionic equation for the reaction that occurs when the solutions of K_2SO_4 and $BaCl_2$ are mixed.

The student filters and dries the precipitate of $BaSO_4$ (molar mass 233.4 g/mol) and records the data in the table below.

Volume of K_2SO_4 solution	50.0 mL
Volume of 1.0 M $BaCl_2$ added	100.0 mL
Mass of $BaSO_4$ precipitate collected	1.17 g

Q112
Determine the number of moles of K_2SO_4 in the original 50.0 mL of solution.

Q113
The student realizes that the precipitate was not completely dried and claims that as a result, the calculated K_2SO_4 molarity is too high. Do you agree with the student's claim? Justify your answer.

Q114
After the precipitate forms and is filtered, the liquid that passed through the filter is tested to see if it can conduct electricity. What would be observed? Justify your answer.

Q115-Q117

Propene, $C_3H_6(g)$ (molar mass 42.1 g/mol), can be prepared by the dehydration of 1-propanol, $C_3H_7OH(g)$ (molar mass 60.1 g/mol), using a solid catalyst. The equation for the dehydration reaction is given below.

$$C_3H_7OH(g) + \text{catalyst} \rightarrow C_3H_6(g) + H_2O(g)$$

A student added a 0.250 g sample of $C_3H_7OH(l)$ to a test tube. The student heated the test tube gently with a Bunsen burner until all of the $C_3H_7OH(l)$ evaporated and gas generation stopped. When the reaction stopped, the volume of collected gas was 0.102 L at 0.900 atm and 298 K. (The vapor pressure of water at 298 K is 23.8 torr.)

Q115
Calculate the number of moles of $C_3H_6(g)$ that are actually produced in the experiment and measured in the gas collection tube.

Q116
Calculate the number of moles of $C_3H_6(g)$ that would be produced if the dehydration reaction went to completion.

Q117
Calculate the percent yield of $C_3H_6(g)$) in the experiment.

Q118- Q121
A student dissolved a 0.150 g sample of ascorbic acid ($C_6H_8O_6$) in water in an Erlenmeyer flask. Then the student titrated the $C_6H_8O_6$ solution in the flask with a solution of I_2 in KI, which has a dark brown color. The balanced chemical equation for the reaction that occurred during the titration is shown below:

$$C_6H_8O_6 \text{ (aq)} + I_2\text{(aq)} \rightarrow C_6H_6O_6 \text{ (aq)} + 2\ HI\text{(aq)}$$

Q118
Identify the species that was oxidized in the titration reaction. Justify your answer in terms of oxidation numbers.

Q119
The student used a 50.00 mL buret to add the I_2 solution to the $C_6H_8O_6$(aq) until the dark brown color was no longer visible in the flask, indicating that the end point of the titration had been reached. The initial volume reading of the solution in the buret was 2.50 mL, and the final reading was 26.85 mL. Calculate the volume of I_2 (aq) that was added during the titration.

Q120
Given that the concentration of I_2(aq) was 0.0150 M, calculate the number of moles of I_2 that completely reacted with the $C_6H_8O_6$.

Q121
The student proposes to perform another titration using a 0.150 g sample of $C_6H_8O_6$, but this time using 0.00750 M I_2(aq) in the buret. Would this titrant concentration be a reasonable choice to use if the student followed the same procedure and used the same equipment as before? Justify your response with calculation.

Q122-Q125

A student performs an experiment to produce a copper(II) salt of unknown composition, Cu_xCl_y, and determine its empirical formula. The student places a sample of copper metal, Cu(s), in a beaker containing excess hydrochloric acid, HCl(aq), as represented by the following equation.

$$x\ Cu(s) + y\ HCl(aq) \rightarrow Cu_xCl_y(aq) + \frac{y}{2}\ H_2(g)$$

The student heats the resulting mixture until only Cu_xCl_y (s) remains in the beaker. The data are given in the following table.

Measurement	mass
Mass of empty beaker	50.145 g
Mass of beaker and Cu(s)	51.280 g
Mass of beaker and Cu_xCl_y (s) after heating to constant mass	52.671 g

Q122
Calculate the mass of copper (Cu) used in the experiment.

Q123
Calculate the mass of chlorine (Cl) in the sample of Cu_xCl_y (s) remaining in the beaker.

Q124
Calculate the number of moles of Cl in the sample of Cu_xCl_y (s) remaining in the beaker.

Q125
The student determines that 0.0178 mol of Cu was used in the experiment. Use the data to determine the empirical formula of Cu_xCl_y (s).

Q126-Q130

3 Fe(NO$_3$)$_2$(aq) + 2 K$_2$Cr$_2$O$_7$(aq) + 16 HNO$_3$ (aq)
$\rightarrow$ 3 Fe(NO$_3$)$_3$(aq) + 4 KNO$_3$(aq) + 2 Cr(NO$_3$)$_3$(aq) + 7 H$_2$O(l)

Q126
Determine the oxidation number of Cr in K$_2$Cr$_2$O$_7$.

Q127
Determine the oxidation number of Fe in Fe(NO$_3$)$_3$.

Q128
Calculate the number of grams of K$_2$Cr$_2$O$_7$ needed to prepare 250.00 mL of 0.200 M K$_2$Cr$_2$O$_7$ (aq).

In the experiment, the student uses the solutions shown in the table below.

	Concentration (M)	Volume (mL)
$Fe(NO_3)_2(aq)$	0.200	25.00
$K_2Cr_2O_7(aq)$	0.100	50.00
$HNO_3(aq)$	1.00	75.00

Q129
Using the balanced equation for the oxidation-reduction reaction and the information in the table above, determine which reactant is the limiting reactant. Justify your answer.

Q130
Write the balanced net ionic equation for the given reaction.

Worked solution with answer for Topic 4

A101
$2\ MnO_4^-(aq) + 5\ H_2O_2\ (aq) + 6\ H^+(aq) \rightarrow 2\ Mn^{2+}(aq) + 5\ O_2\ (g) + 8\ H_2O(l)$

A102
Initial volume = 1.00 mL
Final volume = 24.50 mL
Volume of $KMnO_4$ (aq) added = 24.50 mL - 1.00 mL = 23.50 mL

A103
Molarity of $KMnO_4$ = 0.0200 M
Volume of $KMnO_4$ = 23.50 mL = 0.02350 L
Moles of $KMnO_4$ = Molarity × Volume = 0.0200 M × 0.02350 L = 4.70×10^{-4} moles $KMnO_4$
Moles of H_2O_2 = 4.70×10^{-4} moles $KMnO_4$ × $\frac{5\ mol\ H_2O_2}{2\ mol\ MnO_4^-}$ = 1.18×10^{-3} moles H_2O_2

A104
Using 0.0100 M $KMnO_4$ (aq) would double the volume required to reach the endpoint.
This would require about 47.00 mL of titrant, which is still within the capacity of the buret.
Therefore, the concentration is reasonable.

A105
The mass after the second and third heating is nearly identical, indicating no more water is being lost. Thus, the hydrate was heated a sufficient number of times.

A106
(a)
Mass of water lost = 33.920 g - 32.131 g = 1.789 g
Moles of water lost = 1.789 g / 18.02 g/mol = 0.0993 mol

(b)
Moles of $CaSO_4$ = (32.131 g - 30.455 g) / 136.14 g/mol = 0.0123 mol
Ratio of moles of H_2O to $CaSO_4$ = 0.0993 mol / 0.0123 mol ≈ 8
Formula: $CaSO_4 \cdot 8\ H_2O$

A107
The calculated mass of water lost by the hydrate will be too large because the mass of the solid that was lost will be assumed to be water when it actually include some $CaSO_4$ as well.

A108
$Ba^{2+}(aq) + SO_4^{2-}(aq) \rightarrow BaSO_4\ (s)$

A109
1. Add $BaCl_2(aq)$ to the solution containing SO_4^{2-}.
2. Filter the solution to collect the precipitate using filter paper and funnel.
3. Wash the precipitate with distilled water (three times).
4. Dry the precipitate to a constant mass (about three times).
5. Weigh the precipitate ($BaSO_4$).

A110
(a)
Moles of $BaSO_4$ = 4.68 g / 233.4 g/mol = 0.02005 mol
Moles of $CaSO_4$ = 0.02005 mol

(b)
Mass of $CaSO_4$ = 0.02005 mol × 136.14 g/mol = 2.73 g
% Mass of $CaSO_4$ = (2.73 g / 3.25 g) × 100% = 84.0%

A111
$Ba^{2+}(aq) + SO_4^{2-}(aq) \rightarrow BaSO_4(s)$

A112
Mass of $BaSO_4$ precipitate = 1.17 g
Moles of $BaSO_4$ = 1.17 g / 233.4 g/mol = 5.01×10^{-3} mol
Moles of K_2SO_4 = Moles of $BaSO_4$ = 5.01×10^{-3} mol

A113
Agree.
If the precipitate was not completely dried, the measured mass would be higher than the actual mass, leading to an overestimation of the number of moles of K_2SO_4. Therefore, the calculated molarity would be too high.

A114
The filtrate would conduct electricity because it contains excess K^+ and Cl^- ions from KCl, which are dissociated in solution and Ba^{2+} from excess $BaCl_2$ solution. These ions are free to move in the solution, allowing the solution to conduct electricity.

A115
P = Ptotal − Pwater
= 0.900 atm − (23.8 torr / (760 torr/atm)) = 0.869 atm
PV = nRT
(0.869 atm)(0.102 L) = n(0.08206 L·atm/mol·K)(298 K)
n = 0.0036 mol

A116
If the reaction went to completion, all of the 0.250 g of C_3H_7OH would convert to $C_3H_6(g)$.
n = mass / molar mass = 0.250 g / 60.1 g/mol = 0.00416 mol
0.00416 mol of $C_3H_6(g)$ would be produced if the reaction went to completion because ratio of $C_3H_7OH : C_3H_6$ is 1 : 1.

A117
Percent yield = (actual yield / theoretical yield) x 100
Percent yield = (0.0036 mol / 0.00416 mol) x 100 = 86.5%

A118
In the titration reaction, $C_6H_8O_6$ (ascorbic acid) is oxidized. Oxidation involves the loss of electrons, which corresponds to an increase in oxidation number. In this reaction, the oxidation number of carbon in $C_6H_8O_6$ increases from +0.67 to +1 as it converts to $C_6H_6O_6$.

Oxidation number of C in $C_6H_8O_6$
$6x + 8 - 12 = 0$
$x = 4/6 = +0.67$
Oxidation number of C in $C_6H_6O_6$
$6x + 6 - 12 = 0$
$x = +1$

A119
Volume of I_2(aq) added = Final volume - Initial volume
= 26.85 mL - 2.50 mL = 24.35 mL

A120
Number of moles = Molarity x Volume (in liters)
Number of moles of I_2 = (0.0150 M)(0.02435 L) = 0.000365 mol

A121
To determine if this concentration is appropriate, calculate the volume of 0.00750 M I_2 needed:
Moles of I_2 required = 0.000365 mol (as previously calculated).
Volume needed = Moles / Molarity = 0.000365 mol / 0.00750 M = 0.0487 L = 48.7 mL.

This volume is close to the maximum capacity of the buret (50.00 mL), making it a reasonable choice, but it could be close to the limit, so care must be taken.

A122
Mass of copper = Mass of beaker and Cu(s) - Mass of empty beaker
Mass of copper = 51.280 g - 50.145 g = 1.135 g

A123
Mass of Cu_xCl_y (s) = Mass of beaker and Cu_xCl_y (s) after heating - Mass of empty beaker
Mass of Cu_xCl_y (s) = 52.671 g - 50.145 g = 2.526 g
Mass of Cl = Mass of Cu_xCl_y (s) - Mass of Cu
Mass of Cl = 2.526 g - 1.135 g = 1.391 g

A124
Molar mass of Cl = 35.45 g/mol
Number of moles of Cl = Mass / Molar mass
Number of moles of Cl = 1.391 g / 35.45 g/mol = 0.0392 mol

A125
Moles of Cu = 0.0178 mol
Moles of Cl = 0.0392 mol
Ratio of moles of Cl to moles of Cu = 0.0392 mol / 0.0178 mol = 2.2:1
Since the ratio should be a whole number, approximate the ratio as 2:1.
Thus, the empirical formula is $CuCl_2$.

A126
The oxidation number of Cr in $K_2Cr_2O_7$ is +6.
In $K_2Cr_2O_7$, the oxidation number of K is +1, and oxygen is -2. The sum of the oxidation numbers in the compound must equal 0. Let the oxidation number of Cr be x.

$2(+1) + 2(x) + 7(-2) = 0$
$2 + 2x - 14 = 0$
$2x = 12$
$x = +6$

A127

The oxidation number of Fe in $Fe(NO_3)_3$ is +3.
In $Fe(NO_3)_3$, the oxidation number of NO_3 is -1, and the compound is neutral, so the sum of the oxidation numbers must equal 0.
Let the oxidation number of Fe be x.
$x + 3(-1) = 0$
$x - 3 = 0$
$x = +3$

A128

Molar mass of $K_2Cr_2O_7$ = 294.2 g/mol
Number of moles required = Molarity x Volume (in liters)
Number of moles = 0.200 M x 0.250 L = 0.0500 mol
Mass = Moles x Molar mass = 0.0500 mol x 294.2 g/mol = 14.71 g

A129

To determine the limiting reactant, calculate the moles of each reactant:
Moles of $Fe(NO_3)_2$ = 0.200 M x 0.025 L = 0.00500 mol
Moles of $K_2Cr_2O_7$ = 0.100 M x 0.050 L = 0.00500 mol
According to the balanced equation, 3 moles of $Fe(NO_3)_2$ react with 2 moles of $K_2Cr_2O_7$.
Moles of $Fe(NO_3)_2$ required = (3/2) x Moles of $K_2Cr_2O_7$ = 3/2 x 0.00500 mol = 0.00750 mol
Since only 0.00500 mol of $Fe(NO_3)_2$ is available, $Fe(NO_3)_2$ is the limiting reactant.

A130

$3\ Fe^{2+}(aq) + 2\ Cr_2O_7^{2-}(aq) + 16\ H^+(aq) \rightarrow 3\ Fe^{3+}(aq) + 2\ Cr^{3+}(aq) + 7\ H_2O(l)$

Topic _5
Kinetics

Exam Weighting : 7-9%

Topic 5 Key Point Review

Rate law
- Expresses the relationship between the rate of a chemical reaction and the concentration of the reactants.
$$\text{Rate} = k[A]^m[B]^n$$
(n, m = determined by experiments)
- The overall order of the reaction is the sum of the exponents m + n.

Collision theory
- Reactants must collide with enough energy (activation energy) to react.
- Collisions must occur with the correct orientation.
- Increasing temperature or concentration increases the number of effective collisions, thus increasing the reaction rate.

Integrated rate law
- Describes how the concentration of reactants changes over time.
- Zero order
  - $[A] = -kt + [A]_0$
  - Plot of [A] vs. time is linear
- First order
  - $\ln[A] = -kt + \ln[A]_0$
  - Plot of ln[A] vs. time is linear
  - constant half life = $\ln 2 / k$
- Second order
  - $\frac{1}{[A]} = kt + \frac{1}{[A]_0}$
  - Plot of 1/[A] vs. time is linear

Mechanism
- The series of elementary steps that describe how a chemical reaction occurs at the molecular level.
- The slowest step in the mechanism is the rate-determining step.
- Coefficients of reactants in the rate-determining step often determine the order of the reaction (for elementary steps only).
- The overall reaction's rate law can often be derived from the rate-determining step.
- Intermediates are species that are formed in one step and consumed in another, and catalysts are used and regenerated during the reaction.

True/False Questions

Read the following statements carefully and determine whether each one is true or false. Place a tick (✔) in the appropriate box. If the statement is false, correct the incorrect part of the statement.

	Statement	True	False
Q136	The rate of a reaction generally increases as the concentration of reactants increases because higher concentrations of reactants lead to an increased number of molecules in a given volume, which raises the likelihood of collisions and thus increases the reaction rate.		
Q137	Increasing the temperature of a reaction always increases the reaction rate because the activation energy is lowered, allowing more molecules to react.		
Q138	A catalyst speeds up a reaction by lowering the activation energy, which provides an alternative reaction pathway with a lower energy requirement.		
Q139	In a reaction where the rate law is Rate=$k[A]^2[B]$, the reaction is second order with respect to [A] so that the second order overall because the exponents in the rate law indicate the reaction order.		
Q140	The half-life of a first-order reaction is constant and does not depend on the initial concentration of the reactant because the rate of a first-order reaction is directly proportional to the concentration of one reactant.		
Q141	The rate-determining step in a reaction mechanism is the fastest step because it involves the highest energy transition state, which controls the overall reaction rate.		
Q142	According to collision theory, for a reaction to occur, reactant molecules must collide with sufficient energy and the correct orientation because only effective collisions can lead to product formation.		
Q143	The order of a reaction can be determined by analyzing graphs of concentration versus time, and the corresponding straight line will indicate whether the reaction is zero-order, first-order, or second-order because different reaction orders produce different graphical relationships.		
Q144	In an elementary reaction, the order of the reaction is equal to the stoichiometric coefficient of the reactant in the balanced chemical equation.		
Q145	According to collision theory, for a reaction to occur, reactant molecules must collide with sufficient energy, and the orientation of the molecules during the collision is not important because any collision with enough energy will lead to a successful reaction.		

Concept Check Questions

When solving Free-Response Questions (FRQs), it is essential to clearly and accurately explain your reasoning. Make sure to outline the steps in your solution process thoroughly, showing all calculations with appropriate numbers and units. This demonstrates a full understanding of the problem and ensures that your answer is both correct and complete.

Q146
Explain how increasing the temperature affects the rate of a chemical reaction, considering the concept of activation energy and the distribution of molecular kinetic energy.

Q147
Consider the following elementary reaction: $A_2 + B_2 \rightarrow 2\ AB$. Using the principles of collision theory, explain why not every collision between A_2 and B_2 molecules leads to the formation of AB molecules. What factors must be met for a successful reaction to occur, and how do these factors relate to the concepts of sufficient energy and proper orientation?

Q148
Consider a reaction between a solid reactant and a liquid reactant. Describe how the rate of this reaction would be affected by the following factors, and explain why each factor influences the reaction rate:
- Surface Area of the solid reactant
- Temperature of the reaction mixture

Q149
You are studying the reaction 2A+B→C and have conducted a series of experiments to determine the rate law.
The following data were collected at a constant temperature:

Experiment	[A] (M)	[B] (M)	Initial rate (M/s)
1	0.10	0.10	1.0×10^{-3}
2	0.20	0.10	4.0×10^{-3}
3	0.10	0.20	1.0×10^{-3}

Based on this data:
(a) Determine the order of the reaction with respect to A and B.

(b) Write the experimental rate law for the reaction.

(c) Calculate the rate constant k using the data from any one experiment.

Q150
You are given an unknown reaction A →products and need to determine the rate law. Describe the steps you would take to determine the order of the reaction using graphical methods. What graphs would you plot, and how would you interpret the results to identify whether the reaction is zero-order, first-order, or second-order with respect to A?

Q151
Explain why increasing the temperature of a reaction generally leads to a faster reaction rate. Provide two distinct reasons based on chemical kinetics and collision theory.

Q152
Explain how a catalyst increases the rate of a chemical reaction. Your answer should include an explanation based on the Maxwell-Boltzmann distribution and the concept of an alternative pathway with lower activation energy.

Q153
Explain how the rate law differs between an elementary reaction and a complex reaction. Why can you directly use stoichiometric coefficients in an elementary reaction to determine the reaction order, but not in a complex reaction?

Q154

How does an increase in pressure affect the rate of a reaction involving gaseous reactants? Consider a reaction where the number of moles of gas changes during the reaction.

Q155

Consider a reaction

$$A + B \rightarrow \text{products}.$$

Explain how changing the concentration of reactant A while keeping the concentration of B constant affects the reaction rate. Assume the reaction is first-order with respect to A and zero-order with respect to B.

Multiple Choice Questions

The following questions are multiple-choice.
Choose the correct answer and explain why the other options are incorrect.

Q156
The decomposition of hydrogen peroxide (H_2O_2) in aqueous solution is catalyzed by iodide ion (I^-). The reaction is represented by the following balanced equation:

$$2\ H_2O_2\ (aq) + I^-(aq) \rightarrow 2\ H_2O(l) + O_2(g) + I^-\ (aq)$$

The following data were collected for the reaction at a certain temperature.

Experiment	[H_2O_2] (M)	[I^-] (M)	Initial rate (M/s)
1	0.010	0.010	2.5×10^{-6}
2	0.020	0.010	5.0×10^{-6}
3	0.020	0.020	1.0×10^{-5}

Based on the data, what is the rate law for this reaction?

A) Rate = $k[H_2O_2][I^-]$
B) Rate = $k[H_2O_2]^2[I^-]$
C) Rate = $k[H_2O_2][I^-]^2$
D) Rate = $k[H_2O_2][I^-]^2$

Q157
The following data were obtained for the reaction of nitrogen dioxide (NO_2) and carbon monoxide (CO):

$$NO_2\ (g) + CO\ (g) \rightarrow NO\ (g) + CO_2\ (g)$$

Experiment	[NO_2] (M)	[CO] (M)	Initial rate (M/s)
1	0.100	0.100	1.3×10^{-4}
2	0.200	0.100	5.2×10^{-4}
3	0.100	0.200	1.3×10^{-4}

What is the order of the reaction with respect to NO_2?

A) Zero
B) First
C) Second
D) Third

Q158
The reaction A → B follows first-order kinetics. A plot of ln[A] versus time gives a straight line with a slope of - 0.358 s^{-1}.
What is the half-life of the reaction?

A) 0.693 s
B) 1.00 s
C) 1.44 s
D) 1.94 s

Q159
For the reaction 2A + B → C, the rate law is found to be:

$$\text{Rate} = k[A]^2[B]$$

If the concentration of A is doubled and the concentration of B is halved, how does the rate of the reaction change?

A) The rate remains the same.
B) The rate is halved.
C) The rate is doubled.
D) The rate is quadrupled.

Q160
A reaction has the following rate law:

$$\text{Rate} = k[NO]^2[O_2]$$

If the rate constant k is 2.5×10^{-3} M^{-2}s^{-1}, and the concentrations of NO and O_2 are 0.030 M and 0.020 M, respectively, what is the initial rate of the reaction?

A) 1.5×10^{-7} M/s
B) 4.5×10^{-7} M/s
C) 7.5×10^{-7} M/s
D) 1.2×10^{-6} M/s

Q161
The decomposition of ozone (O_3) is believed to occur via the following mechanism:

$$\text{Step 1}: O_3 \rightarrow O_2 + O \quad \text{(slow)}$$
$$\text{Step 2}: O + O_3 \rightarrow 2\,O_2 \quad \text{(fast)}$$

What is the rate law for the decomposition of ozone based on this mechanism?

A) Rate = $k[O_3]^2$
B) Rate = $k[O_3]$
C) Rate = $k[O]$
D) Rate = $k[O_2]$

Q162
The following reaction mechanism is proposed for the formation of hydrogen iodide (HI) from hydrogen and iodine:

$$\text{Step 1}: N_2O \rightleftharpoons N_2 + O \quad \text{(fast equilibrium)}$$
$$\text{Step 2}: O + N_2O \rightarrow N_2 + O_2 \quad \text{(slow)}$$

What is the rate law for the overall reaction according to this mechanism?

A) Rate = $k[N_2O]^2[O]$
B) Rate = $k[N_2O]^2[N_2]^{-1}$
C) Rate = $k[N_2O]^{1/2}[O]^{3/2}$
D) Rate = $k[N_2]$

Q163

The reaction between nitrogen monoxide (NO) and chlorine (Cl_2) is proposed to occur via the following mechanism:

$$\text{Step 1: } NO + Cl_2 \rightarrow NOCl_2 \quad \text{(fast)}$$
$$\text{Step 2: } NOCl_2 + NO \rightarrow 2\, NOCl \quad \text{(slow)}$$

What is the overall rate law for this reaction based on the proposed mechanism?

A) Rate = $k[NO][Cl_2]$
B) Rate = $k[NOCl_2]$
C) Rate = $k[NO]^2[Cl_2]$
D) Rate = $k[NOCl]^2$

Q164

In the reaction between nitrogen monoxide (NO) and ozone (O_3), the following mechanism is proposed:

$$NO + O_3 \rightarrow NO_2 + O$$

Which of the following statements best describes why not every collision between NO and O_3 results in a reaction?

A) Not all collisions have sufficient energy to overcome the activation energy.
B) The molecules must collide with a specific orientation for the reaction to occur.
C) Only collisions that meet both the energy and orientation requirements will lead to a reaction.
D) The reaction does not depend on either energy or orientation.

Q165
Which of the following best explains why a catalyst increases the rate of a chemical reaction according to collision theory?

A) A catalyst increases the frequency of collisions between reactant molecules.
B) A catalyst lowers the activation energy, so more collisions have sufficient energy to result in a reaction.
C) A catalyst ensures that all collisions occur with the proper orientation.
D) A catalyst increases the energy of the reactant molecules, making all collisions successful.

Worked solution with answer for Topic 5

	Statement	True	False
A136	The rate of a reaction generally increases as the concentration of reactants increases because higher concentrations of reactants lead to an increased number of molecules in a given volume, which raises the likelihood of collisions and thus increases the reaction rate.	v	
A137	Increasing the temperature of a reaction always increases the reaction rate because ~~the activation energy is lowered, allowing more molecules to react~~ **it increases the average kinetic energy of the molecules, allowing more molecules to have sufficient energy to overcome the activation energy.**		v
A138	A catalyst speeds up a reaction by lowering the activation energy, which provides an alternative reaction pathway with a lower energy requirement.	v	
A139	In a reaction where the rate law is Rate=k[A]^2[B], the reaction is second order with respect to [A] so that the ~~second~~ **third** order overall because the exponents in the rate law indicate the reaction order.		v
A140	The half-life of a first-order reaction is constant and does not depend on the initial concentration of the reactant because the rate of a first-order reaction is directly proportional to the concentration of one reactant.	v	
A141	The rate-determining step in a reaction mechanism is the ~~fastest~~ **slowest** step because it involves the highest energy transition state, which controls the overall reaction rate.		v
A142	According to collision theory, for a reaction to occur, reactant molecules must collide with sufficient energy and the correct orientation because only effective collisions can lead to product formation.	v	
A143	The order of a reaction can be determined by analyzing graphs of concentration versus time, and the corresponding straight line will indicate whether the reaction is zero-order, first-order, or second-order because different reaction orders produce different graphical relationships.	v	
A144	In an elementary reaction, the order of the reaction is equal to the stoichiometric coefficient of the reactant in the balanced chemical equation.	v	
A145	According to collision theory, for a reaction to occur, reactant molecules must collide with sufficient energy **and the correct orientation,** ~~and the orientation of the molecules during the collision is not important because any collision with enough energy will lead to a successful reaction.~~ **because only collisions with the correct orientation and sufficient energy will lead to a successful reaction.**		v

A146
Increasing the temperature increases the average kinetic energy of the molecules, which means greater proportion of molecules have energy greater than the activation energy. This results in more frequent and effective collisions, thereby increasing the reaction rate.

A147
Not every collision between A_2 and B_2 molecules leads to the formation of AB molecules because, according to collision theory, two key conditions must be satisfied for a successful reaction:

Sufficient Energy: The colliding molecules must have enough kinetic energy to overcome the activation energy barrier of the reaction. If the molecules do not possess enough energy, they will not be able to break the bonds within A_2 and B_2 to form the new AB bonds.

Proper Orientation: The molecules must collide with the correct orientation, meaning that the reactive parts of the molecules (i.e., the atoms that need to bond) must align correctly during the collision. For A_2 and B_2, this means that the bond between the A and B atoms must be able to form, which requires a specific geometric arrangement during the collision.

A148
Surface Area:
Increasing the surface area of the solid reactant (e.g., by grinding it into a fine powder) increases the rate of the reaction. This is because a larger surface area allows more reactant particles to be exposed to the liquid reactant, leading to more frequent collisions between the reactants. The increased number of effective collisions per unit time results in a higher reaction rate.

Temperature:
Increasing the temperature of the reaction mixture increases the rate of the reaction. Higher temperatures provide reactant molecules with more kinetic energy, which means that a greater proportion of the molecules will have enough energy to overcome the activation energy barrier. Additionally, higher temperatures increase the frequency of collisions between reactant molecules, both of which contribute to a faster reaction rate.

A149
(a)
Order of Reaction with Respect to A:
Compare experiments 1 and 2, where the concentration of B is constant, but the concentration of A is doubled.
The rate increases by a factor of 4 when [A] is doubled
Therefore, the reaction is second order with respect to A.
Order of Reaction with Respect to BB:
Compare experiments 1 and 3, where the concentration of A is constant, but the concentration of B is doubled.
The rate does not change when [B] is doubled.
Therefore, the reaction is zero order with respect to B.

(b) Experimental Rate Law:
Rate=$k[A]^2$

(c) Calculation of Rate Constant k

1.0×10^{-3} M/s = k(0.10 M)^2

k = $\frac{1.0 \times 10^{-3} \text{ M/s}}{(0.10 \text{ M})^2}$ = 0.10 M^{-1} s^{-1}

A150

To determine the order of the reaction using graphical methods, follow these steps:
Collect Data:
Measure the concentration of reactant A at different times as the reaction proceeds.
Record the concentration of A at regular intervals to generate data for [A] versus time.

Plot Three Different Graphs:
Zero-Order Test
- Plot [A] (concentration of A) versus time.
- If the plot of [A] versus time is a straight line with a negative slope, the reaction is zero-order with respect to A.

First-Order Test
- Plot ln[A] (natural logarithm of [A]) versus time.
- If the plot of ln[A] versus time is a straight line with a negative slope, the reaction is first-order with respect to A.
- If the plot shows constant half life, this indicates that the reaction is first-order with respect to A. ($t_{1/2}$ = 0.693/k)

Second-Order Test
- Plot 1/[A] (inverse of [A]) versus time.
- If the plot of 1/[A] versus time is a straight line with a positive slope, the reaction is second-order with respect to A.

A151

Increased Kinetic Energy of Molecules
As the temperature increases, the average kinetic energy of the reactant molecules also increases. This means that a greater proportion of the molecules move faster and with greater average kinetic energy. According to collision theory, for a reaction to occur, molecules must collide with sufficient energy to overcome the activation energy barrier. At higher temperatures, more molecules have enough energy to surpass this barrier, leading to a higher frequency of effective collisions and thus a faster reaction rate.

More Frequent Collisions
Higher temperatures result in an increased frequency of collisions between reactant molecules. When the molecules move faster (due to higher kinetic energy), they collide more often in a given time period. Although not every collision results in a reaction, the increased number of collisions raises the overall chance of successful collisions that lead to product formation, thereby increasing the reaction rate.

A152

A catalyst increases the rate of a reaction by shifting the Maxwell-Boltzmann distribution so that a greater number of molecules have the necessary energy to react, and providing an alternative pathway with a lower activation energy, which makes it easier for more reactant molecules to convert into products.

A153

Elementary Reaction: In an elementary reaction, the rate law can be directly written from the balanced chemical equation because the reaction occurs in a single step. The stoichiometric coefficients of the reactants in the balanced equation directly correspond to the reaction orders in the rate law.

Complex Reaction: In a complex reaction, the overall reaction consists of multiple steps. The rate law for the overall reaction must be determined experimentally because it depends on the rate-determining step, which may not reflect the stoichiometric coefficients of the overall balanced equation.

A154

Increasing the pressure in a system with gaseous reactants generally increases the reaction rate, particularly when the reaction involves a decrease in the number of moles of gas (example : 2 A→B). Higher pressure increases the concentration of gaseous molecules, leading to more frequent collisions and a faster reaction rate.

A155

Effect of Concentration of A:
Since the reaction is first-order with respect to A, the reaction rate is directly proportional to the concentration of A. This means that if the concentration of A is increased, the reaction rate will also increase proportionally. For example, doubling the concentration of A will double the reaction rate.

Effect of Concentration of B:
Since the reaction is zero-order with respect to B, changes in the concentration of B do not affect the reaction rate. The reaction rate is independent of the concentration of B.
Doubling the concentration of A doubles the reaction rate because the reaction is first-order with respect to A. The reaction rate does not change with the concentration of B since it is zero-order with respect to B.

Therefore, the overall reaction rate becomes 2 times the original rate when the concentration of is doubled, regardless of any change in the concentration of B.

A156 (A)

From the data, when the concentration of $[H_2O_2]$ is doubled while $[I^-]$ remains constant, the rate doubles. This indicates a first-order reaction with respect to $[H_2O_2]$. Similarly, when $[I^-]$ is doubled while $[H_2O_2]$ is constant, the rate also doubles, indicating first-order with respect to $[I^-]$. Therefore, the rate law is Rate = $k[H_2O_2][I^-]$.

A157 (C)

When $[NO_2]$ is doubled (from experiment 1 to 2), the rate increases by a factor of 4, indicating that the reaction is second-order with respect to NO_2.

A158 (B)

For a first-order reaction, the half-life ($t_{1/2}$) is related to the rate constant k by $t_{1/2} = 0.693 / k$. Given that the slope (k) is 0.358 s^{-1}, the half-life is 1.94 s.

A159 (C)
The rate law is Rate = $k[A]^2[B]$. Doubling [A] increases the rate by a factor of 4, and halving [B] decreases the rate by a factor of 2. Therefore, the overall rate is doubled.

A160 (B)
Using the rate law Rate = $k[NO]^2[O_2]$, and substituting the given values:
Rate = $(2.5 \times 10^{-3} \text{ M}^{-2}\text{s}^{-1}) * (0.030 \text{ M})^2 * (0.020 \text{ M}) = 4.5 \times 10^{-7}$ M/s.

A161 (B)
Since the first step is the slow, rate-determining step, the rate law is determined by the concentration of O_3, so Rate = $k[O_3]$.

A162 (B)
Second step is RDS → Rate = $k[O][N_2O]$
Since O is an intermediate, it should not be in overall rate law.
Use fast equilibrium first reaction, rate = $kf[N_2O] = kr [N_2][O]$
$[O] = k1 [N_2O]/ [N_2]$ (when $k1 = kf / kr$)
Insert [O] to overall rate law, rate = $k \cdot k1[N_2O] [N_2O]/ [N_2]$
= $k [N_2O]^2 [N_2]^{-1}$

A163 (C)
The rate-determining step involves $NOCl_2$ and NO, but since $NOCl_2$ is formed from NO and Cl_2, the rate law is Rate = $k[NO]_2[Cl_2]$.

A164 (C)
According to collision theory, both sufficient energy and proper orientation are necessary for a successful reaction

A165 (B)
Catalysts lower the activation energy, allowing more molecules to have sufficient energy to overcome the activation barrier, thus increasing the reaction rate.

Topic _6
Thermochemistry

Exam Weighting : 7-9%

Topic 6 Key Point Review

Exothermic reaction
- A reaction that releases energy in the form of heat.
- $\Delta H < 0$ (negative enthalpy change).
- Products have lower energy than reactants.
- Temperature increases.
- Required energy for bond breaking < Released energy for bond making

Endothermic reaction
- A reaction that absorbs energy from the surroundings.
- $\Delta H > 0$ (positive enthalpy change).
- Products have higher energy than reactants.
- Temperature decreases.
- Required energy for bond breaking > Released energy for bond making

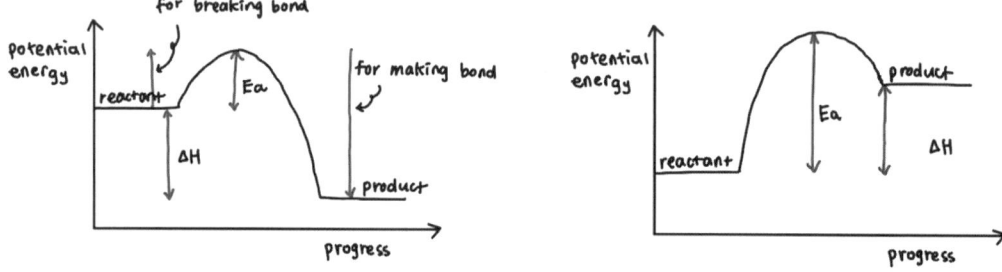

Calorimeter
A device used to measure the heat change (ΔH) during a chemical or physical process.
$q = c\, m\, \Delta T$

Hess's law
The total enthalpy change of a reaction is the same regardless of the path taken, as long as the initial and final states are the same.
$\Delta H = \Delta H_1 + \Delta H_2$

Enthalpy change calculation
$\Delta H° = \Sigma\, \Delta H°_f(\text{products}) - \Sigma\, \Delta H°_f(\text{reactants})$
$= \Sigma\, \text{Bond Energy (broken)} - \Sigma\, \text{Bond Energy (formed)}$
$= -q / \text{mol}_{rxn}$

Entropy change
$\Delta S° = \Sigma S°(\text{products}) - \Sigma S°(\text{reactants})$
- $\Delta S° < 0$: Decrease in entropy (less disorder)
- $\Delta S° > 0$: Increase in entropy (more disorder)

Gibbs free energy change
$\Delta G° = \Sigma G°_f(\text{products}) - \Sigma G°_f(\text{reactants})$
$= -RT \ln K_{eq}$
$= -nFE°_{Cell}$
- $\Delta G° < 0$: Reaction is spontaneous
- $\Delta G° > 0$: Reaction is non-spontaneous
- $\Delta G° = 0$: System is at equilibrium

True/False Questions

Read the following statements carefully and determine whether each one is true or false. Place a tick (✓) in the appropriate box. If the statement is false, correct the incorrect part of the statement.

	Statement	True	False
Q166	In an exothermic reaction, the system releases energy in the form of heat, which increases the temperature of the surroundings, and the enthalpy change (ΔH) for the reaction is always negative. This type of reaction is spontaneous under all conditions.		
Q167	Endothermic processes, such as the melting of ice, involve the absorption of energy from the surroundings, which leads to a decrease in temperature of the surroundings. The enthalpy change (ΔH) is positive, and these processes are non-spontaneous at low temperatures but can become spontaneous at high temperatures due to the influence of entropy (ΔS).		
Q168	When a solution forms, if the energy required to break solute-solute and solvent-solvent bonds is greater than the energy released from solute-solvent interactions, the overall process is endothermic. However, if solute-solvent interactions are much stronger, the solution formation becomes exothermic.		
Q169	During a phase change, such as vaporization, the temperature of the substance remains constant as the system absorbs energy. This energy only contributes to overcoming intermolecular forces rather than increasing kinetic energy.		
Q170	Calorimetry is a technique used to measure the heat absorbed or released during a chemical or physical process.		
Q171	On a heating curve, the slope of the graph is inversely proportional to the specific heat capacity of the substance. Therefore, a steeper slope indicates a lower specific heat capacity, meaning less energy is required to raise the temperature by 1°C per unit mass.		
Q172	The standard enthalpy change of a reaction refers to the enthalpy change when all reactants and products are in their standard states (1 atm pressure and 298 K temperature) and 1 mole of the substance is involved, regardless of the state of matter or physical conditions of the reaction.		

Q173	The standard enthalpy change of combustion is defined as the enthalpy change when one mole of a substance undergoes complete combustion in oxygen under standard conditions, with all reactants and products in their standard states. This process always releases energy, meaning the enthalpy change is negative.		
Q174	The heat of formation of a compound is defined as the energy change when 1 mole of a compound is formed from its constituent elements in their standard states under standard conditions. For elements in their standard states, the enthalpy of formation is always zero.		
Q175	Bond enthalpy represents the energy required to break one mole of bonds in the gas phase. Bond breaking is always an endothermic process, requiring energy input, while bond formation is exothermic and releases energy.		
Q176	Hess's Law states that the total enthalpy change for a reaction is independent of the pathway taken, meaning it can be calculated by summing the enthalpy changes of individual steps. However, if you reverse a reaction, the enthalpy change must also be reversed in sign, but it does not need to be scaled if the coefficients change.		
Q177	Entropy increases when a substance changes from solid to liquid, or from liquid to gas, because the particles in the gas phase have the greatest degree of freedom and randomness.		
Q178	Gibbs free energy (ΔG) is a thermodynamic potential that can predict the spontaneity of a process. If ΔG is negative, the process is spontaneous under the given conditions, while if ΔG is positive, the process is non-spontaneous. When ΔG is zero, the system is at equilibrium.		
Q179	A process can become spontaneous at high temperatures if the enthalpy change (ΔH) is positive, and the entropy change (ΔS) is also positive. This is because the temperature-dependent term, $-T\Delta S$, will eventually dominate and make Gibbs free energy negative.		
Q180	When both the enthalpy change (ΔH) and entropy change (ΔS) are negative, the process is spontaneous at all temperatures because the decreasing entropy is always outweighed by the release of energy as heat.		

Concept Check Questions

When solving Free-Response Questions (FRQs), it is essential to explain your reasoning clearly and accurately. Make sure to outline the steps in your solution process thoroughly, showing all calculations with appropriate numbers and units. This demonstrates a full understanding of the problem and ensures that your answer is both correct and complete.

Q181

A chemical reaction is classified as exothermic.

(a)
Explain what it means for a reaction to be exothermic and describe the energy flow between the system and the surroundings.

(b)
Using a diagram, explain the difference in potential energy between the reactants and the products in an exothermic reaction. Indicate whether the potential energy of the products is higher or lower than that of the reactants.

(c)
Describe how the temperature of the surroundings changes as a result of an exothermic reaction. Explain why this temperature change occurs in terms of energy transfer.

Q182

A chemical reaction is classified as endothermic.

(a)
Explain what it means for a reaction to be endothermic, and describe the energy flow between the system and the surroundings.

(b)
Using a diagram, explain the difference in potential energy between the reactants and the products in an endothermic reaction. Indicate whether the potential energy of the products is higher or lower than that of the reactants.

(c)
Describe how the temperature of the surroundings changes as a result of an endothermic reaction. Explain why this temperature change occurs in terms of energy transfer.

Q183

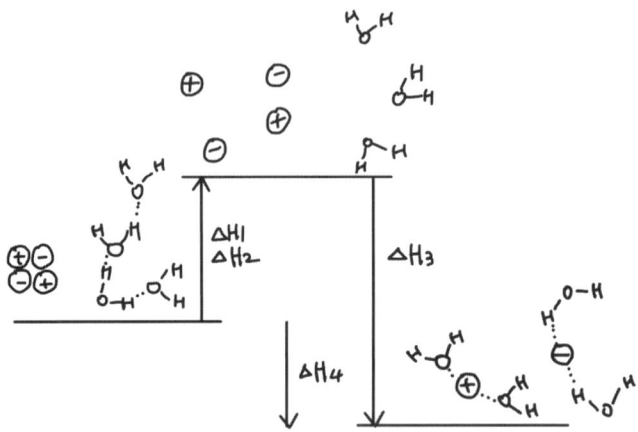

ΔH1	Enthalpy change for bond breaking in ionic compound
ΔH2	Enthalpy change for bond breaking in water solvent
ΔH3	Enthalpy change for ion-dipole bond forming
ΔH4	Overall enthalpy change in solution making process

Consider a solution process that is overall exothermic as depicted in the diagram provided.

(a)
Explain why the solution process is classified as overall exothermic despite involving both endothermic and exothermic steps.

(b)
Describe the significance of ΔH1, ΔH2, and ΔH3 in the diagram. Explain how the relationship between these enthalpy changes results in an overall exothermic reaction.

Q184

A piece of iron metal at 100°C is placed in contact with water at 25°C. Describe the process through which the metal and water reach thermal equilibrium, focusing on the particle-level interactions.

(a)
Explain thermal equilibrium in the context of this scenario.

(b)
Describe the initial state of the particles in the iron metal and the water before they are brought into contact.

(c)
Explain the energy transfer process from the iron to the water, including details about how the kinetic energy of the particles changes.

(d)
Justify what happens at the particle level as the iron and water approach thermal equilibrium.

Q185
Consider a piece of aluminum (specific heat capacity= 0.89 J/g°C) and an equal mass of water (specific heat capacity = 4.18 J/g°C), each initially at the same temperature. Both substances are subjected to the same amount of heat energy.
Predict the temperature change in both aluminum and water after the same amount of heat is applied, based on their specific heats.

Q186
You place 150. g of water into a foam-cup calorimeter and find that its initial temperature is 24.50°C. You then heat a 60.0 g sample of an unknown metal to 120.0°C and put the metal into the water. Heat flows from the hot metal to the cooler water, and the temperature of the water rises. After a while, the temperature in the calorimeter stabilizes at 28.70°C, which is the final temperature for both the water and the metal. (The specific heat of water is 4.18 J/g°C.)
Calculate the specific heat of the unknown metal.

Q187

A 120.0 g sample of a different metal at 82.0°C is added to 250.0 g of water at 23.0°C. The temperature of the water rises to 25.5°C. Calculate the specific heat capacity of the metal, assuming that all the heat lost by the metal is gained by the water.
(The specific heat of water is 4.18 J/g°C.)

Q188

In a coffee-cup calorimeter, 150.0 mL of 1.5 M KOH and 150.0 mL of 1.5 M HNO_3 are mixed. Both solutions were initially at 25.0°C. After the reaction, the final temperature rises to 32.0°C. Assuming that the solutions have a density of 1.0 g/cm³ and a specific heat capacity of 4.18 J/°C·g, calculate the enthalpy change for the neutralization of HNO_3 by KOH.
Assume no heat is lost to the surroundings or the calorimeter.
(1 cm³ = 1 mL)

Q189

In a coffee-cup calorimeter, 60.0 mL of 0.150 M NaCl and 60.0 mL of 0.150 M Pb(NO$_3$)$_2$ are mixed to yield the following reaction.

$$Pb(NO_3)_2 \,(aq) + 2\,NaCl\,(aq) \rightarrow PbCl_2(s) + 2\,NaNO_3(aq)$$

The two solutions were initially at 21.50°C, and the final temperature is 22.30°C.
Calculate the enthalpy of this reaction in kJ/mol$_{rxn}$. Assume that the combined solution has a mass of 120.0 g and a specific heat capacity of 4.18 J/g°C.

Q190

In a coffee-cup calorimeter, 100. mL of 0.200 M Al(NO$_3$)$_3$ and 75.0 mL of 0.300 M Na$_2$SO$_4$ are mixed to yield the following reaction:

$$2\,Al(NO_3)_3 \,(aq) + 3\,Na_2SO_4\,(aq) \rightarrow Al_2(SO_4)_3\,(s) + 6\,NaNO_3\,(aq)$$

The two solutions were initially at 21.00°C, and the final temperature is 24.50°C.
Calculate enthalpy of this reaction in kJ/mol$_{rxn}$. Assume that the combined solution has a mass of 150.0 g and a specific heat capacity of 4.18 J/g°C.

Q191

A coffee-cup calorimeter initially contains 150.0 g of water at 24.5°C. Sodium chloride (12.0 g), also at 24.5°C, is added to the water, and after the NaCl dissolves, the final temperature is 19.8°C.
Calculate the enthalpy change for dissolving the salt in J/g and kJ/mol.
Assume that the specific heat capacity of the solution is 4.18 J/°C·g and that no heat is transferred to the surroundings or the calorimeter.
Molar mass of NaCl (Mr) = 58.44 g/mol

Q192

A coffee-cup calorimeter initially contains 180 g of water at 23.0°C. Calcium chloride ($CaCl_2$) weighing 15.0 g, also at 23.0°C, is added to the water, and after the $CaCl_2$ dissolves, the final temperature rises to 27.8°C.
Calculate the enthalpy change for dissolving the salt in J/g and kJ/mol.
Assume that the specific heat capacity of the solution is 4.18 J/°C·g and that no heat is transferred to the surroundings or the calorimeter.
Molar mass of $CaCl_2$ (Mr) = 110.98 g/mol

Q193
Consider the dissolution of KI:

$$KI\,(s) \rightarrow K^+(aq) + I^-(aq) \qquad \Delta H = -58.9 \text{ kJ/mol}$$

A 25.0 g sample of KI is dissolved in 150 g of water, with both substances at 25.0°C.
Calculate the final temperature of the solution assuming no heat loss to the surroundings and assuming the solution has a specific heat capacity of 4.18 J/°C·g.
Molar mass of KI (Mr) = 166.00 g/mol

Q194
Copper metal can be recycled from scrap metal by melting the metal to evaporate impurities. Calculate the amount of heat needed to purify 1.00 mole of Cu originally at 298 K by melting it. The melting point of Cu is 1356 K. The molar heat capacity of Cu is 25 J/(mol·K), and the heat of fusion of Cu is 13.0 kJ/mol.

Q195

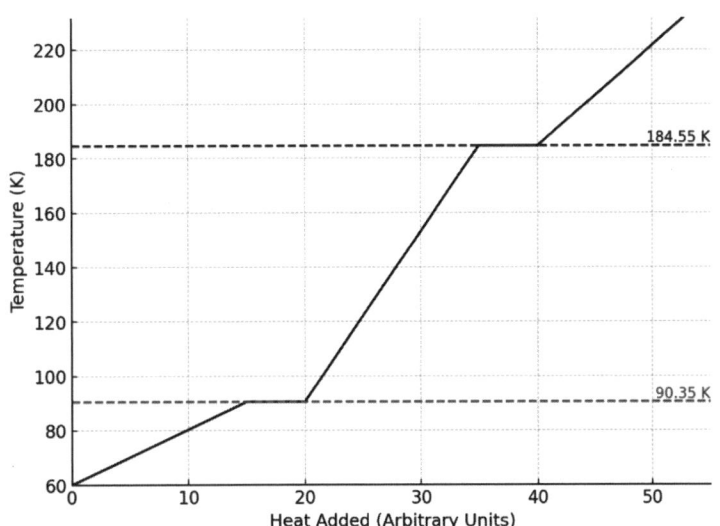

Ethane undergoes various phase transitions when heat is added at different temperatures. Answer the following questions based on the provided heating curve for ethane.

(a)
Calculate the amount of energy required to melt 25g of ethane at 90.35 K.
(The molar mass of ethane is 30.07 g/mol, and the heat of fusion of ethane is 2.44 kJ/mol.)

(b)
Explain why more energy is required to vaporize ethane at 184.55 K compared to melting it at 90.35 K. In your explanation, describe the differences in the energy changes associated with phase transitions such as melting and vaporization, and how intermolecular forces play a role in these processes.

Q196

A student is tasked with determining the mass of propane, $C_3H_8(g)$, required to heat a 2000. g beaker of water from 25.0°C to 100.0°C using the setup shown below.

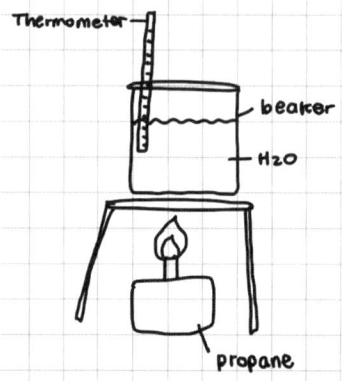

(a)
Calculate the amount of heat energy needed to raise the temperature of the beaker of water by 75°C. Assume that all the heat energy from the burner is transferred to the beaker of water and that the specific heat capacity of water is 4.18 J/(g·°C).

(b)
The student runs the experiment and collects the data shown in the table below:

Description	Data
Mass of beaker and water	2000. g
Mass of propane burner before combustion	250.00 g
Mass of propane burner after combustion	242.50 g
Initial temperature of the water	25.0 °C
Final temperature of the water	100.0 °C

Calculate the number of moles of propane that was used in the experiment.
Report your answer to the appropriate number of significant figures.

Q197

Propanol (C_3H_7OH) is burned in oxygen according to the following chemical equation:

$$2\ C_3H_7OH\ (g) + 9\ O_2\ (g) \rightarrow 6\ CO_2\ (g) + 8\ H_2O\ (g)$$

The heat from the combustion reaction is directed into a container of water. Data from this experiment are shown in the table below.

Description	Data
Mass of beaker and water	75.0 g
Initial temperature of the water	22.0 °C
Final temperature of the water	65.0 °C
Initial mass of burner with propanol	135.0 g
Final mass of burner with propanol	132.0 g

Calculate the enthalpy of combustion for propanol based on the data provided. Assume that all the heat energy from the burner is transferred to the beaker of water and that the specific heat capacity of water is 4.18 J/(g·°C).

Q198

The reaction between zinc metal and hydrochloric acid can be represented by the following equation:

$$Zn(s) + 2\ HCl(aq) \rightarrow ZnCl_2(aq) + H_2(g)$$

Using the information in the table below, calculate the value of $\Delta H°_{rxn}$, the standard enthalpy change for the reaction, in kJ/mol$_{rxn}$.

Substance	Standard heat of formation, $\Delta H°_f$ (kJ/mol)
HCl (aq)	- 167
$ZnCl_2$(aq)	- 415

Q199

The approximate values of the average bond enthalpies, in kJ per mole, for four different bonds are shown in the table below:

Bond	Average bond enthalpy (kJ/mol)
N-H	391
N=N	470
N-N	158
N≡N	945
H-H	436

Using this information, calculate the enthalpy change of the following reactions:

(a)
Reaction 1: $2\ NH_3 \rightarrow 3\ H_2 + N_2$
Calculate the enthalpy change of this reaction.

(b)
Reaction 2: $2\ N_2H_4 \rightarrow 2\ NH_3 + N_2$
Calculate the enthalpy change of this reaction.

Q200

Reaction: $2\ NO_2(g) \rightleftarrows 2\ NO(g) + O_2(g)$ $\Delta H° = -114\ kJ/mol_{rxn}$

The bond enthalpy of the nitrogen-oxygen bond in NO(g) is 607 kJ/mol.
The bond enthalpy of the oxygen-oxygen bond in $O_2(g)$ is 498 kJ/mol.

Based on the enthalpy of the reaction represented above, calculate the average bond enthalpy, in kJ/mol, of a nitrogen-oxygen bond in NO_2.

Q201

Equations	ΔH (kJ/mol)
$2\ O_3(g) \rightarrow 3\ O_2(g)$	−427
$O_2(g) \rightarrow 2\ O(g)$	+495
$NO(g) + O_3(g) \rightarrow NO_2(g) + O_2(g)$	−199

Calculate ΔH for the reaction.
$NO(g) + O(g) \rightarrow NO_2(g)$

Q202
Find the ΔH for the reaction below.

$$4 NH_3 (g) + 5 O_2 (g) \rightarrow 4 NO (g) + 6 H_2O (g)$$

Equations	ΔH (kJ/mol)
$N_2(g) + O_2(g) \rightarrow 2 NO(g)$	+ 180.6
$N_2(g) + 3 H_2(g) \rightarrow 2 NH_3(g)$	− 91.8
$2 H_2(g) + O_2(g) \rightarrow 2 H_2O(g)$	− 483.7

Q203

$$KBr(s) \rightarrow K^+(g) + Br^-(g)$$

Chemical reaction	Type of reaction	ΔH° (kJ/mol)	Endo or Exo
$K(s) + 1/2\ Br_2(g) \rightarrow KBr(s)$	Heat of formation	−395	Exo
$K(s) \rightarrow K(g)$	Heat of sublimation	+89	Endo
$K(g) \rightarrow K^+(g) + e$	First ionization energy	+419	Endo
$Br_2(g) \rightarrow 2Br(g)$	Bond dissociation energy	+190	Endo
$Br(g) + e \rightarrow Br^-(g)$	First electron affinity	−325	Exo

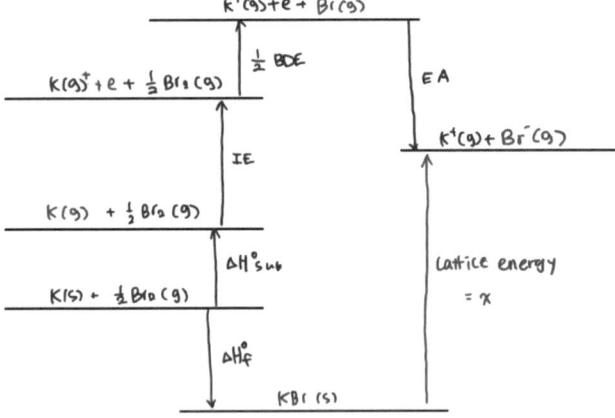

Determine the lattice enthalpy of potassium bromide using the Born-Haber cycle.

Q204

The Born-Haber cycle data of potassium oxide Na_2O is shown below.

Chemical reaction	Type of reaction	ΔH° (kJ/mol)	Endo or Exo
$2Na(s) + 1/2\ O_2(g) \rightarrow Na_2O(s)$	Heat of formation	x	Exo
$Na(s) \rightarrow Na(g)$	Heat of sublimation	+107	Endo
$Na(g) \rightarrow Na^+(g) + e$	First ionization energy	+496	Endo
$O_2(g) \rightarrow 2O(g)$	Bond dissociation energy	+498	Endo
$O(g) + e \rightarrow O^-(g)$	First electron affinity	-141	Exo
$O^-(g) + e \rightarrow O^{2-}(g)$	Second electron affinity	+753	Endo
$Na_2O(s) \rightarrow 2\ Na^+(g) + O^{2-}(g)$	Lattice enthalpy	+2528	Endo

Calculate the heat of formation in kJ/mol.

Q205

Draw Born Haber cycle of MgO.

Q206

Predict the entropy change (ΔS) for the following reactions or processes (increase / decrease / remain the same):

(a)
$2 H_2O_2 (l) \rightarrow 2 H_2O(l) + O_2 (g)$
Entropy Change:

(b)
$4 Fe(s) + 3 O_2 (g) \rightarrow 2 Fe_2O_3(s)$
Entropy Change:

(c)
$C_6H_{12}O_6(s) \rightarrow 6 C(s) + 6 H_2(g) + 3 O_2(g)$
Entropy Change:

(d)
$H_2O(s) \rightarrow H_2O(l)$
Entropy Change:

(e)
$N_2(g) + O_2(g) \rightarrow 2 NO(g)$
Entropy Change:

Q207
The reaction below shows the formation of aluminum oxide from aluminum metal and oxygen gas:

$$4\ Al(s) + 3\ O_2(g) \rightarrow 2\ Al_2O_3(s)$$

Use the data in the table below to determine the standard entropy change, $\Delta S°_{rxn}$, in J/K mol for the reaction.

Substance	Absolute entropy at 298 K (J/K mol)
Al(s)	28.3
$O_2(g)$	205.0
$Al_2O_3(s)$	50.9

Q208
Given the values of ΔH and ΔS, determine whether the following changes will be spontaneous at constant T and P by calculating ΔG (Gibbs free energy).

(a)
ΔH = +25 kJ, ΔS = +50.0 J/K, T = 400 K

(b)
ΔH = +50 kJ, ΔS = +200.0 J/K, T = 500 K

(c)
ΔH = −10 kJ, ΔS = +30.0 J/K, T = 298 K

(d)
ΔH = −15 kJ, ΔS = −70.0 J/K, T = 273 K

Q209

Consider the reaction:

$$2NO_2(g) \rightarrow 2\,NO(g) + O_2(g)$$

(a)

Calculate ΔG° for this reaction.

The $\Delta G°_f$ values for $NO_2(g)$, $NO(g)$, and $O_2(g)$ are +51.3 kJ/mol, +87.6 kJ/mol, and 0 kJ/mol, respectively.

(b)

Is this reaction spontaneous under standard conditions at 298 K?

Q210

Questions (a)-(g) refer to the following combinations of enthalpy changes (ΔH) and entropy changes (ΔS) for chemical reactions.

    I. $\Delta H > 0, \Delta S > 0$
    II. $\Delta H > 0, \Delta S < 0$
    III. $\Delta H < 0, \Delta S > 0$
    IV. $\Delta H < 0, \Delta S < 0$

(a)
Must be true for a reaction that is spontaneous at low temperatures only.

(b)
True for the condensation of water at 100 °C and 1 atm.

(c)
True for the sublimation of carbon dioxide.

(d)
True for the combustion of liquid pentane, $C_5H_{12}(l)$, to form H_2O (g) and CO_2 (g) at 1 atm.

(e)
Must be true for a reaction that is **never** spontaneous, regardless of temperature.

(f)
True for the freezing of liquid water at 0°C and 1 atm.

(g)
Must be true for a reaction that is spontaneous at high temperatures but non-spontaneous at low temperatures.

Multiple Choice Questions

The following questions are multiple-choice.
Choose the correct answer and explain why the other options are incorrect.

Q211
In an experiment to determine the enthalpy of the reaction between monoprotic lactic acid ($C_3H_6O_3$) and barium hydroxide ($Ba(OH)_2$), 150.0 mL of a 0.300 M lactic acid solution is combined with 200.0 mL of a 0.700 M barium hydroxide solution. The initial temperature of both solutions is 25.0°C and the final temperature after mixing in a calorimeter is 28.6°C. Assuming the density of each solution is 1.00 g/mL and the specific heat capacity of the solution is 4.18 J/(g·°C), calculate the molar enthalpy of the reaction (kJ/mol).

A) – 95.0 kJ/mol
B) – 117 kJ/mol
C) – 125 kJ/mol
D) – 150. kJ.mol

Q212
A coffee-cup calorimeter contains 200.0 g of water at 22.0°C. When 8.0 g of potassium nitrate (KNO_3) is dissolved in the water, the final temperature of the solution is 17.5°C. Calculate the enthalpy change for dissolving KNO_3 in J/g and kJ/mol. Assume the specific heat capacity of the solution is 4.18 J/°C·g and no heat is lost to the surroundings or the calorimeter. The molar mass of KNO_3 is 101.10 g/mol.

A) +392 J/g and + 49 kJ/mol
B) -489 J/g and – 49 kJ/mol
C) - 392 J/g and - 49 kJ/mol
D) +489 J/g and + 49 kJ/mol

Q213
In an experiment, 120.0 mL of 0.400 M acetic acid (CH_3COOH) solution is mixed with 180.0 mL of 0.500 M potassium hydroxide (KOH) solution in a calorimeter. The initial temperature of both solutions is 23.0°C, and the final temperature after the neutralization reaction is 29.5°C. Assuming the density of each solution is 1.00 g/mL and the specific heat capacity is 4.18 J/(g·°C), calculate the molar enthalpy of the reaction.

A) – 814 kJ/mol
B) + 814 kJ/mol
C) – 170 kJ/mol
D) + 170 kJ/mol

Q214
A 200 g sample of a gold was heated to 150°C and then quickly transferred to an insulated container holding 150 g of water at 20°C. The temperature of the water increased and reached a final temperature of 30°C. Which of the following can be concluded?

A) The specific heat capacity of gold is higher than that of water, but the metal lost the same amount of thermal energy as the water gained.
B) The specific heat capacity of gold is lower than that of water, but the metal lost the same amount of thermal energy as the water gained.
C) The specific heat capacity of gold is equal to that of water, as the metal lost the same amount of thermal energy as the water gained.
D) No conclusion about the specific heat capacities can be drawn without additional information about the heat capacities.

Q215
Consider the following reaction:

$$2\ C_2H_6(g) + 7\ O_2(g) \rightarrow 4\ CO_2(g) + 6\ H_2O(g)$$

If the standard molar heats of formation of ethane, $C_2H_6(g)$, carbon dioxide, $CO_2(g)$, and gaseous water, $H_2O(g)$, are -85 kJ/mol, -394 kJ/mol, and -242 kJ/mol, respectively, what is the value of $\Delta H°_{298}$ for the reaction represented above?

A) -1,100 kJ/mol
B) -1,560 kJ/mol
C) -2,031 kJ/mol
D) -2,858 kJ/mol

Q216
What is the enthalpy change when 40.0 mL of 0.250 M phosphoric acid reacts with 30.0 mL of 0.500 M sodium hydroxide?

$$H_3PO_4(aq) + 3\ NaOH(aq) \rightarrow Na_3PO_4(aq) + 3\ H_2O(l)$$
$$\Delta H° = -134.5\ kJ/mol_{rxn}$$

A) - 0.450 kJ
B) - 0.673 kJ
C) - 44.8 kJ
D) - 22.4 kJ

Q217

Consider the following reaction:

$$C_4H_9OH(l) + 6\ O_2(g) \rightarrow 4\ CO_2(g) + 5\ H_2O(l) \qquad \Delta H = -2{,}650\ \text{kJ/mol}$$

For the combustion of butanol as described in the above equation, which of the following is true?

I. The reaction releases heat.
II. The enthalpy change would be different if water vapor was produced instead of liquid water.
III. The reaction is not a redox reaction.
IV. The volume of the products is bigger than the volume of the reactants.

A) I, II
B) I, II, IV
C) II, III, IV
D) I, III

Q218

$$Zn(s) + 2\ HCl(aq) \rightarrow ZnCl_2(aq) + H_2(g) \qquad \Delta H°rxn = -120\ \text{kJ/mol}_{rxn}$$

In an experiment, a student places a 5.0 g sample of Zn(s) into 100.0 mL of 1.5 M HCl(aq), where it reacts according to the equation above.
Which of the following shows the limiting reactant and the amount of heat released, q, for the experiment?

	Limiting reactant	q (kJ)
A)	Zn	9.0
B)	Zn	18.0
C)	HCl	9.0
D)	HCl	18.0

Q219

$$3 \text{ Fe(s)} + 4 \text{ H}_2\text{O(l)} \rightarrow \text{Fe}_3\text{O}_4\text{(s)} + 4 \text{ H}_2\text{(g)} \qquad \Delta H°_{rxn} = -160 \text{ kJ/mol}_{rxn}$$

In an experiment, a student places a 16.8 g sample of iron into 150.0 mL of water, where it reacts according to the equation above.

Which of the following shows the limiting reactant and the amount of heat released, q, for the experiment?

	Limiting reactant	q (kJ)
A)	Fe	16.05
B)	Fe	160
C)	H$_2$O	16.05
D)	H$_2$O	160

Q220

$$\text{N}_2\text{H}_4\text{(aq)} \rightarrow \text{N}_2\text{(g)} + 2 \text{ H}_2\text{(g)} \qquad \Delta H° = -990 \text{ kJ/mol}_{rxn}$$

Assume that the bond enthalpies of the nitrogen-hydrogen bonds in H$_2$(g) are not significantly different from those in N$_2$H$_4$(aq). Based on the value of ΔH° of the reaction, which of the following could be the bond enthalpies (in kJ/mol) for the bonds broken and formed in the reaction?

	N-N in N$_2$H$_4$	N≡N in N$_2$	N-H
A)	400	950	390
B)	300	900	400
C)	200	850	410
D)	150	800	420

Q221

The heating curve for a sample of pure water is provided. As a 60.0 g sample of solid water (ice) was heated at a constant rate, the temperature was recorded. In the heating curve, Segment A represents the heating of water vapor, while Segment B represents the heating of liquid water. The slope of Segment A is greater than the slope of Segment B.
(Hint : draw the heating curve by yourself)
Which of the following explains why the slope of Segment A is greater than the slope of Segment B?

A) The heat of vaporization of water is less than the heat of fusion of water.
B) The heat of vaporization of water is greater than the heat of fusion of water.
C) The specific heat capacity of the gaseous water (steam) is less than the specific heat capacity of liquid water.
D) The specific heat capacity of the gaseous water (steam) is greater than the specific heat capacity of liquid water.

Q222

$\Delta G°_{298}$	+ 21 kJ/mol
$\Delta H°_{298}$	+ 20 kJ/mol
$\Delta S°_{298}$	- 5 J/K mol

Under which of the following temperature conditions is the reaction thermodynamically favored?

A) It is only favored at high temperatures.
B) It is only favored at low temperatures.
C) It is favored at all temperatures.
D) It is not favored at any temperature.

Q223
When hydrogen gas is released into the air at room temperature, it does not react with oxygen. However, when a spark is introduced, the hydrogen combusts, producing a visible flame as heat is continuously released. Why is a spark required for this reaction to occur?

A) The reaction has an unfavorable entropy
B) The reaction has an unfavorable enthalpy
C) The reaction is thermodynamically unfavorable
D) The reaction has a high activation energy

Q224
Which of the following processes involve an increase in the entropy of the system?
Select all that apply.

A) Melting of a solid
B) Sublimation
C) Freezing
D) Mixing
E) Separation
F) Boiling

Q225
Consider the reaction:

$$2\ SOCl_2(g) \rightarrow 2\ SO_2(g) + Cl_2(g)$$

(a)
Calculate ΔG° for this reaction. The ΔG°$_f$ values for SOCl$_2$ (g) and SO$_2$ (g) are 340 kJ/mol and 300 kJ/mol, respectively.

(b)
Is this reaction spontaneous under standard conditions at 298 K?

(c)
The value of ΔS° for this reaction is 220 J/Kmol. At what temperatures is this reaction spontaneous at standard conditions? Assume that ΔH° and ΔS° do not depend on temperature.

	(a)	(b)	(c)
A)	− 80 kJ/mol	Yes	Above 65.6 K
B)	+ 80 kJ/mol	No	Below 65.6 K
C)	− 80 kJ/mol	Yes	Above 0.064 K
D)	+ 80 kJ/mol	No	Above 0.064 K

Worked solution with answer for Topic 6

	Statement	True	False
A166	In an exothermic reaction, the system releases energy in the form of heat, which increases the temperature of the surroundings, and the enthalpy change (ΔH) for the reaction is always negative. ~~This type of reaction is spontaneous under all conditions.~~ **This type of reaction is not always spontaneous under all conditions because spontaneity depends on both enthalpy (ΔH) and entropy (ΔS), as well as temperature.**		v
A167	Endothermic processes, such as the melting of ice, involve the absorption of energy from the surroundings, which leads to a decrease in temperature of the surroundings. The enthalpy change (ΔH) is positive, and these processes are non-spontaneous at low temperatures but can become spontaneous at high temperatures due to the influence of entropy (ΔS).	v	
A168	When a solution forms, if the energy required to break solute-solute and solvent-solvent bonds is greater than the energy released from solute-solvent interactions, the overall process is endothermic. However, if solute-solvent interactions are much stronger, the solution formation becomes exothermic.	v	
A169	During a phase change, such as vaporization, the temperature of the substance remains constant as the system absorbs energy. This energy only contributes to overcoming intermolecular forces rather than increasing kinetic energy.	v	
A170	Calorimetry is a technique used to measure the heat absorbed or released during a chemical or physical process.	v	
A171	On a heating curve, the slope of the graph is inversely proportional to the specific heat capacity of the substance. Therefore, a steeper slope indicates a lower specific heat capacity, meaning less energy is required to raise the temperature by 1°C per unit mass.	v	
A172	The standard enthalpy change of a reaction refers to the enthalpy change when all reactants and products are in their standard states (1 atm pressure and 298 K temperature) and 1 mole of the substance is involved, ~~regardless of the state of matter or physical conditions of the reaction.~~ **taking into account the state of matter of the substances.**		v
A173	The standard enthalpy change of combustion is defined as the enthalpy change when one mole of a substance undergoes complete combustion in oxygen under standard conditions, with all reactants and products in their standard states. This process always releases energy, meaning the enthalpy change is negative.	v	

A174	The heat of formation of a compound is defined as the energy change when 1 mole of a compound is formed from its constituent elements in their standard states under standard conditions. For elements in their standard states, the enthalpy of formation is always zero.	v	
A175	Bond enthalpy represents the energy required to break one mole of bonds in the gas phase. Bond breaking is always an endothermic process, requiring energy input, while bond formation is exothermic and releases energy.	v	
A176	Hess's Law states that the total enthalpy change for a reaction is independent of the pathway taken, meaning it can be calculated by summing the enthalpy changes of individual steps. However, if you reverse a reaction, the enthalpy change must also be reversed in sign, but ~~it does not need to be scaled if the coefficients change.~~ **it must be scaled proportionally if the coefficients change.**		v
A177	Entropy increases when a substance changes from solid to liquid, or from liquid to gas, because the particles in the gas phase have the greatest degree of freedom and randomness.	v	
A178	Gibbs free energy (ΔG) is a thermodynamic potential that can predict the spontaneity of a process. If ΔG is negative, the process is spontaneous under the given conditions, while if ΔG is positive, the process is non-spontaneous. When ΔG is zero, the system is at equilibrium.	v	
A179	A process can become spontaneous at high temperatures if the enthalpy change (ΔH) is positive and the entropy change (ΔS) is also positive. This is because the temperature-dependent term, $-T\Delta S$, will eventually dominate and make Gibbs free energy negative.	v	
A180	When both the enthalpy change (ΔH) and entropy change (ΔS) are negative, the process is spontaneous ~~at all temperatures because the decreasing entropy is always outweighed by the release of energy as heat.~~ **only at low temperatures, as at higher temperatures the negative entropy term ($-T\Delta S$) becomes dominant and can result in a non-spontaneous process (positive ΔG).**		v

A181

(a)
An exothermic reaction is one in which the system releases energy, typically in the form of heat, to the surroundings. The enthalpy change (ΔH) for the reaction is negative because the energy of the products is lower than the energy of the reactants.

(b)
In an exothermic reaction, the potential energy of the products is lower than the potential energy of the reactants. The difference in energy is released to the surroundings as heat. A labeled diagram should show the reactants at a higher energy level and the products at a lower energy level, with an arrow indicating the release of energy.

(c)
The temperature of the surroundings increases as a result of an exothermic reaction because the system releases heat into the surroundings. This heat transfer increases the kinetic energy of the particles in the surroundings, causing the temperature to rise.

A182

(a)
An endothermic reaction is one in which the system absorbs energy, typically in the form of heat, from the surroundings. The enthalpy change (ΔH) for the reaction is positive because the energy of the products is higher than the energy of the reactants.

(b)
In an endothermic reaction, the potential energy of the products is higher than the potential energy of the reactants. The difference in energy is absorbed from the surroundings. A labeled diagram should show the reactants at a lower energy level and the products at a higher energy level, with an arrow indicating the absorption of energy.

(c)
The temperature of the surroundings decreases as a result of an endothermic reaction because the system absorbs heat from the surroundings. This heat transfer reduces the kinetic energy of the particles in the surroundings, causing the temperature to drop.

A183

(a)
The process is classified as overall exothermic due to the net release of energy. While energy is absorbed to break strong ionic bonds in the solute (ΔH1) and hydrogen bonds in the solvent (ΔH2), more energy is released when new ion-dipole interactions form between the solute ions and water molecules (ΔH3). This energy release surpasses the absorbed energy, leading to an overall exothermic reaction.

(b)
ΔH1: Energy required to break ionic bonds, which are very strong and thus highly endothermic.
ΔH2: Energy needed to disrupt hydrogen bonds between water molecules; these are moderately strong and endothermic.
ΔH3: Energy released by forming ion-dipole forces between solute ions and water, which, although not as strong as ionic bonds, release enough energy to outweigh ΔH1 and ΔH2.

A184

(a)
Thermal equilibrium occurs when two objects at different temperatures come into contact and exchange energy until they reach the same temperature, at which point no further net heat transfer occurs. In this scenario, thermal equilibrium between the iron metal and the water will be achieved when both reach a common temperature, and the rate of heat transfer from the iron to the water equals the rate of heat transfer from the water back to the iron.

(b)
Iron Metal: The iron atoms at 100°C are highly energized, exhibiting vigorous vibrations and movements due to their high kinetic energy. This higher energy state reflects the metal's higher temperature.
Water: At 25°C, the water molecules have significantly lower kinetic energy compared to the iron atoms. They move slower and with less intensity, indicative of the cooler temperature of the water.

(c)
Heat flows from the hotter iron to the cooler water due to the temperature difference. The high-energy iron atoms transfer kinetic energy to the lower-energy water molecules through collisions. This transfer raises the kinetic energy of the water molecules while reducing that of the iron atoms, gradually balancing their temperatures.

(d)
As the temperature difference narrows, the rate of energy transfer slows. Eventually, iron atoms and water molecules reach similar kinetic energy levels. Thermal equilibrium is achieved when no further net heat transfer occurs, indicated by stable and equal temperatures for both substances.

A185

When aluminum (specific heat = 0.89 J/g°C) and water (specific heat = 4.18 J/g°C) are subjected to the same amount of heat energy, aluminum will experience a larger temperature increase than water. This is because aluminum has a lower specific heat, meaning it requires less energy to raise its temperature compared to water.
For the same amount of heat:
- Aluminum's temperature will increase significantly due to its low specific heat.
- Water's temperature will increase only slightly because its high specific heat allows it to absorb more energy without a large temperature change.

For example, if 1000 J of heat is applied to 100 g of both substances:

- Aluminum's temperature increases by approximately 11.24°C.
- Water's temperature increases by only about 2.39°C.

This shows how specific heat affects the rate of temperature change.

A186

Heat gained by water:
Use the formula q = m c ΔT to calculate the heat gained by water.
q_{water} = 150. g × 4.18 J/g°C × (28.70°C−24.50°C) = 2,630 J

Heat lost by metal:
The heat lost by the metal equals the heat gained by water (since no heat is lost to the surroundings).
q_{metal} = −q_{water} = −2,630 J

Find the specific heat of the metal:
Using q = m c ΔT, solve for c.
−2,630 J = (60.0 g) (c) (28.70°C − 120.0°C)
c = 0.48 J/g°C

A187

Heat gained by water:
Use the formula q = m c ΔT to calculate the heat gained by water.
q_{water} = 250 g × 4.18 J/g°C × (25.5°C−23.0°C) = 2,613 J

Heat lost by metal:
The heat lost by the metal equals the heat gained by the water, assuming no heat loss to the surroundings:
q_{metal} = −q_{water} = −2,613 J

Find the specific heat of the metal:
Using q = m c ΔT, solve for c.
−2,613 J = (120.0 g) (c) (25.5°C − 82.0°C)
c = 0.385 J/g°C

A188

Calculate the total mass of the solution:
Since the density is 1.0 g/cm³ and 1 cm³ = 1 mL, the mass of the solution is equal to the volume in milliliters.
Total volume = 150.0 mL of KOH + 150.0 mL of HNO_3 = 300.0 mL
Therefore, total mass of the solution = 300.0 g

Calculate the heat absorbed by the solution:
Use the formula q = m c ΔT
where:

m = 300.0 g (mass of the solution)
c = 4.18 J/g°C (specific heat capacity)
ΔT = 32.0°C − 25.0°C = 7.0°C (temperature change)
q = (300.0 g) × (4.18 J/g°C) × (7.0 °C) = 8778 J
Therefore, the heat absorbed by the solution is 8,778 J.

Calculate the moles of KOH or HNO_3:
Moles of KOH (or HNO_3) = M V = 1.5 M × 0.150 L = 0.225 mol

Calculate the enthalpy change per mole of reaction:
Overall equation : HNO_3 + KOH → H_2O + KNO_3
The heat absorbed by the solution corresponds to the heat released by the reaction.

$$\Delta H = - \frac{q}{\text{mol of limiting} * \frac{\text{mol rxn}}{\text{coefficient of limiting}}} = - \frac{8778 \text{ J}}{0.225 \text{ mol KOH} * \frac{\text{mol rxn}}{1 \text{ mol KOH}}}$$

= − 39 kJ / mol_{rxn}

A189

Calculate the heat absorbed by the solution:
Use the formula q = m c ΔT
where:
m = 120.0 g (mass of the solution)
c = 4.18 J/g°C (specific heat capacity)
ΔT = 22.30°C − 21.50°C = 0.80°C (temperature change)
q = (120.0 g) × (4.18 J/g°C) × (0.80°C) = 401.3 J
Therefore, the heat absorbed by the solution is 401.3 J.

Determine the limiting reagent:
Moles of NaCl = 0.150M × 0.0600L = 0.00900 mol
Moles of $Pb(NO_3)_2$ = 0.150 M × 0.0600 L = 0.00900 mol
According to the balanced equation, 1 mole of $Pb(NO_3)_2$ reacts with 2 moles of NaCl to form 1 mole of $PbCl_2$. Since both reactants are present in a 1:2 ratio, NaCl is the limiting reagent.

Calculate the enthalpy change per mole of NaCl:
The heat released by the reaction corresponds to the heat absorbed by the solution. The enthalpy change per mole of NaCl is:

$$\Delta H = - \frac{q}{\text{mol of limiting} * \frac{\text{mol rxn}}{\text{coefficient of limiting}}} = - \frac{401.3 \text{ J}}{0.00900 \text{ mol NaCl} * \frac{\text{mol rxn}}{2 \text{ mol NaCl}}}$$

= − 44.6 kJ / mol_{rxn}

A190

Calculate the heat absorbed by the solution:
Use the formula q = m c ΔT
where:

m = 150.0 g (mass of the solution)
c = 4.18 J/g°C (specific heat capacity)
ΔT = 24.50°C − 21.00°C = 3.50°C (temperature change)
q = (150.0 g) × (4.18 J/g°C) × (3.50°C) = 2194.5 J
Therefore, the heat absorbed by the solution is 2194.5 J.

Determine the limiting reagent:
Moles of $Al(NO_3)_3$ = 0.200 M × 0.100 L = 0.0200 mol
Moles of Na_2SO_4 = 0.300 M × 0.0750 L = 0.0225 mol
According to the reaction stoichiometry (2:3 ratio), Na_2SO_4 is the limiting reagent.

Calculate the enthalpy change per mole of **Na_2SO_4**:
The heat released by the reaction corresponds to the heat absorbed by the solution. The enthalpy change per mole of Na_2SO_4 is:

$$\Delta H = - \frac{q}{\text{mol of limiting} * \frac{\text{mol rxn}}{\text{coefficient of limiting}}} = - \frac{2194.5 \text{ J}}{0.0225 \text{ mol } Na_2SO_4 * \frac{\text{mol rxn}}{3 \text{ mol } Na_2SO_4}}$$

= − 293 kJ / mol$_{rxn}$

A191

Calculate the heat absorbed by the water:
Use the formula q = m c ΔT
where:
m = (150.0 + 12.0) g (mass of the solution)
c = 4.18 J/g°C (specific heat capacity)
ΔT = 19.8°C − 24.50°C = − 4.7 °C (temperature change)
q = (167.0 g) × (4.18 J/g°C) × (− 4.7 °C) = − 3183 J
Therefore, the heat absorbed by the solution is − 3183 J.

Calculate the enthalpy change per mole of NaCl:
The heat absorbed by the solution corresponds to the heat required to dissolve the sodium chloride

$$\Delta H = - \frac{-3183 \text{ J}}{12.0 \text{ g NaCl}}$$

= + 265 J/g

$$\Delta H = - \frac{-3183 \text{ J}}{12.0 \text{ g NaCl} * \frac{1 \text{ mol NaCl}}{58.44 \text{ g NaCl}}}$$

= + 16 kJ/mol

A192

Calculate the heat released by the water:
Use the formula q = m c ΔT
where:
m = (180.0 + 15.0) g (mass of the solution)
c = 4.18 J/g°C (specific heat capacity)
ΔT = 27.8°C − 23.0°C = 4.8 °C (temperature change)

q = (195.0 g) × (4.18 J/g°C) × (4.8 °C) = + 3912 J
Therefore, the heat released by the solution is +3912 J.

Calculate the enthalpy change per mole of $CaCl_2$:
The heat released by the solution corresponds to the heat released by dissolving the calcium chloride

$\Delta H = - \dfrac{+3912 \text{ J}}{15.0 \text{ g } CaCl_2}$

= - 261 J/g

$\Delta H = - \dfrac{+3912 \text{ J}}{15.0 \text{ g } CaCl_2 * \dfrac{1 \text{ mol } CaCl_2}{110.98 \text{ g } CaCl_2}}$

= - 28.9 kJ/mol

A193

Calculate the moles of KI dissolved:
Mol of KI = (25.0 g) / (166.00 g/mol) = 0.1506 mol

Calculate the heat released by the dissolution of KI:

$\Delta H = - 58.9 \text{ kJ/mol} = - \dfrac{q \text{ kJ}}{0.1506 \text{ mol KI}}$

q = + 8.87 kJ

Calculate the temperature change:
q = c m ΔT = (4.18 J/g°C) (150 g + 25.0 g) (ΔT) = 8870 J
ΔT = 12.12 °C

Calculate the final temperature:
Initial temperature = 25.0°C
Final temperature = 12.12 + 25.0 = 37.12 °C

A194

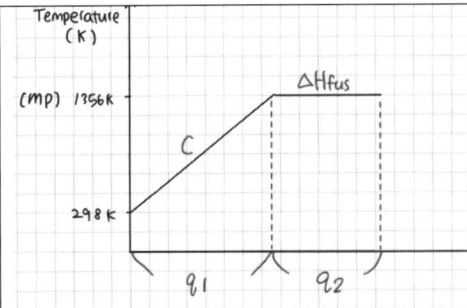

Calculate the heat required to raise the temperature of 1.00 mole of copper from 298 K to its melting point (1356 K):
q1 = c m ΔT
= (25 J/mol K) (1.00 mol) (1356 K – 298 K) = 26.5 kJ

Calculate the heat required to melt the copper at 1356 K:
q2 = ΔH_{fus} m
= (13.0 kJ/mol) (1.00 mol) = 13.0 kJ

Calculate the total heat required:
q_{total} = q1 + q2 = 26.5 kJ + 13.0 kJ = 39.5 kJ

A195

(a)
Calculate the moles of ethane:
Mol of ethane = (25.0 g) / (30.07g/mol) = 0.831 mol

Calculate the heat required using the heat of fusion:
q = ΔH_{fus} m
= (2.44 kJ/mol) (0.831 mol) = 2.03 kJ

(b)
Vaporizing ethane at 184.55 K requires more energy than melting it at 90.35 K because vaporization involves completely overcoming intermolecular forces to change from liquid to gas, whereas melting only partially loosens these forces as ethane transitions from solid to liquid. This distinction in the degree of intermolecular force disruption explains the greater energy needed for vaporization.

A196

(a)
Use the formula q = m c ΔT
= (2000. g) × (4.18 J/g°C) × (75 °C) = 627 kJ

(b)
Calculate the Moles of Propane Burned
Mass of propane used = 250.00 - 242.50 = 7.50 g
Mole of propane used = (7.50 g) (1 mol / 44.094 g) = 0.170 mol

A197

Calculate the amount of heat transferred to the water
Use the formula q = m c ΔT
= (75.0 g) × (4.18 J/g°C) × (43.0 °C) = +13481 J
Therefore, the heat released by the solution is +13481 J

Calculate the Amount of Propanol Burned
Mass of propanol used = 135.0 g – 132.0 g = 3.0 g
Mole of propanol used = (3.0 g) (1 mol / 60.09 g) = 0.050 mol

Calculate the Enthalpy of Combustion per Mole of Propanol

$$\Delta H = -\frac{13.481 \text{ kJ}}{0.050 \text{ mol propanol}}$$
$= -270$ kJ/mol

A198

Calculate $\Delta H°rxn$:
$\Delta H°rxn = \sum \Delta H°_f \text{(products)} - \sum \Delta H°_f \text{(reactants)}$
$= [\Delta H°_f (ZnCl_2) + \Delta H°_f (H_2)] - [\Delta H°_f (Zn) + 2 \Delta H°_f (HCl)]$
$= [(-415 \text{ kJ/mol}) + (0 \text{ kJ/mol})] - [(0 \text{ kJ/mol}) + 2 \times (-167 \text{ kJ/mol})]$
$= -81$ kJ/mol

A199

(a)

Bonds broken : 2 x (3 N-H bonds in NH_3)
Bonds formed : 3 x (H-H bond) + (N≡N)
$\Delta H°rxn = \sum \Delta$Bond energy (broken) $- \sum$Bond energy (formed)
$= [6 (391) \text{ kJ/mol}] - [3 (436) \text{ kJ/mol} + 945 \text{ kJ/mol}]$
$= +93$ kJ/mol

(b)

Bonds broken : 2 x (4 N-H bonds in N_2H_4) + 2 x ((N-N) in bonds in N_2H_4)
Bonds formed : 2 x (3 N-H bonds in NH_3) + (N≡N)
$\Delta H°rxn = \sum \Delta$Bond energy (broken) $- \sum$Bond energy (formed)
$= [8 (391) \text{ kJ/mol} + 2 (158) \text{ kJ/mol}] - [6 (391) \text{ kJ/mol} + 945 \text{ kJ/mol}]$
$= 153$ kJ/mol

A200

$$2 \left[\ddot{O}=\dot{N}-\ddot{O}\!: \;\leftrightarrow\; :\!\ddot{O}-\dot{N}=\ddot{O} \right] \rightleftarrows 2 \cdot \dot{N}=\ddot{O} \;+\; O=O$$

Bonds broken : 2 x (2 N-O bonds in NO_2)
Bonds formed : 2 x (N-O bonds in NO) + (O-O bond in O_2)
$\Delta H°rxn = \sum \Delta$Bond energy (broken) $- \sum$Bond energy (formed)
$= [4 (x) \text{ kJ/mol}] - [2 (607) \text{ kJ/mol} + 498 \text{ kJ/mol}]$
$= -114$ kJ/mol
x = N-O bonds in NO_2
$= +399.5$ kJ/mol

A201

Equation 1 x (-1) x (1/2) = + 213.5
Equation 2 x (-1) x (1/2) = - 247.5

Equation 3 = - 199
Summation = (+213.5) + (-247.5) + (-199) = - 233 kJ/mol

A202

Equation 1 x (2) = 361.2
Equation 2 x (-1) x (2) = 183.6
Equation 3 x (3) = -1451.1
Summation = (361.2) + (183.6) + (-1451.1) = - 906.3 kJ/mol

A203

$(-\Delta H°_f) + (\Delta H°_{sub}) + (IE) + (1/2\ BDE) + EA = \Delta H°_{lattice}$
$(- (-395) kJ/mol) + (+89\ kJ/mol) + (419\ kJ/mol) + (1/2\ (190)\ kJ/mol) + (-325\ kJ/mol)$
$= \Delta H°_{lattice}$
$= + 673\ kJ/mol$

A204

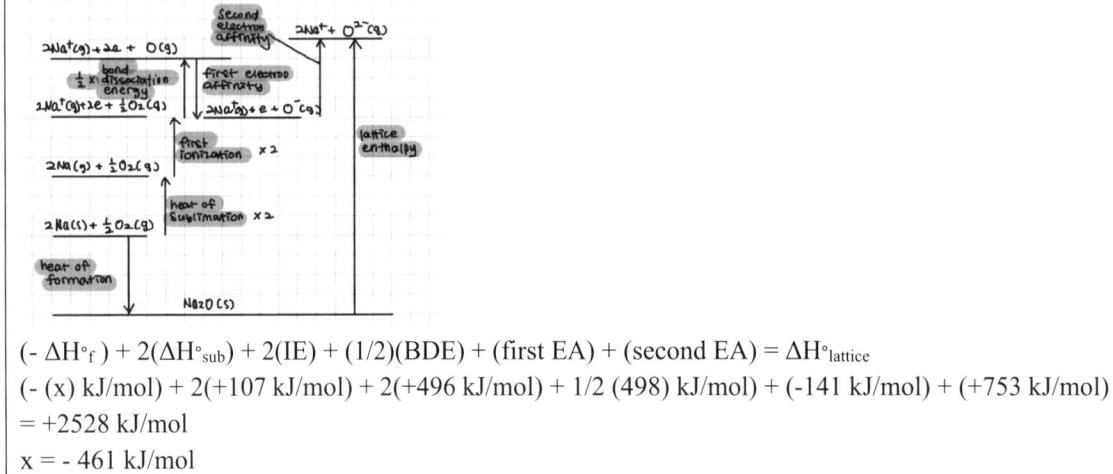

$(-\Delta H°_f) + 2(\Delta H°_{sub}) + 2(IE) + (1/2)(BDE) + (first\ EA) + (second\ EA) = \Delta H°_{lattice}$
$(- (x)\ kJ/mol) + 2(+107\ kJ/mol) + 2(+496\ kJ/mol) + 1/2\ (498)\ kJ/mol) + (-141\ kJ/mol) + (+753\ kJ/mol)$
$= +2528\ kJ/mol$
$x = - 461\ kJ/mol$

A205

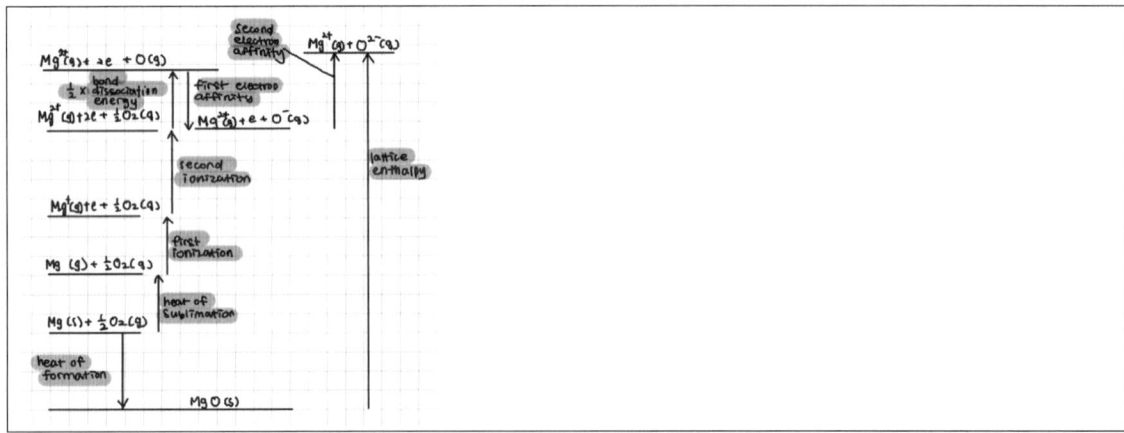

A206

(a) increase
(b) decrease
(c) increase
(d) increase
(e) remain the same

A207

$\Delta S°_{rxn} = \sum S°$ (products) $- \sum S°$ (reactants)
= 2 (+50.9 J/mol K) – [4 (+28.3 J/mol K) + 3 (+205.0 J/mol K)]
= – 626.4 J/mol K

A208

(a)
$\Delta G = \Delta H - T \Delta S$
= (+25 kJ) – (400 K)(+50.0/1000 kJ / K)
= +5 kJ
Nonspontaneous

(b)
$\Delta G = \Delta H - T \Delta S$
= (+50 kJ) – (500 K)(+200.0/1000 kJ / K)
= – 50 kJ
Spontaneous

(c)
$\Delta G = \Delta H - T \Delta S$
= (–10 kJ) – (298 K)(+30/1000 kJ / K)
= – 18.94 kJ
Spontaneous

(d)
$\Delta G = \Delta H - T \Delta S$
= (–15 kJ) – (273 K)(–70/1000 kJ / K)
= +4.11 kJ
Nonspontaneous

A209

(a)
$\Delta G°_f(NO_2(g)) = +51.3 \text{ kJ/mol}$
$\Delta G°_f(NO(g)) = +87.6 \text{ kJ/mol}$
$\Delta G°_f(O_2(g)) = 0 \text{ kJ/mol}$ (since it's in its elemental state)
The formula to calculate $\Delta G°$ for the reaction is:
$\Delta G° = \sum \Delta G°_f(\text{products}) - \sum \Delta G°_f(\text{reactants})$
$= [2(+87.6 \text{ kJ/mol}) + (0 \text{ kJ/mol})] - [2(+51.3 \text{ kJ/mol})]$
$= +72.6 \text{ kJ/mol}$

(b)
For a reaction to be spontaneous, $\Delta G°$ must be negative. Since we calculated $\Delta G°_{rxn} = +72.6 \text{ kJ/mol}$, the reaction is not spontaneous under standard conditions at 298 K.

A210

(a) IV
At low temperatures, the ΔH term dominates in $\Delta G = \Delta H - T\Delta S$. For a reaction to be spontaneous only at low temperatures, ΔH should be negative (favorable enthalpy change), and ΔS should be negative (entropy decreases with temperature).

(b) IV
Condensation is an exothermic process ($\Delta H < 0$) where entropy decreases ($\Delta S < 0$) because gas is converted to liquid.

(c) I
Sublimation is an endothermic process ($\Delta H > 0$) with an increase in entropy ($\Delta S > 0$) because a solid is converted to gas.

(d) III
Combustion is an exothermic reaction ($\Delta H < 0$), and the formation of gases increases entropy ($\Delta S > 0$).

(e) II
For a reaction to never be spontaneous, ΔG must always be positive, which requires both $\Delta H > 0$ and $\Delta S < 0$.

(f) IV
Freezing is exothermic ($\Delta H < 0$), and the entropy decreases as the system becomes more ordered ($\Delta S < 0$).

(g) I
At high temperatures, the $-T\Delta S$ term dominates, so for the reaction to be spontaneous at high temperatures but non-spontaneous at low temperatures, $\Delta H > 0$ and $\Delta S > 0$.

A211 (B)

$C_3H_6O_3 = HA$
$2HA + Ba(OH)_2 \rightarrow 2H_2O + BaA_2$

Determine the limiting reactant
Lactic acid = MV = (0.300M) (0.150L) = 0.0450 mol

Barium hydroxide = MV = (0.700M) (0.2000L) = 0.140 mol
→ limiting reactant is lactic acid

Calculate the heat
q = c m ΔT = (4.18 J/g °C) (350 g) (28.6 °C – 25.0 °C) = 5.284 kJ

Calculate molar enthalpy (ΔH)

$$\Delta H = - \frac{q}{\text{mol of limiting} * \frac{\text{mol rxn}}{\text{coefficient of limiting}}} = - \frac{5.284 \text{ kJ}}{0.0450 \text{ mol lactic acid} * \frac{\text{mol rxn}}{2 \text{ mol lactic acid}}}$$

= - 117 kJ/mol$_{rxn}$

A212 (D)

Calculate the heat
q = c m ΔT = (4.18 J/g °C) (208 g) (17.5 °C – 22.0 °C) = - 3.912 kJ

Enthalpy change for dissolving KNO$_3$ in J/g

$$\Delta H = - \frac{q}{\text{g of solute}} = - \frac{-3912 \text{ J}}{8.0 \text{ g}}$$

= + 489 J/g

Enthalpy change for dissolving KNO$_3$ in kJ/mol

$$\Delta H = - \frac{q}{\text{mol of solute}} = - \frac{-3.912 \text{ kJ}}{8.0 \text{ g} * \frac{\text{mol}}{101.10 \text{ g}}}$$

= + 49 kJ/mol

A213 (C)

Acetic acid is monoprotic acid = HA
HA + KOH → H$_2$O + KA

Determine the limiting reactant
Acetic acid = MV = (0.400M) (0.1200L) = 0.0480 mol
potassium hydroxide = MV = (0.500M) (0.1800L) = 0.0900 mol
→ limiting reactant is acetic acid

Calculate the heat
q = c m ΔT = (4.18 J/g °C) (300 g) (29.5 °C – 23.0 °C) = + 8151 J = + 8.151 kJ
Enthalpy change

$$\Delta H = - \frac{q}{\text{mol of limiting} * \frac{\text{mol rxn}}{\text{coefficient of limiting}}} = - \frac{+8.151 \text{ kJ}}{0.0480 \text{ mol acetic acid} * \frac{\text{mol rxn}}{1 \text{ mol acetatic acid}}}$$

= - 170 kJ/mol

A214 (B)

Heat lost by metal = Heat gained by water
- c m ΔT = + c m ΔT
- (specific heat of metal) (200 g) (30 °C - 150 °C)
            = + (specific heat of water) (150 g) (30 °C – 20 °C)
- (specific heat of metal) (- 24000) = + (specific heat of water) (1500)
specific heat of metal < specific heat of water

A215 (D)

Calculate ΔH°rxn:
ΔH°rxn = ∑ΔHf°(products) − ∑ΔHf°(reactants)
= [4 ΔHf°(CO_2) + 6 ΔHf°(H_2O)] − [2ΔHf°(C_2H_6) + 7 ΔHf°(O_2)]
= [4 (-394 kJ/mol) + 6 (- 242 kJ/mol)] – [2 (-85 kJ/mol) + 7 x (0 kJ/mol)]
= - 2858 kJ/mol

A216 (B)

Determine the limiting reactant
Phosphoric acid acid = MV = (0.250M) (0.0400L) = 0.0100 mol
Sodium hydroxide = MV = (0.500M) (0.0300L) = 0.0150mol
→ limiting reactant is sodium hydroxide
$\Delta H° = (\frac{-134.5 \text{ kJ}}{1 \text{mol rxn}})(\frac{1 \text{ mol rxn}}{3 \text{ mol NaOH}})(0.0150 \text{mol NaOH}) = -0.673 \text{ kJ}$

A217 (A)

I – true because ΔH has negative sign.
II – true because the enthalpy of vapor is greater than the enthalpy of liquid water.
III – false because the oxidation number of O in O_2 is 0 and the oxidation number in O in water is -2.
IV – false because the coefficient of the gas product is 4, which is smaller than that of the reactant.

A218 (C)

Determine the limiting reactant
Zind = (5.0 g) (65.38 g /mol) = 0.0765 mol
Hydrochloric acid = MV = (1.5M) (0.1000L) = 0.150mol
→ limiting reactant is hydrochloric acid

Calculate the amount of heat released
$\Delta H°_{rxn} = -120 \text{ kJ/mol} = -\frac{q}{0.150 \text{ mol HCl} * \frac{1 \text{ mol rxn}}{2 \text{ mol HCl}}}$
q = 9.0 kJ

A219 (A)

Determine the limiting reactant
Iron = (16.8 g) (55.85 g /mol) = 0.301 mol
Water = (150.0 g) (18.02 g /mol) = 8.324 mol

→ limiting reactant is Fe

Calculate the amount of heat released
$\Delta H°_{rxn} = -160 \text{ kJ/mol} = -\dfrac{q}{0.301 \text{ mol Fe} * \dfrac{1 \text{ mol rxn}}{3 \text{ mol Fe}}}$

q = 16.05 kJ

A220 (C)

Bonds broken : (N-N bonds in N_2H_4) + 4 x (N-H bonds in N_2H_4)
Bonds formed : (N≡N)
$\Delta H°_{rxn} = \Sigma\Delta$Bond energy (broken) − ΣBond energy (formed)
A) 400 + 4(390) – (950) = 1010
B) 300 + 4(400) – 900 = 1000
C) 200 + 4(410) – 850 = 990
D) 150 + 4(420) – 800 = 1030

A221 (C)

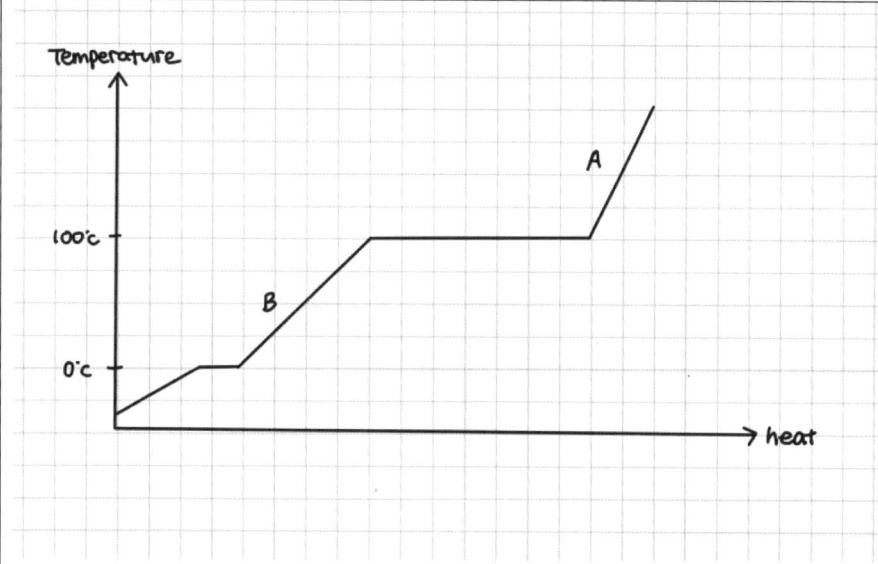

In the heating curve, the equation q = cmΔT can be rearranged to $\Delta T = \dfrac{q}{cm}$, which is similar to the equation of a line y = ax, where the slope **a** is determined by 1/cm. This shows that the temperature change (ΔT) depends on the amount of heat added (q) and the specific heat capacity (c) of the substance.

The lower the specific heat capacity (c), the larger the value of 1/cm, resulting in a steeper slope on the heating curve. Therefore, substances with lower specific heat capacity heat up more quickly for the same amount of heat added, as shown in the curve where the slope of segment A (vapor) is steeper than segment B (liquid).

Slope : A > B
Specific heat capacity : A < B

A222 (D)

Since ΔG°₂₉₈ = +21kJ/mol, which is positive, the reaction is not thermodynamically favored under standard conditions at 298 K. A reaction with a positive ΔG means it is non-spontaneous and will not proceed without external energy.

A223 (D)

The reaction between hydrogen and oxygen is under kinetic control, meaning that although the reaction is thermodynamically favorable (it releases energy), it does not occur spontaneously at room temperature due to the high activation energy. A spark is needed to provide enough energy to overcome this activation barrier and initiate the reaction.

A224

A)B)D)F)

A225 (A)

(a)

$\Delta G°_f$ for $SOCl_2(g)$ = +340 kJ/mol

$\Delta G°_f$ for $SO_2(g)$ = +300 kJ/mol

$\Delta G°_f$ for $Cl_2(g)$ = 0 kJ/mol (since it's in its elemental form)

The formula to calculate ΔG° for the reaction is:

$\Delta G° = \sum \Delta G°_f(\text{products}) - \sum \Delta G°_f(\text{reactants})$

= [2(+300 kJ/mol) + (0 kJ/mol)] − [2(+340 kJ/mol)]

= − 80 kJ/mol

(b)

Since ΔG° is negative, the reaction is spontaneous under standard conditions at 298 K.

(c)

$\Delta G° = \Delta H° - T \Delta S°$

For spontaneous reaction, ΔG° < 0

ΔH° - T ΔS° < 0

$T > \frac{\Delta H°}{\Delta S°} = \frac{-14.44 \text{ kJ/mol}}{0.220 \text{ kJ/mol K}} = 65.6 \text{ K}$

Above 65.6 K

Topic _7
Equilibrium

Exam Weighting : 7-9%

Topic 7 Key Point Review

Equilibrium constant
- A ratio that expresses the concentrations of products and reactants at equilibrium for a reversible reaction.

$$K = \frac{[\text{Product}]^{\text{coefficient}}}{[\text{Reactant}]^{\text{coefficient}}}$$

- Include gas and aqueous solution only.
- Exclude solid and liquid.
- K value depends on the reaction temperature.
- K > 1: Products are favored at equilibrium.
- K < 1: Reactants are favored at equilibrium.

Q vs. K
- Reaction Quotient (Q): Similar to the equilibrium constant (K), but uses initial concentrations instead of equilibrium concentrations.
- Q < K : The reaction will proceed forward (toward products) to reach equilibrium.
- Q > K : The reaction will proceed backward (toward reactants) to reach equilibrium.
- Q = K : The system is at equilibrium.

Le Chatelier's principle
- If a system at equilibrium is disturbed, it will shift to counteract the disturbance and restore equilibrium.
- Concentration
    - Increasing reactants shifts equilibrium toward products
    - Increasing products shifts toward reactants
- Temperature
    - For exothermic reactions, increasing temperature shifts equilibrium toward reactants
    - For endothermic reactions, increasing temperature shifts equilibrium toward products.
- Pressure (for gases): Increasing pressure shifts equilibrium toward the side with fewer moles of gas.
- Adding catalyst
    - No effect on equilibrium position.
    - Catalysts speed up the rate of both the forward and reverse reactions but do not shift the equilibrium.
- Adding Solids or Pure Liquids:
    - Adding solids or pure liquids does not affect the equilibrium position, as their concentrations are constant and do not appear in the equilibrium expression.
- Addition of Distilled Water (Dilution)
    - Adding water dilutes the solution, decreasing the concentration of all aqueous species.
    - The system will shift in the direction that increases the number of dissolved particles (moles) to counteract the effect of dilution.
    - Typically, the equilibrium shifts toward the side with more moles of dissolved species (aqueous ions or molecules) to increase concentration.

Precipitation
- The process by which a solid forms from a solution during a chemical reaction.
- Occurs when: The concentration of ions in a solution exceeds the solubility product (Ksp), causing a solid to form.
- Ksp: Solubility product constant, specific for sparingly soluble salts.
- If Q > Ksp, precipitation occurs.
- If Q < Ksp, no precipitation occurs (solution remains unsaturated)

True/False Questions

Read the following statements carefully and determine whether each one is true or false. Place a tick (✔) in the appropriate box. If the statement is false, correct the incorrect part of the statement.

	Statement	True	False
Q226	Dynamic equilibrium is a state in which the rate of the forward reaction and the rate of the reverse reaction occur at the same pace, leading to no observable changes in the concentrations of reactants and products over time, even though the reactions continue to take place.		
Q227	The equilibrium constant expression includes the concentrations of pure solids and liquids, which are taken into account when calculating the value of the equilibrium constant.		
Q228	When the value of the equilibrium constant (K) is greater than 1, this indicates that the equilibrium lies to the right, favoring the formation of products over reactants in the chemical reaction.		
Q229	At dynamic equilibrium, the concentrations of reactants and products must always be equal, which is necessary for the system to maintain its state of balance without any further changes.		
Q230	The reaction quotient (Q) is used to determine the direction in which a reaction will proceed to reach equilibrium by comparing the current concentration ratios of reactants and products to the equilibrium constant (K).		
Q231	According to Le Chatelier's Principle, when the pressure of a system at equilibrium is increased by reducing the volume, the system will shift toward the side with more moles of gas to counteract the change.		
Q232	Le Chatelier's Principle states that for an exothermic reaction, increasing the temperature will shift the equilibrium to the left, favoring the reactants, because the system will absorb the added heat to reduce the disturbance.		
Q233	The solubility product constant (Ksp) reflects the maximum concentration of ions in a solution at equilibrium, and adding more solid to the solution will increase the value of Ksp.		
Q234	The common ion effect increases the solubility of a salt in solution, as the presence of a common ion reduces the ion concentration imbalance, thus shifting the equilibrium to favor more dissolution of the salt.		
Q235	When the value of Q is greater than the equilibrium constant (K), the reaction will shift in the reverse direction to re-establish equilibrium, as there are too many products compared to the reactants.		

Q236	The common ion effect refers to the decrease in solubility of an ionic compound when a salt that contains one of the ions in the compound is added to the solution, shifting the equilibrium and reducing the dissolution of the compound.		
Q237	The relationship between the solubility product constant (Ksp) and Gibbs free energy ($\Delta G°$) is expressed by the equation $\Delta G° = -RT\ln(Ksp)$, where a more negative $\Delta G°$ indicates a more spontaneous dissolution process, and thus a higher Ksp value.		
Q238	The equilibrium constant (K) is entirely independent of temperature, meaning that changing the temperature of a reaction will not affect the position of equilibrium or the relative concentrations of reactants and products.		
Q239	Adding water to a saturated solution leads to dilution, which decreases the ion concentration and causes the reaction quotient (Q) to drop below the solubility product constant (Ksp), thereby shifting the equilibrium towards the dissolution of more solid to restore balance.		
Q240	When additional reactant is added to a system at equilibrium, Le Chatelier's Principle predicts that the system will shift toward the reactants, resulting in a decrease in the concentration of products to balance the added substance.		

Concept Check Questions

When solving Free-Response Questions (FRQs), it is essential to clearly and accurately explain your reasoning. Make sure to outline the steps in your solution process thoroughly, showing all calculations with appropriate numbers and units. This demonstrates a full understanding of the problem and ensures that your answer is both correct and complete.

Q241
A chemical system is initially at equilibrium with the following balanced equation:

$$N_2(g) + 3H_2(g) \rightleftharpoons 2NH_3(g)$$

The equilibrium constant, K, for this reaction at a given temperature is 6.0. The initial concentrations of N_2, H_2, and NH_3 are 0.5 M, 1.5 M, and 1.0 M, respectively.

(a)
Calculate the reaction quotient Q for this system.

(b)
Based on the value of Q and K, predict which direction the reaction will shift to reach equilibrium.

Q242

Consider the following exothermic reaction at equilibrium:

$$CO(g) + 2\,H_2(g) \rightleftharpoons CH_3OH(g) \qquad \Delta H > 0$$

(a)
According to Le Chatelier's Principle, describe how the system will respond if the concentration of CO is increased.

(b)
How will the system respond to a decrease in temperature? Justify your answer using Le Chatelier's Principle.

(c)
Explain what will happen to the equilibrium position if the pressure of the system is increased by reducing the volume.

Q243

A saturated solution of AgCl(s) is at equilibrium with its ions in water according to the equation:

$$AgCl(s) \rightleftarrows Ag^+(aq) + Cl^-(aq)$$

(a)

Predict and explain how the addition of NaCl to the solution would affect the solubility of AgCl, using the concept of the common ion effect.

(b)

Describe how an decrease in temperature would affect the solubility of AgCl if the dissolution process is endothermic.

Q244

The equilibrium constant Kc for the following reaction at 400°C is 0.65:

$$2\ SO_2(g) + O_2(g) \rightleftarrows 2\ SO_3(g)$$

In an experiment, the initial concentrations are as follows:
$[SO_2] = 0.30$ M
$[O_2] = 0.40$ M
$[SO_3] = 0.50$ M

(a)
Calculate the reaction quotient Qc for this system.

(b)
Compare Qc to Kc and predict and explain the direction in which the reaction will shift to reach equilibrium.

(c)
Predict what would happen to the concentrations of SO_2, O_2, and SO_3 as the system moves toward equilibrium.

Q245

Consider the following equilibrium in a solution:

$$CaCO_3\,(s) \rightleftarrows Ca^{2+}(aq) + CO_3^{2-}(aq)$$

The solubility product constant Ksp for $CaCO_3$ at 25°C is 3.3×10^{-9}.
Suppose the concentrations of Ca^{2+} and CO_3^{2-} in a solution are 1.0×10^{-5} M and 3.0×10^{-4} M, respectively.

(a)
Calculate the reaction quotient Q for this system.

(b)
Compare Q to Ksp and determine whether a precipitate will form or not.

(c)
Explain how the system would respond if additional CO_3^{2-} ions were added to the solution.

Q246

Consider the following two sparingly soluble salts and their solubility equilibria:

$CaF_2(s) \rightleftharpoons Ca^{2+}(aq) + 2\,F^-(aq)$ $K_{sp} = 3.9 \times 10^{-11}$

$BaSO_4(s) \rightleftharpoons Ba^{2+}(aq) + SO_4^{2-}(aq)$ $K_{sp} = 1.1 \times 10^{-10}$

(a)
Write the Ksp expression for each salt based on the given balanced chemical equations.

(b)
Calculate the molar solubility of each salt in pure water. For CaF_2, assume the concentration of fluoride ions is twice the concentration of calcium ions due to its dissociation stoichiometry.

(c)
Compare the molar solubilities of CaF_2 and $BaSO_4$, and explain which salt is more soluble in water. Consider both the Ksp values and the difference in the stoichiometric coefficients of the ions.

Q247

The chromate (CrO_4^{2-}) and dichromate ($Cr_2O_7^{2-}$) ions exist in equilibrium in aqueous solution according to the following equation:

$$Cr_2O_7^{2-}(aq) + 3\, H_2O(l) \rightleftharpoons 2\, CrO_4^{2-}(aq) + 2\, H_3O^+(aq)$$

The dichromate ion is orange and the chromate ion is yellow. Initially, the solution has equal concentrations of chromate and dichromate ions.

(a)
Explain the effect of adding a strong acid, such as hydrochloric acid, to this equilibrium system. What happens to the equilibrium position?

(b)
Predict the resulting color of the solution after the addition of 6.0 M hydrochloric acid.

Q248
Consider the Haber process for the synthesis of ammonia:

$$N_2(g) + 3\,H_2(g) \rightleftarrows 2\,NH_3(g)$$

The change in enthalpy (ΔH°) for this reaction is −92.4 kJ/mol, indicating that the reaction is exothermic. A student hypothesizes that increasing the temperature of the equilibrium mixture will result in more ammonia production. Indicate whether you agree or disagree with the hypothesis.
Justify your answer.

Q249
Three different calcium salts—calcium fluoride (CaF_2), calcium carbonate ($CaCO_3$), and calcium sulfate ($CaSO_4$)—are each dissolved in separate solutions to form saturated solutions at 25°C. The solubility product constants (Ksp) for each salt at this temperature are given as follows:

- Calcium fluoride (CaF_2): Ksp = 3.9×10^{-11}
- Calcium carbonate ($CaCO_3$): Ksp = 4.8×10^{-9}
- Calcium sulfate ($CaSO_4$): Ksp = 2.4×10^{-5}

(a)
Write the dissolution reaction for each of the calcium salts.

(b)
Calculate the molar solubility of each salt in water based on their Ksp values.

Q250

A 1.0 L solution of calcium nitrate, $Ca(NO_3)_2$(aq), and magnesium nitrate, $Mg(NO_3)_2$(aq), has a Ca^{2+} concentration of 0.050 M and a Mg^{2+} concentration of 0.030 M. A 0.0020 mol sample of sodium carbonate (Na_2CO_3) is added to the solution. The solubility product constants (Ksp) at 298 K for the possible precipitates are as follows:

- Calcium carbonate ($CaCO_3$): Ksp = 4.8×10^{-9}
- Magnesium carbonate ($MgCO_3$): Ksp = 6.8×10^{-6}

(a)
Write the dissolution reactions for calcium carbonate and magnesium carbonate.

(b)
Predict whether calcium carbonate or magnesium carbonate will precipitate when A 0.0020 mol sample of sodium carbonate (Na_2CO_3) is added to the solution. Show your calculations for the ion product of each salt.

Q251

$$2\ SO_3(g) \rightleftarrows 2\ SO_2(g) + O_2(g)$$

Sulfur dioxide decomposes into sulfur trioxide and oxygen gas according to the equation above. A pure sample of sulfur dioxide is placed in a rigid, evacuated 1.00 L container. The initial pressure of the SO_2 (g) is 1.00 atm. The temperature is held constant until the SO_2 (g) reaches equilibrium with its decomposition products. The table below show the initial and equilibrium conditions of the system.

Initial	Equlibrium
$SO_2(g)$	$SO_3(g)$, $O_2(g)$
Ptotal = 1.00 atm	Ptotal = 1.40 atm

(a)
If the decomposition reaction were to go to completion, calculate the total pressure in the container.

(b)
If the decomposition reaction reaches equilibrium, calculate the partial pressure of each component in the container.

(c)
Which of the following statements about Kp, the equilibrium constant for the reaction, is correct?

A) Kp>1
B) Kp<1
C) Kp=1
D) It cannot be determined whether Kp > 1, Kp < 1, or Kp = 1 without additional information.

Q252

Given the solubility product constant (Ksp) for barium sulfate (BaSO$_4$) as 1.1×10^{-10}, you are asked to analyze a solution containing 0.010 M of barium nitrate (Ba(NO$_3$)$_2$).

Calculate the minimum concentration of sulfate ions (SO$_4^{2-}$) required to initiate precipitation of BaSO$_4$ from a solution containing 0.010 M Ba^{2+} ions derived from Ba(NO$_3$)$_2$. Use the Ksp value provided and explain your calculation process clearly.

Q253

Given the solubility product constant (Ksp) for calcium fluoride (CaF$_2$) as 3.9×10^{-11} at 298 K, and considering the dissolution reaction:

$$CaF_2 \text{ (s)} \rightleftharpoons Ca^{2+}\text{(aq)} + 2\, F^-\text{(aq)}$$

(a)
Calculate the Gibbs free energy change ($\Delta G°$) for the dissolution of CaF$_2$ using the given Ksp.

(b)
Using your result from part (a), explain whether the dissolution of CaF$_2$ is spontaneous under standard conditions at 298 K.

Q254

The dissolution of calcium hydroxide in water is described by the following reaction.

$$Ca(OH)_2(s) \rightleftharpoons Ca^{2+}(aq) + 2\,OH^-(aq)$$

To create a saturated solution, a student continuously adds $Ca(OH)_2$ to pure water, stirring until the solid no longer dissolves. It is found that the concentration of Ca^{2+} is 0.015 M.

(a)
Determine the concentration of OH^- ions in this solution.

(b)
Calculate the Ksp for $Ca(OH)_2$ based on the concentrations found in the solution.

Q255

A 1.0 L solution containing zinc sulfate, $ZnSO_4$(aq), and copper(II) sulfate, $CuSO_4$ (aq), has a Zn^{2+} concentration of 0.040 M and a Cu^{2+} concentration of 0.0025 M. A 0.0030 mol sample of sodium phosphate (Na_3PO_4) is added to the solution. The solubility product constants (Ksp) at 298 K for the possible precipitates are as follows:

- Zinc phosphate ($Zn_3(PO_4)_2$): Ksp = 2.5×10^{-17}
- Copper(II) phosphate ($Cu_3(PO_4)_2$): Ksp = 1.4×10^{-29}

(a)
Write the dissolution reactions for zinc phosphate and copper(II) phosphate.

(b)
Calculate the concentration of phosphate ions (PO_4^{3-}) introduced by the sodium phosphate addition. Assume that sodium phosphate fully dissociates and that the volume change of the solution is negligible.

(c)
Using the initial ion concentrations and the calculated phosphate concentration, determine whether $Zn_3(PO_4)_2$ or $Cu_3(PO_4)_2$, or both, will precipitate. Show your calculations for the ion product of each salt.

Multiple Choice Questions

The following questions are multiple-choice.
Choose the correct answer and explain why the other options are incorrect.

Q256
If a reaction has a very large Keq value, what does this indicate?

A) The concentration of reactants is much higher than the concentration of products at equilibrium.
B) The concentration of products is much higher than the concentration of reactants at equilibrium.
C) The reaction is slow and barely reaches equilibrium.
D) The reaction does not reach equilibrium.

Q257
Which of the following expressions correctly represents the equilibrium constant (Keq) for the reaction:

$$2\ NO_2\ (g) \rightleftarrows N_2O_4(g)$$

A) $Keq = \dfrac{[NO2]^2}{[N2O4]}$

B) $Keq = \dfrac{[N2O4]}{[NO2]^2}$

C) $Keq = \dfrac{2[NO2]}{[N2O4]}$

D) $Keq = \dfrac{[NO2]}{[N2O4]^2}$

Q258
Which factor can change the value of Keq for a given reaction?

A) Pressure
B) Volume
C) Temperature
D) Concentration of reactants

Q259
The following equilibrium pressures were observed at a certain temperature for the reaction:

$$2\ NO_2(g) \rightleftarrows 2\ NO(g) + O_2(g)$$

$P_{NO_2} = 0.55$ atm
$P_{NO} = 6.5 \times 10^{-5}$ atm
$P_{O_2} = 4.5 \times 10^{-5}$ atm

What is the value of the equilibrium constant Kp at this temperature?

A) 3.2×10^{-13}
B) 5.2×10^{-14}
C) 6.3×10^{-13}
D) 7.3×10^{-14}

Q260
For the reaction:

$$2 H_2O(g) \rightleftarrows 2 H_2(g) + O_2(g)$$

The equilibrium constant K is 3.5×10^{-3} at a given temperature.
At equilibrium in a 3.0 L container, it is found that $[H_2O(g)] = 1.3 \times 10^{-1}$ M and $[H_2(g)] = 2.1 \times 10^{-2}$ M.
What is the number of moles of $O_2(g)$ present under these conditions?

A) 0.203 mol
B) 0.402 mol
C) 0.531 mol
D) 0.784 mol

Q261
A 10.0 L flask was filled with 3.00 moles of gaseous SO_2 and 3.00 moles of gaseous NO_2, and the mixture was heated. After equilibrium was reached, it was found that 2.50 moles of gaseous NO were present. Assume that the following reaction occurs under these conditions:

$$SO_2(g) + NO_2(g) \rightleftarrows SO_3(g) + NO(g)$$

What is the value of the equilibrium constant K for this reaction?

A) 20
B) 25
C) 30
D) 35

Q262

At a given temperature, the equilibrium constant K is 1.3×10^{-2} for the following reaction:

$$N_2(g) + 3\,H_2(g) \rightleftarrows 2\,NH_3(g)$$

What is the value of the equilibrium constant K for each of the following reactions at the same temperature?

(a)

$$\tfrac{1}{2} N_2(g) + \tfrac{3}{2} H_2(g) \rightleftarrows NH_3(g)$$

A) 0.011
B) 0.114
C) 0.030
D) 0.056

(b)

$$2\,NH_3(g) \rightleftarrows N_2(g) + 3\,H_2(g)$$

A) 23
B) 45
C) 59
D) 77

(c)

$$NH_3(g) \rightleftharpoons \frac{1}{2} N_2(g) + \frac{3}{2} H_2(g)$$

A) 8.77
B) 9.15
C) 7.80
D) 6.90

(d)

$$2 N_2(g) + 6 H_2(g) \rightleftharpoons 4 NH_3(g)$$

A) 1.69×10^{-4}
B) 1.12×10^{-4}
C) 1.56×10^{-4}
D) 1.69×10^{-2}

Q263
Consider the following system at 450 K:

$$N_2O_4(g) \rightleftharpoons 2\,NO_2(g), \quad K_c = 4.5 \times 10^{-3}$$

Initially, the concentrations are $[N_2O_4] = 0.020$ mol/L and $[NO_2] = 0.100$ mol/L.
Which of the following best predicts what will occur as the system approaches equilibrium at 450 K?

A) The amount of $NO_2(g)$ will increase, because $Q > K_c$
B) The amount of $NO_2(g)$ will decrease, because $Q > K_c$
C) The amount of $NO_2(g)$ will increase, because $Q < K_c$
D) The amount of $NO_2(g)$ will decrease, because $Q < K_c$

Q264
Consider the following system at 350 K:

$$CO(g) + Cl_2(g) \rightleftharpoons COCl_2(g), \quad K_c = 6.5 \times 10^2$$

Initially, the concentrations are $[CO] = 0.080$ mol/L and $[Cl_2] = 0.080$ mol/L, and $[COCl_2] = 0.200$ mol/L.
Which of the following best predicts what will occur as the system approaches equilibrium at 350 K?

A) The amount of $CO(g)$ will increase, because $Q > K_c$
B) The amount of $CO(g)$ will decrease, because $Q > K_c$
C) The amount of $CO(g)$ will increase, because $Q < K_c$
D) The amount of $CO(g)$ will decrease, because $Q < K_c$

Q265

The student reads in a reference text that NO(g) and NO_2(g) will react as represented by the equation below. Thermodynamic data for the reaction are also provided.

$$NO(g) + NO_2(g) \rightleftarrows N_2O_3(g), \qquad \Delta H° = -40.4 \text{ kJ/mol}_{rxn}$$

The student hypothesizes that increasing the temperature will increase the amount of N_2O_3(g) in the equilibrium mixture.
Which of the following is the best response to the student's hypothesis?

A) Disagree, because the reaction is exothermic, and increasing temperature will favor the reverse reaction.
B) Disagree, because the reaction is endothermic, and increasing temperature will favor the reverse reaction.
C) Agree, because the reaction is exothermic, and increasing temperature will favor the forward reaction.
D) Agree, because the reaction is endothermic, and increasing temperature will favor the forward reaction.

Q266

Consider the following equilibrium system:

$$Co(H_2O)_6^{2+}(aq) + 4\ Cl^-(aq) \rightleftarrows CoCl_4^{2-}(aq) + 6\ H_2O(l)$$
$$\text{Pink} \qquad\qquad\qquad\qquad\qquad \text{Blue}$$

The equilibrium system initially contains equal concentrations of $Co(H_2O)_6^{2+}$ (pink) and $CoCl_4^{2-}$ (blue). Which of the following statements correctly predicts the result of adding a sample of 6.0 M HCl(aq) to the system and provides an explanation?

A) The mixture will become more blue because Cl^-(aq) will oxidize Co^{2+} in $CoCl_4^{2-}$.
B) The mixture will become more blue because Cl^-(aq) will shift the equilibrium toward the formation of $CoCl_4^{2-}$.
C) The color of the mixture will not change because HCl(aq) does not affect the equilibrium.
D) The mixture will become more pink because Cl^-(aq) will shift the equilibrium toward reactants.

Q267
Consider the following reaction for the formation of sulfur trioxide:

$$2\ SO_2(g) + O_2(g) \rightleftarrows 2\ SO_3(g)$$

For this reaction, the equilibrium constant Kp at different temperatures is:

8.50×10^{-2} at 400°C
1.72×10^{-3} at 500°C
3.58×10^{-4} at 600°C

Based on this information, is the reaction exothermic or endothermic?

A) Exothermic, because the value of Kp decreases as temperature increases.
B) Endothermic, because the value of Kp decreases as temperature increases.
C) Exothermic, because the value of Kp increases as temperature increases.
D) Endothermic, because the value of Kp increases as temperature increases.

Q268
Which of the following represents an incorrect balanced equation and solubility product (Ksp) expression for the dissolution of a solid?

A) For $BaSO_4(s)$, balanced equation is $BaSO_4(s) \rightleftarrows Ba^{2+}(aq) + SO_4^{2-}(aq)$
Ksp=$[Ba^{2+}][SO_4^{2-}]$

B) For AgCl(s), balanced equation is $PbCl_2(s) \rightleftarrows Pb^{2+}(aq) + 2Cl^-(aq)$
Ksp=$[Pb^{2+}][2Cl^-]$

C) For $Ca(OH)_2(s)$, balanced equation is $Ca(OH)_2(s) \rightleftarrows Ca^{2+}(aq) + 2\ OH^-(aq)$
Ksp=$[Ca^{2+}][OH^-]^2$

D) For $Al_2(SO_4)_3(s)$, balanced equation is $Al_2(SO_4)_3(s) \rightleftarrows 2\ Al^{3+}(aq) + 3\ SO_4^{2-}(aq)$
Ksp=$[Al^{3+}]^2[SO_4^{2-}]^3$

Q269
The solubility product constant (Ksp) of $Al(OH)_3$ is 2.0×10^{-32}.
What is the molar solubility of $Al(OH)_3$ in water?

A) 1.2×10^{-8} mol/L
B) 2.7×10^{-9} mol/L
C) 5.2×10^{-9} mol/L
D) 1.5×10^{-7} mol/L

Q270
Given the solubility product constants (Ksp) for the following solids:

$$CaF_2 \text{ (s), Ksp} = 4.0 \times 10^{-11}$$
$$BaF_2 \text{(s), Ksp} = 2.4 \times 10^{-5}$$

Which of the following correctly identifies the solid with the smallest molar solubility and provides an explanation?

A) CaF_2, because it has a smaller Ksp value.
B) BaF_2, because it has a smaller Ksp value.
C) CaF_2, because it has a larger Ksp value.
D) BaF_2, because it has a larger Ksp value.

Q271
Given the solubility product constants (Ksp) for the following solids:

$$Ca_3(PO_4)_2 \text{ (s)}, K_{sp} = 1.3 \times 10^{-32}$$
$$FePO_4 \text{ (s)}, K_{sp} = 1.0 \times 10^{-22}$$

Which solid has the smallest molar solubility?

A) $Ca_3(PO_4)_2$, because it has a smaller Ksp value than $FePO_4$.
B) $FePO_4$, because it has a smaller Ksp value than $Ca_3(PO_4)_2$.
C) $Ca_3(PO_4)_2$, because after calculating the molar solubility, it releases fewer ions into solution compared to $FePO_4$.
D) $FePO_4$, because after calculating the molar solubility, it releases fewer ions into solution compared to $Ca_3(PO_4)_2$.

Q272
The value of Ksp for PbI_2(s) is 7.1×10^{-9}.
The concentration of I^-(aq) in a solution is 0.10 M.
What is the molar solubility of PbI_2(s) in this solution?

A) 7.1×10^{-8} mol/L
B) 7.1×10^{-7} mol/L
C) 3.6×10^{-8} mol/L
D) 3.6×10^{-9} mol/L

Q273
Calculate the solubility of solid $Mg_3(PO_4)_2$ in a 0.15 M Na_3PO_4 solution. $Ksp = 6.4 \times 10^{-30}$.

A) 2.2×10^{-10} mol/L
B) 8.3×10^{-11} mol/L
C) 5.7×10^{-12} mol/L
D) 3.4×10^{-11} mol/L

Q274
A solution is prepared by mixing 100.0 mL of 1.5×10^{-2} M $Ca(NO_3)_2$ and 100.0 mL of 2.0×10^{-3} M $NaSO_4$.
Will $CaSO_4(s)$ precipitate if $Ksp = 2.4 \times 10^{-5}$?

A) Yes, because calculate Q is 7.5×10^{-6} which is less than Ksp.
B) No, because calculate Q is 7.5×10^{-6} which is less than Ksp.
C) Yes, because calculate Q is 3.0×10^{-5} which is greater than Ksp.
D) No, because calculate Q is 3.0×10^{-5} which is greater than Ksp.

Q275
Consider the reaction:

$$N_2(g) + 3\,H_2(g) \rightleftharpoons 2\,NH_3(g)$$

The Gibbs free energy change ($\Delta G°$) for the reaction is related to the equilibrium constant K by the equation:
$\Delta G° = -\,R\,T\,\ln K$

Given that $\Delta G°$ is negative for this reaction, which of the following statements is correct?

A) K > 1, and the reaction favors the formation of products at equilibrium.
B) K < 1, and the reaction favors the formation of reactants at equilibrium.
C) K > 1, and the reaction is at equilibrium with no net formation of products or reactants.
D) K < 0, and the reaction does not proceed in either direction.

Worked solution with answer for Topic 7

	Statement	True	False
A226	Dynamic equilibrium is a state in which the rate of the forward reaction and the rate of the reverse reaction occur at the same pace, leading to no observable changes in the concentrations of reactants and products over time, even though the reactions continue to take place.	v	
A227	The equilibrium constant expression ~~includes~~ exclude the concentrations of pure solids and liquids, which are taken into account when calculating the value of the equilibrium constant.		v
A228	When the value of the equilibrium constant (K) is greater than 1, this indicates that the equilibrium lies to the right, favoring the formation of products over reactants in the chemical reaction.	v	
A229	At dynamic equilibrium, the concentrations of reactants and products ~~must always~~ do not have to be equal, which is necessary for the system to maintain its state of balance without any further changes.		v
A230	The reaction quotient (Q) is used to determine the direction in which a reaction will proceed to reach equilibrium by comparing the current concentration ratios of reactants and products to the equilibrium constant (K).	v	
A231	According to Le Chatelier's Principle, when the pressure of a system at equilibrium is increased by reducing the volume, the system will shift toward the side with ~~more~~ fewer moles of gas to counteract the change.		v
A232	Le Chatelier's Principle states that for an exothermic reaction, increasing the temperature will shift the equilibrium to the left, favoring the reactants, because the system will absorb the added heat to reduce the disturbance.	v	
A233	The solubility product constant (Ksp) reflects the maximum concentration of ions in a solution at equilibrium, ~~and adding more solid to the solution will increase the value of Ksp.~~ Adding more solid does not change the value of Ksp because Ksp is constant for a given temperature and does not depend on the amount of solid present.		v
A234	The common ion effect ~~increases~~ decreases the solubility of a salt in solution~~, as the presence of a common ion reduces the ion concentration imbalance, thus shifting the equilibrium to favor more dissolution of the salt.~~ Because the presence of a common ion shifts the equilibrium toward the formation of more solid, reducing dissolution.		v
A235	When the value of Q is greater than the equilibrium constant (K), the reaction will shift in the reverse direction to re-establish equilibrium, as there are too many products compared to the reactants.	v	

A236	The common ion effect refers to the decrease in solubility of an ionic compound when a salt that contains one of the ions in the compound is added to the solution, shifting the equilibrium and reducing the dissolution of the compound.	v	
A237	The relationship between the solubility product constant (Ksp) and Gibbs free energy (ΔG°) is expressed by the equation, ΔG° = -RTln(Ksp), where a more negative ΔG° indicates a more spontaneous dissolution process, and thus a higher Ksp value.	v	
A238	The equilibrium constant (K) is entirely ~~independent of~~ **dependent on** temperature, meaning that changing the temperature of a reaction will not affect the position of equilibrium or the relative concentrations of reactants and products.		v
A239	Adding water to a saturated solution leads to dilution, which decreases the ion concentration and causes the reaction quotient (Q) to drop below the solubility product constant (Ksp), thereby shifting the equilibrium towards the dissolution of more solid to restore balance.	v	
A240	When additional reactant is added to a system at equilibrium, Le Chatelier's Principle predicts that the system will shift toward the ~~reactants~~ **products**, resulting in a ~~decrease~~ **increase** in the concentration of products to balance the added substance.		v

A241

(a)

The reaction quotient Q is calculated using the expression for K but with the initial concentrations of the reactants and products:

$$Q = \frac{[NH_3]^2}{[N_2][H_2]^3}$$

Substituting the given initial concentrations:

$[N_2] = 0.5$ M

$[H_2] = 1.5$ M

$[NH_3] = 1.0$ M

$$Q = \frac{[1.0]^2}{[0.5][1.5]^3} = 0.59$$

(b)

Since Q < K, this indicates that the reaction will shift towards the products to reach equilibrium. The concentration of NH_3 needs to increase, and the concentrations of N_2 and H_2 need to decrease.

A242

(a)

Stress	Response	Shift	K value
CO increases	CO decreases	Forward shift	No change

According to Le Chatelier's Principle, if the concentration of a reactant (in this case, CO) is increased, the system will respond by trying to counteract this change. The system will shift the equilibrium to the right (toward the formation of more products) to reduce the increased concentration of CO. As a result, more CH_3OH will be produced as the reaction shifts to the right.

(b)

Stress	Response	Shift	K value
T decreases	T increases	Toward exothermic (reverse shift)	Decreases

According to Le Chatelier's Principle, if the temperature decreases, the system will try to counteract this change by increasing the temperature, causing the equilibrium to shift toward the exothermic direction. Since the reaction is endothermic, it will shift in the reverse direction, toward the reactants, resulting in a decrease in the equilibrium constant (K).

(c)

Stress	Response	Shift	K value
P increases	P decreases (# moles of gas decreases) (3 mol → 1 mol)	Forward shift	No change

According to Le Chatelier's Principle, if the pressure increases, the system will try to counteract this change by decreasing the pressure, shifting the equilibrium in the direction where the number of gas moles decreases (in this case, from 3 moles to 1 mole). This results in a forward shift; however, the equilibrium constant (K) remains unchanged.

A243

(a)

Stress	Response	Shift	Solubility
Cl^- increases	Cl^- decreases	reverse shift	decreases

The addition of NaCl reduces the solubility of AgCl due to the common ion effect, as the system shifts to reduce the increased Cl^- concentration. This happens because the increased Cl^- makes Q > Ksp, causing the equilibrium to shift left to precipitate more AgCl.

(b)

Stress	Response	Shift	solubility
T decreases	T increases	Toward exothermic (reverse shift)	decreases

According to Le Chatelier's Principle, if the temperature decreases, the system will try to counteract this change by increasing the temperature, causing the equilibrium to shift toward the exothermic direction. Since the reaction is endothermic, it will shift in the reverse direction, toward the reactants, resulting in a decrease in the solubility of AgCl.

A244

(a)

$$Q = \frac{[SO_3]^2}{[O_2][SO_2]^2}$$

Substituting the given initial concentrations:
$[SO_2] = 0.30$ M
$[O_2] = 0.40$ M
$[SO_3] = 0.50$ M

$$Q = \frac{[0.50]^2}{[0.40][0.30]^2} = 6.9$$

(b)
Since Q (6.9) > K (0.65), this indicates that the reaction will shift towards the reactants to reach equilibrium, as the system will attempt to reduce the concentrations of the products and re-establish the balance. This shift helps decrease the value of Q until it equals K.

(c)
The concentration of SO_3 needs to decreases, and the concentrations of O_2 and SO_2 need to increases.

A245

(a)
$Q = [Ca^{2+}][CO_3^{2-}] = [1.0 \times 10^{-5}][3.0 \times 10^{-4}] = 3.0 \times 10^{-9}$

(b)
Since Q (3.0×10^{-9}) < Ksp (3.3×10^{-9}), the reaction will shift towards the products to increase their concentrations and reach equilibrium. This shift will continue until Q equals Ksp, meaning more $CaCO_3$ can dissolve. Therefore, no precipitate will form.

(c)

Stress	Response	Shift	Solubility
CO_3^{2-} increases	CO_3^{2-} decreases	reverse shift	decreases

The addition of CO_3^{2-} reduces the solubility of $CaCO_3$ due to the common ion effect, as the system shifts to reduce the increased Cl^- concentration. This happens because the increased CO_3^{2-} makes Q>Ksp, causing the equilibrium to shift left to precipitate more $CaCO_3$.

A246

(a)
$K_{sp} = [Ca^{2+}][F^-]^2$
$K_{sp} = [Ba^{2+}][SO_4^{2-}]$

(b)
Let x = molar solubility (M)

	$CaF_2(s)$	⇌	$Ca^{2+}(aq)$	$2 F^-(aq)$
Initial (I)				
Change (C)	-x		+x	+2x
Equilibrium (E)			x	2x

$K_{sp} = [Ca^{2+}][F^-]^2$
$= (x)(2x)^2 = 4x^3 = 3.9 \times 10^{-11}$
$x = 2.1 \times 10^{-4}$ M

(c)
Let x = molar solubility (M)

	$BaSO_4(s)$	⇌	$Ba^{2+}(aq)$	$SO_4^{2-}(aq)$
Initial (I)				
Change (C)	-x		+x	+x
Equilibrium (E)			x	x

$K_{sp} = [Ba^{2+}][SO_4^{2-}]$
$= (x)(x) = x^2 = 1.1 \times 10^{-10}$
$x = 1.0 \times 10^{-5}$ M

Since the molar solubility of CaF_2 (2.1×10^{-4} M) is greater than that of $BaSO_4$ (1.0×10^{-5} M), CaF_2 is more soluble in water.

A247

(a)
Adding the strong acid hydrochloric acid to an equilibrium system has the effect of introducing H_3O^+ ions.

Stress	Response	Shift
H_3O^+ increases	H_3O^+ decreases	reverse shift

According to Le Chatelier's Principle, if the concentration of a product (in this case, H_3O^+) is increased, the system will respond by trying to counteract this change. The system will shift the equilibrium to the left (toward the formation of more reactants) to reduce the increased concentration of H_3O^+.

(b)
The resulting color of the solution after the addition of 6.0 M hydrochloric acid will be orange because the equilibrium shifts to the left.

A248

I disagree with the student's hypothesis.

Stress	Response	Shift
T increases	T decreases	Toward endothermic (reverse shift)

Since the reaction is exothermic (ΔH°=−92.4kJ/mol), increasing the temperature will add heat to the system, which shifts the equilibrium to favor the reactants according to Le Chatelier's Principle. To counteract the added heat, the system will shift in the endothermic direction (toward the reactants, N_2 and H_2), resulting in less ammonia production. Therefore, increasing the temperature will decrease the production of ammonia.

A249

(a)
$CaF_2(s) \rightleftharpoons Ca^{2+}(aq) + 2\,F^-(aq)$
$CaCO_3(s) \rightleftharpoons Ca^{2+}(aq) + CO_3^{2-}(aq)$
$CaSO_4(s) \rightleftharpoons Ca^{2+}(aq) + SO_4^{2-}(aq)$

(b)
Let x = molar solubility (M)

	$CaF_2(s)$	$\rightleftharpoons$	$Ca^{2+}(aq)$	$2\,F^-(aq)$
Initial (I)				
Change (C)	-x		+x	+2x
Equilibrium (E)			x	2x

$Ksp = (x)(2x)^2 = 4x^3 = 3.9 \times 10^{-11}$
Molar solubility = x = 2.1×10^{-4} M

	$CaCO_3(s)$	$\rightleftharpoons$	$Ca^{2+}(aq)$	$CO_3^{2-}(aq)$
Initial (I)				
Change (C)	-x		+x	+x
Equilibrium (E)			x	x

$Ksp = (x)(x) = x^2 = 4.8 \times 10^{-9}$
Molar solubility = x = 6.9×10^{-5} M

	$CaSO_4(s)$	$\rightleftharpoons$	$Ca^{2+}(aq)$	$SO_4^{2-}(aq)$
Initial (I)				
Change (C)	-x		+x	+x
Equilibrium (E)			x	x

$Ksp = (x)(x) = x^2 = 2.4 \times 10^{-5}$
Molar solubility = $x = 4.9 \times 10^{-3}$ M

A250

(a)
$CaCO_3 (s) \rightleftarrows Ca^{2+}(aq) + CO_3^{2-}(aq)$
$MgCO_3 (s) \rightleftarrows Mg^{2+}(aq) + CO_3^{2-}(aq)$

(b)
$Q = [Ca^{2+}][CO_3^{2-}] = [0.050][0.002] = 0.0001 = 1.0 \times 10^{-4} > Ksp$
$Q = [Mg^{2+}][CO_3^{2-}] = [0.030][0.002] = 0.00006 = 6.0 \times 10^{-5} > Ksp$
Both $CaCO_3$ and $MgCO_3$ will precipitate.

A251

(a)

	2 SO_3 (g)	$\rightleftarrows$	2 SO_2 (g)	O_2 (g)
Initial (I)	1.00 atm			
Change (C)	-1.00 atm		+1.00 atm	+0.50 atm
End	0.00		1.00	0.50

Total pressure is 1.50 atm.

(b)

	2 SO_3 (g)	$\rightleftarrows$	2 SO_2 (g)	O_2 (g)
Initial (I)	1.00 atm			
Change (C)	-2x atm		+2x atm	+x atm
End	1.00-2x		2x	x

$(1.00-2x) + (2x) + (x) = 1.40$ atm
$x = 0.40$ atm
Partial pressure of SO_3 is 0.2 atm.
Partial pressure of SO_2 is 0.8 atm.
Partial pressure of O_2 is 0.4 atm.

(c)
$Kp = \dfrac{(PO2)(PSO2)^2}{(PSO3)^2} = \dfrac{(0.40)(0.80)^2}{(0.20)^2} = 6.4$

A252

If $Q > Ksp$, precipitation occurs. Therefore, by calculating when $Q = Ksp$, we can determine the minimum concentration of sulfate needed to initiate precipitation.
$Q = [Ba^{2+}][SO_4^{2-}] = [0.010][x] = 1.1 \times 10^{-10}$
Concentration of SO_4^{2-} is 1.1×10^{-8} M.

A253

(a)

$\Delta G° = -RT \ln K$
$= -(8.314 \text{ J/mol K})(298 \text{ K}) \ln(3.9 \times 10^{-11})$
$= +59 \text{ kJ/mol}$

(b)

Since $\Delta G° > 0$, the dissolution of CaF_2 is non-spontaneous.

A254

(a)

$[OH^-] = 2 \times 0.015$
$= 0.030 \text{ M}$

(b)

$K_{sp} = [Ca^{2+}][OH^-]^2 = (0.015)(0.030)^2$
$= 1.4 \times 10^{-5}$

A255

(a)

$Zn_3(PO_4)_2(s) \rightleftarrows 3 Zn^{2+}(aq) + 2 PO_4^{3-}(aq)$
$Cu_3(PO_4)_2(s) \rightleftarrows 3 Cu^{2+}(aq) + 2 PO_4^{3-}(aq)$

(b)

	$Na_3PO_4(aq)$	$\rightarrow$	$3 Na^+(aq)$	$PO_4^{3-}(aq)$
Initial	0.0030 M			
Change	-0.0030M		+0.0090M	+0.0030M
End	0		0.0090	0.0030

Concentration of phosphate ions = 0.0030 M

(c)

$Q = [Zn^{2+}]^3[PO_4^{3-}]^2 = [0.040]^3[0.0030]^2 = 5.8 \times 10^{-10} > K_{sp} (2.5 \times 10^{-17})$
$Q = [Cu^{2+}]^3[PO_4^{3-}]^2 = [0.0025]^3[0.0030]^2 = 1.4 \times 10^{-13} > K_{sp} (1.4 \times 10^{-29})$
Both will precipitate because $Q > K_{sp}$.

A256(B)

$K_{eq} > 1$: If K_{eq} is greater than 1, products are favored at equilibrium.
$K_{eq} < 1$: If K_{eq} is less than 1, reactants are favored at equilibrium.

A256 (B)

Products over Reactants: The equilibrium constant expression is written as the concentration of the products raised to the power of their coefficients, divided by the concentration of the reactants raised to the power of their coefficients.

Exclude Solids and Pure Liquids: Solids and pure liquids (like water in some cases) are not included in the Keq expression because their concentrations are constant.
Gases and Aqueous Species Only: Only include species that are in the gaseous or aqueous states in the Keq expression.

A258 (C)
Keq value depends on temperature.

A259 (C)
$K = \dfrac{(PNO)^2(PO2)}{(PNO2)^2} = \dfrac{[6.5*10^{-5}]^2[4.5*10^{-5}]}{[0.55]^2} = 6.3 \times 10^{-13}$

A260 (B)
$K = \dfrac{[H2]^2[O2]}{[H2O]^2} = \dfrac{[2.1*10^{-2}]^2[O2]}{[1.3*10^{-1}]^2} = 3.5 \times 10^{-3}$

$[O_2] = 0.134 M = \dfrac{x\ mol}{3\ L}$

x = 0.204 mol

A261 (B)
Make ICE chart to solve the problem.

	SO$_2$(g)	NO$_2$ (g)	⇌	SO$_3$(g)	NO(g)
Initial (I)	0.3 M	0.3 M			
Change (C)	-0.25 M	-0.25 M		+0.25 M	+0.25 M
Equilibrium (E)	0.05	0.05		0.25	0.25

$K = \dfrac{[SO3][NO]}{[SO2][NO2]} = \dfrac{[0.25][0.25]}{[0.05][0.05]} = 25$

A262 (B)(D)(A)(A)
(a)
Equation x $\frac{1}{2}$ → $\sqrt{K}$
(b)
Flip equation → $\frac{1}{K}$
(c)
Flip equation x $\frac{1}{2}$ → $\frac{1}{\sqrt{K}}$
(d)
Equation x 2 → K^2

A263 (B)
$Q = \dfrac{[NO2]^2}{[N2O4]} = \dfrac{(0.100)^2}{(0.020)} = 0.5$

Q > K

According to Le Chatelier's Principle, when Q > K, the reaction shifts toward the reverse direction (to the left) in order to reduce the concentration of products and increase the concentration of reactants. This happens because the system tends to counteract the change and move toward equilibrium. As the forward reaction proceeds, the Q value decreases until it reaches the K value.
In summary, when Q > K, the reaction will favor the forward direction to produce more reactants.

A264 (D)

$$Q = \frac{[CoCl2]}{[Co][Cl2]} = \frac{0.200}{(0.080)(0.080)} = 31.25$$

Q < K

According to Le Chatelier's Principle, when Q < K, the reaction shifts toward the forward direction (to the right) in order to reduce the concentration of reactants and increase the concentration of products. This happens because the system tends to counteract the change and move toward equilibrium. As the forward reaction proceeds, the Q value increases until it reaches the K value.
In summary, when Q < K, the reaction will favor the forward direction to produce more products.

A265 (A)

According to Le Chatelier's Principle

Stress	Response	Shift	Amount of N_2O_3
T increases	T decreases	Toward endothermic (reverse shift)	Decrease

Disagree, because the reaction is exothermic, and increasing temperature will favor the reverse reaction.

A266 (B)

Adding HCl is equivalent to adding Cl^- to the reactants.

Stress	Response	Shift	Mixture color
Add Cl^-	Remove Cl^-	Right shift (forward shift)	blue

Therefore, the mixture will become more blue because Cl^-(aq) will shift the equilibrium toward the formation of $CoCl_4^{2-}$.

A267 (A)

As the temperature increased from 400°C to 600°C, the K value became smaller.

Stress	Response	Shift	K value
T increases	T decreases	Toward endothermic (reverse shift)	Decrease

Therefore, the reaction is exothermic reaction.

A268 (B)

$Ksp = [Pb^{2+}][Cl^-]^2$

A269 (C)

Lex x = molar solubility (M)

	Al(OH)$_3$ (s)	⇌	Al^{3+}(aq)	3 OH$^-$(aq)
Initial (I)				
Change (C)	-x		+x	+3x
Equilibrium (E)			x	3x

$K_{sp} = [Al^{3+}][OH^-]^3$
$= (x)(3x)^3 = 27x^4 = 2.0 \times 10^{-32}$
$x = 5.2 \times 10^{-9}$ M

A270 (A)

When the coefficients are same, you can simply compare the Ksp values.

A271 (D)

When the coefficients are different, you can't simply compare the Ksp values; you need to directly calculate the molar solubility.

Lex x = molar solubility (M)
$Ca_3(PO_4)_2$ (s) ⇌ 3 Ca^{2+}(aq) + 2 PO_4^{3-}(aq)
$K_{sp} = [Ca^{2+}]^3[PO_4^{3-}]^2 = (3x)^3(2x)^2 = 108 x^5 = 1.3 \times 10^{-32}$
$x = 1.6 \times 10^{-7}$ M

$FePO_4$ (s) ⇌ Fe^{3+}(aq) + PO_4^{3-}(aq)
$K_{sp} = [Fe^{3+}][PO_4^{3-}] = x^2 = 1.0 \times 10^{-22}$
$x = 1.0 \times 10^{-11}$ M

Compare molar solubility, $Ca_3(PO_4)_2$ has the greater molar solubility.

A272 (B)

Lex x = molar solubility (M)

	PbI$_2$(s)	⇌	Pb^{2+}(aq)	2 I$^-$(aq)
Initial (I)				0.10 M
Change (C)	-x		+x	+2x
Equilibrium (E)			x	0.10 + 2x

$K_{sp} = 7.1 \times 10^{-9} = [Pb^{2+}][I^-]^2$
$= (x)(0.10+2x)^2 \approx (x)(0.10)^2$
Assume that 0.10 + 2x = 0.10 because of small Ksp.
$x = 7.1 \times 10^{-7}$ mol/L

A273 (A)

Let x = molar solubility (M)

	$Mg_3(PO_4)_2(s)$	⇌	$3\ Mg^{2+}(aq)$	$2\ PO_4^{3-}(aq)$
Initial (I)				0.15 M
Change (C)	-x		+3x	+2x
Equilibrium (E)			3x	0.15 + 2x

$Ksp = 6.4 \times 10^{-30} = [Mg^{2+}]^3[PO_4^{3-}]^2$
$= (3x)^3 (0.15 + 2x)^2 \approx (27x^3)(0.15)^2$
Assume that 0.15 + 2x = 0.15 because of small Ksp.
$x = 2.2 \times 10^{-10}$ mol/L

A274 (B)

To determine whether a precipitate will form, calculate Q and compare it with Ksp.
Q > Ksp : precipitate will form
Q < Ksp : precipitate will not form

When two solutions are mixed, the total volume changes, so be careful when considering the concentrations.

$[Ca^{2+}] = \frac{(100\ mL)(1.5 * 10^{-2}\ M)}{200\ mL} = 0.0075$ M

$[SO_4^{2-}] = \frac{(100\ mL)(2.0 * 10^{-3}\ M)}{200\ mL} = 0.001$ M

$Q = [Ca^{2+}][SO_4^{2-}] = (0.0075)(0.001) = 7.5 \times 10^{-6}$
Since Q < Ksp, precipitate will not form.

A275 (A)

Since $\Delta G° = -RT \ln K$, if $\Delta G°$ is negative, lnK must be positive. For lnK to be positive, K must be greater than 1. When K > 1, it means there are more products than reactants at equilibrium. Therefore, the correct answer is A.

Topic _8
Acids and Bases

Exam Weighting : 11–15%

Topic 8 Key Point Review

Acid
- A substance that donates protons (H^+ ions) in an aqueous solution.
- Bronsted-Lowry: Proton donor.
- pH < 7, turns blue litmus paper red.
- Strong acids : 100% dissociate
    - HCl, HBr, HI, HNO_3, H_2SO_4, $HClO_3$, $HClO_4$

Base
- A substance that accepts protons or produces OH^- ions in an aqueous solution.
- Bronsted-Lowry: Proton acceptor.
- pH > 7, turns red litmus paper blue.
- Strong bases : 100% dissociate
    - LiOH, NaOH, KOH, $Ca(OH)_2$, $Ba(OH)_2$, $Sr(OH)_2$

pH calculation
- pH: A measure of the acidity or basicity of a solution.
- $pH = -\log[H^+]$
    - pH of strong acid $= -\log[H^+]$
    - pH of weak acid $= -\log \sqrt{K_a C}$
- $pOH = -\log[OH^-] = 14 - pH$
- $pH + pOH = 14$
- $[H^+][OH^-] = 1.0 \times 10^{-14}$ @ 25 °C

pKa and pKb
- $pK_a = -\log K_a$
- $pK_b = -\log K_b$
- $K_a * K_b = K_w = 1.0 \times 10^{-14}$ @ 25 °C
- $pK_a + pK_b = 14$

Titration curve

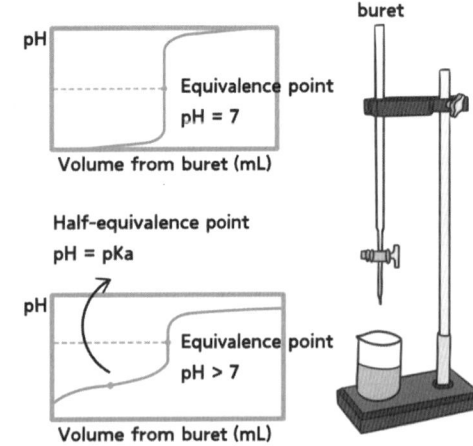

- Strong acid/strong base: Sharp jump in pH near the equivalence point (pH ≈ 7).
- Weak acid/strong base: Equivalence point > 7, with a buffer region and gradual rise.
- Weak base/strong acid: Equivalence point < 7, with a buffer region
- Equivalence Point: Moles of acid = moles of base.
    - $n_a M_a V_a = n_b M_b V_b$
- Buffer region: Flat section before equivalence point where pH changes slowly.

Buffer solution
- A solution that resists changes in pH when small amounts of acid or base are added.
- pH Calculation (Henderson-Hasselbalch equation)

$$pH = pKa + \log \frac{[A^-]}{[HA]}$$

- Best buffer composition
    - Weak acid : its conjugate base = 1 : 1
    - Weak base : its conjugate acid = 1 : 1
    - Strong acid : weak base = 1 : 2
    - Strong base : weak acid = 1 : 2

Salt hydrolysis
- The reaction of a salt with water, which may produce an acidic or basic solution depending on the ions.
    - Hydrolysis reactions occur when the conjugate acid or base reacts with water to produce H^+ or OH^-.
- Salts of strong acids and strong bases: Neutral solution
- Salts of weak acids and strong bases: Basic solution
- Salts of strong acids and weak bases: Acidic solution

True/False Questions

Read the following statements carefully and determine whether each one is true or false. Place a tick (✔) in the appropriate box. If the statement is false, correct the incorrect part of the statement.

	Statement	True	False
Q276	Strong acids completely ionize in aqueous solution, while weak acids partially ionize, meaning they exist primarily as the undissociated form at equilibrium.		
Q277	The acid dissociation constant (Ka) is a measure of the strength of an acid, with larger Ka values indicating weaker acids due to higher levels of dissociation in solution.		
Q278	A solution with a higher concentration of hydronium ions (H_3O^+) than hydroxide ions (OH^-) will have a pH less than 7, indicating an acidic solution.		
Q279	When calculating the pH of a weak acid solution, the equilibrium concentration of H_3O^+ can be approximated using the initial acid concentration and Ka, assuming the degree of ionization is sufficiently small.		
Q380	In pure water at 25°C, the concentration of hydroxide ions (OH^-) is greater than the concentration of hydronium ions (H_3O^+) due to water's self-ionization, leading to a slightly basic solution.		
Q281	In a titration of a strong acid with a strong base, the equivalence point is reached when the moles of acid equal the moles of base, resulting in a neutral solution with a pH of 7.		
Q282	A buffer solution resists pH changes because any added acid combines with the weak acid present, preventing significant changes in the pH of the solution.		
Q283	In a titration curve of a buffer solution, the pH remains relatively stable near the equivalence point due to the buffer's ability to neutralize both added acid and base.		
Q284	In salt hydrolysis, the salt formed from a weak acid and a strong base will hydrolyze in water, resulting in a basic solution due to the production of hydroxide ions.		
Q285	When a solution of a weak acid and its conjugate base is diluted, the pH of the buffer remains relatively unchanged because the ratio of the concentrations of the weak acid to its conjugate base stays the same, regardless of dilution.		

Q286	In a titration of a weak acid with a strong base, the pH at the equivalence point is determined solely by the concentration of the weak acid and is always less than 7, due to the presence of the weak acid's conjugate base.		
Q287	The Henderson-Hasselbalch equation can be used to calculate the pH of a buffer solution at any point during the titration, including when a strong base has been added beyond the buffer's capacity.		
Q288	For a polyprotic acid, the second dissociation constant (K_{a2}) is always significantly smaller than the first dissociation constant (K_{a1}) because it is harder to remove a proton from an already negatively charged species.		
Q289	In a buffer solution, the pH will change more dramatically when a strong acid or base is added if the concentrations of the weak acid and its conjugate base are equal, due to the higher sensitivity at this ratio.		
Q290	In salt hydrolysis, the salt of a weak base and a strong acid will produce a neutral solution because neither the cation nor the anion of the salt significantly reacts with water.		

Concept Check Questions

When solving Free-Response Questions (FRQs), it is essential to clearly and accurately explain your reasoning. Make sure to outline the steps in your solution process thoroughly, showing all calculations with appropriate numbers and units. This demonstrates a full understanding of the problem and ensures that your answer is both correct and complete.

Q291

You are provided with four different solutions as described below:

Solution	Composition
A	0.050 M HI
B	0.10 M HF ($K_a = 6.6 \times 10^{-4}$)
C	0.020 M KOH
D	0.25 M NH_3 ($K_b = 1.8 \times 10^{-5}$)

Calculate the pH of each solutions.

A	
B	
C	
D	

Q292

You are provided with four different solutions as described below:

Solution	Composition
A	0.030 M H_2SO_4
B	0.20 M CH_3COOH ($K_a = 1.8 \times 10^{-5}$)
C	0.040 M $Ca(OH)_2$
D	0.75 M CH_3NH_2 ($K_b = 4.4 \times 10^{-4}$)

Calculate the pH of each solutions.

A	
B	
C	
D	

Q293
A student prepares three different solutions, A, B, and C, as described in the table below:

Solution	Composition
A	100 mL of 0.10 M NaOH (aq) mixed with 100 mL of 0.10 M HCl (aq)
B	100 mL of 0.10 M NaCl (aq) mixed with 100 mL of 0.10 M HCl (aq)
C	100 mL of 0.10 M CH$_3$COOH (aq) mixed with 100 mL of 0.10 M NaOH (aq)

The dissociation constant Ka for acetic acid (CH$_3$COOH) is 1.8×10^{-5}.

(a)
Using the information in the table above, write the letters of the solutions in the boxes below to rank them in order of increasing pH. Explain your reasoning for the ranking.

	<		<	

(b)
Does the pH of Solution B increase, decrease, or remain the same when 100 mL of water is added? Justify your answer.

252 AP Chemistry Power Practice Workbook

Q294

The dissociation of propanoic acid, C_2H_5COOH, is represented by the equation below:

$$C_2H_5COOH(aq) + H_2O(l) \rightleftharpoons H_3O^+(aq) + C_2H_5COO^-(aq)$$

Using a pH probe, the student determines that the pH of the 0.150 M propanoic acid solution is 4.87.

(a)
Using the pH value, calculate the value of Ka for propanoic acid.

(b)
Calculate the percent dissociation of propanoic acid in the 0.150 M solution.

(c)
In a separate experimental procedure, the student titrates 25.0 mL of the 1.500 M propanoic acid with a sodium hydroxide solution of unknown concentration. The student monitors the pH during the titration and constructs a titration curve. Based on the titration data, calculate the molarity of the sodium hydroxide solution if the equivalence point occurs at 30.0 mL of NaOH(aq).

Q295

The molecular formula of benzoic acid, $HC_7H_5O_2$, is similar to acetylsalicylic acid. The dissociation of benzoic acid in water is represented by the equation below:

$$HC_7H_5O_2\,(aq) + H_2O\,(l) \rightleftarrows H_3O^+(aq) + C_7H_5O_2^-\,(aq)$$

The pH of a 0.0020 M $HC_7H_5O_2$ (aq) solution is measured to be 3.12.

(a)
Write the expression for the equilibrium constant, Ka, for the dissociation of benzoic acid.

(b)
Calculate the value of Ka for benzoic acid.

Q296

A buffer solution is prepared using carbonic acid (H_2CO_3) and sodium bicarbonate ($NaHCO_3$). The dissociation constant $Ka1$ for carbonic acid is 4.3×10^{-7}.

(a)
A buffer is made by mixing 0.50 M carbonic acid with 0.50 M sodium bicarbonate in equal volumes. Write the expression for the pH of the buffer using the Henderson-Hasselbalch equation and calculate the pH of this buffer.

(b)
The buffer composition is altered so that the concentration of carbonic acid remains 0.50 M, but the concentration of sodium bicarbonate is changed to 0.25 M. Calculate the new pH of the buffer.

(c)
Describe how the pH of the buffer changes if the concentrations of both carbonic acid and sodium bicarbonate are doubled, while maintaining a 1:1 molar ratio. Will the pH of the buffer increase, decrease, or stay the same? Explain your reasoning.

(d)
For the original buffer (0.50 M carbonic acid and 0.50 M sodium bicarbonate), calculate the pH after adding 0.010 moles of HCl to 1.0 L of the buffer. Assume the total volume of the solution does not change significantly.

(e)
Calculate the pH after adding 0.010 moles of NaOH to 1.0 L of this buffer solution.

(f)
A second buffer is made with the same molar ratio of carbonic acid to sodium bicarbonate as in (a), but the concentrations are both reduced to 0.10 M. Calculate the pH after adding 0.010 moles of HCl to 1.0 L of this buffer.

(g)
Compare the pH change in (d) and (f), and explain how buffer concentration affects the buffer's capacity to resist changes in pH.

Q297

A buffer solution is prepared by mixing 0.200 M benzoic acid (C_6H_5COOH) and 0.150 M sodium benzoate (C_6H_5COONa). The dissociation constant Ka for benzoic acid is 6.3×10^{-5}.

(a)
Write the expression for the Ka of benzoic acid in water and calculate the pKa.

(b)
Using the Henderson-Hasselbalch equation, calculate the pH of the buffer solution.

(c)
If 0.010 moles of HCl is added to 500 mL of this buffer solution, calculate the new pH. Assume no significant volume change.

(d)
If 0.010 moles of NaOH is added to 500 mL of the original buffer solution, calculate the new pH. Again, assume no significant volume change.

(e)
Explain the role of the weak acid and its conjugate base in resisting changes in pH when HCl and NaOH are added to the buffer.

Q298

A student is asked to prepare a buffer solution using equimolar amounts of sodium acetate (CH_3COONa) and acetic acid (CH_3COOH). The student uses 50.00 mL of 0.100 M CH_3COOH, which contains 0.00500 mol of CH_3COOH, to make the buffer.

(a)
The Ka value for acetic acid (CH_3COOH) is 1.8×10^{-5}, and the pH of the buffer the student prepared is 4.74. Calculate the ratio of CH_3COOH and CH_3COO^-.

(b)
The student performs a titration of the acetic acid solution using 0.100 M NaOH.
The initial concentration of CH_3COOH is 0.100 M, and the total volume is 50.00 mL.

Initial pH: Calculate the initial pH of the 0.100 M CH_3COOH solution before the titration begins.	
Half-equivalence point: Determine the volume of NaOH needed to reach the half-equivalence point and calculate the pH at this point.	
Equivalence point: Calculate the volume of 0.100 M NaOH required to reach the equivalence point. What will the pH be at this point?	

Graph: Sketch a titration curve for the addition of NaOH to the CH₃COOH solution, showing the initial pH, the half-equivalence point, and the equivalence point on the graph.

Q299

A student is studying the acid-base properties of oxalic acid ($H_2C_2O_4$), a diprotic acid.
The two-step dissociation of oxalic acid in water is represented by the following reactions:

$H_2C_2O_4 + H_2O \rightleftharpoons HC_2O_4^- + H_3O^+$ $Ka_1 = 5.4 \times 10^{-2}$

$HC_2O_4^- + H_2O \rightleftharpoons C_2O_4^{2-} + H_3O^+$ $Ka_2 = 5.4 \times 10^{-5}$

(a)
Calculate the pKa1 value for the $H_2C_2O_4$ and pKa2 value for the $HC_2O_4^-$ ion.

(b)
A buffer solution with a pH of 4.00 is prepared using $C_2O_4^{2-}$ and $HC_2O_4^-$.
Calculate the ratio of $\dfrac{[C_2O_4^{2-}]}{[HC_2O_4^-]}$ in this solution.

Q300

You are titrating 75.0 mL of an unknown concentration of hydrofluoric acid (HF) with 0.30 M lithium hydroxide (LiOH). After adding 45.0 mL of LiOH, the pH of the solution at the half equivalence point is measured to be 3.17.

(a)
Calculate the pKa and the Ka of hydrofluoric acid.

(b)
In the same titration, right before the half equivalence point, the pH of the solution is 2.90. At this point, is there more HF (acid) or more F^- (conjugate base) in the solution?

(c)
After adding slightly more LiOH, right after the half equivalence point, the pH of the solution is measured to be 3.40. At this point, is there more HF (acid) or more F^- (conjugate base)?

Q301
You are titrating 40.0 mL of 0.20 M hydrobromic acid (HBr) with 0.10 M calcium hydroxide ($Ca(OH)_2$). The goal is to determine the pH at various points during the titration process.

(a)
Calculate the pH of the 0.20 M HBr solution before adding any calcium hydroxide.

(b)
Calculate the pH after 10.0 mL of 0.10 M $Ca(OH)_2$ has been added to the HBr solution.

(c)
Calculate the pH at the equivalence point, where all of the HBr has been neutralized by calcium hydroxide.

(d)
Calculate the pH after 50.0 mL of 0.10 M calcium hydroxide has been added, which is beyond the equivalence point.

Q302

You are titrating 50.0 mL of 0.10 M acetic acid (CH_3COOH) with 0.10 M sodium hydroxide (NaOH). The goal is to determine the pH at several points during the titration process.
The K_a of acetic acid is 1.8×10^{-5}.

(a)
Calculate the pH of the 0.10 M acetic acid solution before adding any NaOH.

(b)
Calculate the pH after 10.0 mL of 0.10 M NaOH has been added to the acetic acid solution.

(c)
Calculate the pH when half of the acetic acid has been neutralized by NaOH.

(d)
Calculate the pH at the equivalence point, where all the acetic acid has been neutralized by NaOH.

(e)
Calculate the pH after 60.0 mL of NaOH has been added, which is beyond the equivalence point.

Q303
You are titrating two different solutions:
- 30.0 mL of 0.200 M HBr (a strong acid)
- 30.0 mL of 0.200 M lactic acid (a weak acid, $K_a = 1.4 \times 10^{-4}$)

Both acids are titrated with 0.500 M KOH. Using this information, describe how the pH changes during the titration of both a strong acid and a weak acid, considering the starting pH, the buffer region for the weak acid, and the sharp rise at the equivalence point. For each acid, identify and include the following on the titration curve:

(a) The initial point (starting pH).
(b) The equivalence point volume.
(c) If applicable, the half-equivalence point.

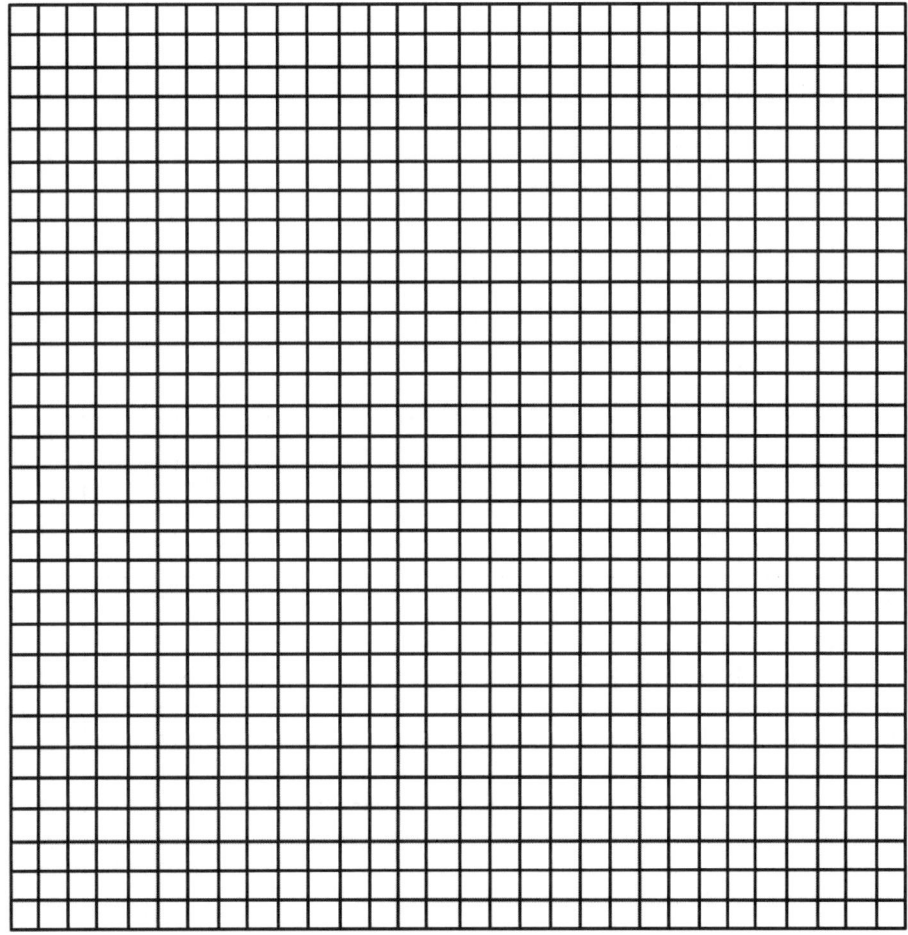

Q304

You are titrating two different solutions:
- 40.0 mL of 0.300 M HI (a strong acid)
- 40.0 mL of 0.300 M H_2SO_4 (a strong acid)

Both acids are titrated with 0.500 M KOH. Using this information, describe how the pH changes during the titration of both a strong acid and a weak acid, considering the starting pH, the buffer region for the weak acid, and the sharp rise at the equivalence point. For each acid, identify and include the following on the titration curve:

(a) The initial point (starting pH).
(b) The equivalence point volume.
(c) If applicable, the half-equivalence point.

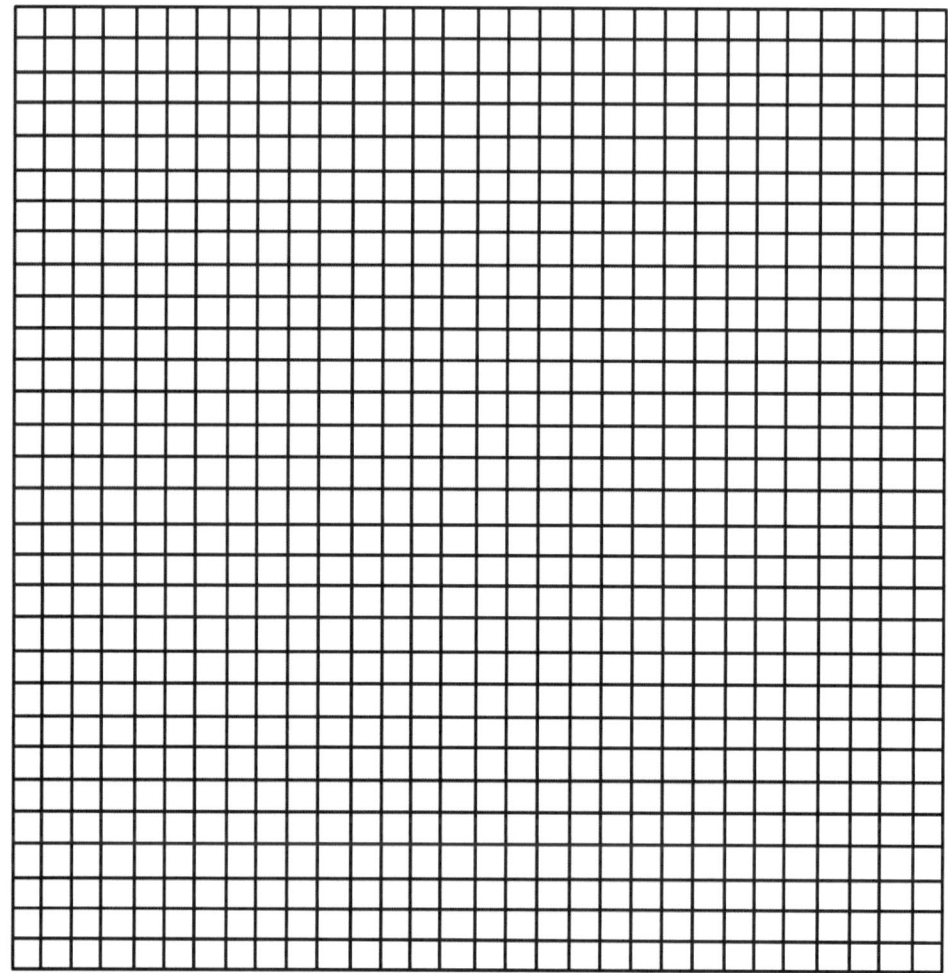

Q305

(a)
You are titrating 25.0 mL of 0.100 M HCl with 0.100 M NaOH. How many milliliters of NaOH are needed to reach the equivalence point?

(b)
50.0 mL of 0.200 M H_2SO_4 is titrated with NaOH. If it takes 100.0 mL of NaOH to reach the equivalence point, what is the molarity of the NaOH solution?

(c)
You are titrating 30.0 mL of 0.150 M HNO_3 with 0.100 M NaOH. After adding 15.0 mL of NaOH, what is the pH of the solution?

(d)
A 35.0 mL sample of acetic acid (CH_3COOH) is titrated with 0.150 M NaOH. It takes 25.0 mL of NaOH to reach the equivalence point. What is the molarity of the acetic acid solution?

(e)
You are titrating 50.0 mL of a diprotic acid, H_2A, with 0.200 M NaOH. If it takes 75.0 mL of NaOH to reach the second equivalence point, what is the molarity of the diprotic acid solution?

Q306
You are tasked with determining the acidity of a fruit juice sample. To achieve this, you perform a titration using 0.10 M Al(OH)$_3$ as the titrant. A 50.0 mL sample of the fruit juice is titrated, and it takes 20.0 mL of Al(OH)$_3$ to reach the equivalence point. Assume that the acid in the juice behaves as a diprotic acid.

Calculate the molarity of the acid present in the fruit juice. Provide your answer with appropriate significant figures and include the necessary steps for your calculation.

Q307
You are tasked with determining the concentration of an unknown base in a household cleaning solution. To do so, you perform a titration using 0.10 M H$_2$SO$_3$ as the titrant. A 25.0 mL sample of the cleaning solution is titrated, and it takes 15.0 mL of H$_2$SO$_3$ to reach the equivalence point. Assume that the base has one hydroxide ion.

Calculate the molarity of the base present in the cleaning solution. Provide your answer with appropriate significant figures and include the necessary steps for your calculation.

Q308
A 0.10 M solution of sodium acetate (NaCH$_3$COO) is prepared by dissolving the salt in water. Acetate ion (CH$_3$COO$^-$) is the conjugate base of acetic acid (CH$_3$COOH), a weak acid with a Ka of 1.8×10^{-5}. Write the hydrolysis reaction for the acetate ion in water and calculate pH of the solution.

Q309
A 0.20 M solution of ammonium chloride (NH$_4$Cl) is prepared by dissolving the salt in water. Ammonium ion (NH$_4^+$) is the conjugate acid of ammonia (NH$_3$), a weak base with a Kb of 1.8×10^{-5}. Write the hydrolysis reaction for the ammonium ion in water and calculate pH of the solution.

Q310
A 0.30 M solution of sodium hydrogen sulfate ($NaHSO_4$) is prepared by dissolving the salt in water. Sodium hydrogen sulfate (HSO_4^-) is the conjugate base of sulfuric acid (H_2SO_4), a diprotic strong acid. The Ka for H_2SO_4 is 1.2×10^{-2}.

Multiple Choice Questions

The following questions are multiple-choice.
Choose the correct answer and explain why the other options are incorrect.

Q311
You have a 0.050 M solution of formic acid (HCOOH), which has a Ka of 1.8×10^{-4}. What is the pH of the solution?

A) 2.02
B) 2.25
C) 2.52
D) 3.00

Q312
A 0.10 M solution of methylamine (CH_3NH_2) has a Kb of 4.4×10^{-4}.
What is the pH of the solution?

A) 11.82
B) 11.12
C) 10.74
D) 9.89

Q313
You are given a 0.070 M solution of sulfurous acid (H_2SO_3), a diprotic acid. The first dissociation constant, K_{a1}, is 1.5×10^{-2}, and the second dissociation constant, K_{a2}, is 6.0×10^{-8}.
What is the approximate pH of the solution, assuming only the first dissociation contributes significantly to the pH?

A) 1.32
B) 1.28
C) 1.49
D) 2.50

Q314
50.0 mL of 0.200 M ammonia (NH_3) is titrated with 25.0 mL of 0.200 M HCl.
The K_b for ammonia is 1.8×10^{-5}. What is the pH of the solution after adding the HCl?

A) 8.90
B) 9.26
C) 9.55
D) 9.80

Q315
A buffer solution is prepared by mixing 100.0 mL of 0.250 M acetic acid (CH_3COOH) and 50.0 mL of 0.250 M sodium acetate (CH_3COONa). The Ka of acetic acid is 1.8×10^{-5}. What is the pH of the buffer solution?

A) 4.14
B) 4.35
C) 4.44
D) 4.75

Q316
A buffer solution is prepared by mixing 50.0 mL of 0.100 M benzoic acid (C_6H_5COOH) and 50.0 mL of 0.050 M sodium benzoate (C_6H_5COONa). The Ka of benzoic acid is 6.3×10^{-5}. What is the pH of the buffer solution?

A) 3.80
B) 3.90
C) 4.40
D) 4.60

Q317
A buffer is made by combining 75.0 mL of 0.300 M ammonia (NH_3) with 25.0 mL of 0.300 M ammonium chloride (NH_4Cl). The Kb for ammonia is 1.8×10^{-5}. What is the pH of this buffer?

A) 8.75
B) 9.38
C) 9.55
D) 9.73

Q318
A buffer is prepared by mixing 100.0 mL of 0.200 M lactic acid ($C_3H_6O_3$) with 50.0 mL of 0.100 M sodium lactate ($C_3H_5O_3Na$). The Ka of lactic acid is 1.4×10^{-4}. What is the pH of the buffer solution?

A) 3.25
B) 3.80
C) 4.00
D) 4.25

Q319
You are titrating two different solutions:
- 50.0 mL of 0.100 M HCl (a strong acid)
- 50.0 mL of 0.100 M acetic acid (a weak acid, $K_a = 1.8 \times 10^{-5}$)

Both are titrated with 0.100 M NaOH. What can you say about the pH at the equivalence points of these two titrations?

A) The pH at the equivalence point will be higher for the acetic acid titration.
B) The pH at the equivalence point will be higher for the HCl titration.
C) The pH at the equivalence point will be the same for both titrations.
D) The pH at the equivalence point will be neutral (pH = 7) for both titrations.

Q320
A 50.0 mL sample of 0.100 M benzoic acid (C_6H_5COOH, $K_a = 6.3 \times 10^{-5}$) is being titrated with 0.100 M NaOH. After 30.0 mL of NaOH has been added, what is the pH of the solution?

A) 4.23
B) 4.38
C) 5.10
D) 5.40

Q321
A 0.100 M solution of a weak acid (HA) with a Ka of 1.5×10^{-5} is titrated with 0.100 M NaOH. If 25.0 mL of NaOH is required to reach the equivalence point, what is the pH when 12.5 mL of NaOH has been added?

A) 4.82
B) 5.00
C) 5.18
D) 5.50

Q322
You are titrating 50.0 mL of 0.100 M acetic acid (CH_3COOH, Ka = 1.8×10^{-5}) with 0.100 M NaOH. Which of the following best describes the pH change as you approach the equivalence point?

A) The pH changes rapidly at the half-equivalence point due to the strong acid-base interaction.
B) The pH remains nearly constant before the equivalence point because the solution acts as a buffer.
C) The pH drops suddenly before the equivalence point due to acetic acid dissociation.
D) The pH remains neutral until the equivalence point, then rises sharply.

Q323
You have two solutions:
- 0.200 M NaOH (a strong base)
- 0.200 M ammonia (NH$_3$, Kb = 1.8×10^{-5})

Which of the following best describes the difference in their initial pH values before titration?

A) The initial pH of the NaOH solution is much higher than the ammonia solution.
B) The initial pH of the NaOH solution is much lower than the ammonia solution.
C) The initial pH of both solutions is the same.
D) The initial pH of the NaOH solution is only slightly higher than the ammonia solution.

Q324
You are titrating two different solutions:
- 50.0 mL of 0.200 M sulfuric acid (H$_2$SO$_4$, a strong diprotic acid)
- 50.0 mL of 0.200 M carbonic acid (H$_2$CO$_3$, a weak diprotic acid, Ka1 =4.3×10^{-7})

Both are titrated with 0.200 M NaOH. What is the pH at the equivalence point for each solution?

A) The pH at the equivalence point will be higher for the sulfuric acid titration.
B) The pH at the equivalence point will be neutral for both titrations.
C) The pH at the equivalence point will be the same for both titrations, but not neutral.
D) The pH at the equivalence point will be higher for the carbonic acid titration.

Q325
You are titrating two different solutions:
- 50.0 mL of 0.200 M NaOH (a strong base)
- 50.0 mL of 0.200 M ammonia (NH$_3$, Kb = 1.8×10^{-5})

Both are titrated with 0.200 M HCl. What is the pH at the equivalence point for each solution?

A) The pH at the equivalence point will be higher for the ammonia titration.
B) The pH at the equivalence point will be neutral for both titrations.
C) The pH at the equivalence point will be higher for the NaOH titration.
D) The pH at the equivalence point will be the same for both titrations, but not neutral.

Q326
A 50.0 mL solution of 0.100 M methylamine (CH$_3$NH$_2$, Kb = 4.4×10^{-4}) is titrated with 0.100 M HCl. What will the pH be at the equivalence point?

A) 3.28
B) 5.92
C) 7.00
D) 9.28

Q327

The student uses the 0.20 M lithium hydroxide solution to titrate unknown monoprotic acid solution, a buret, a pH meter, and a 100 mL Erlenmeyer flask to titrate a 25.0 mL sample of the unknown acid solution. The student's data are shown in the following graph.

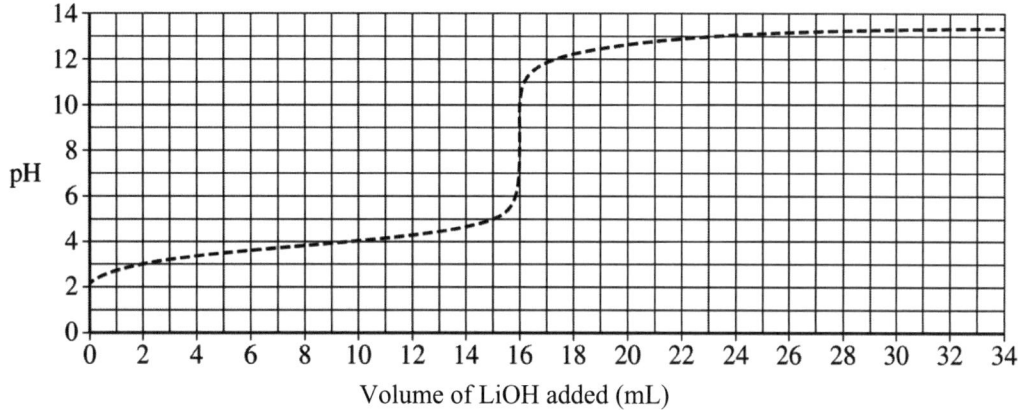

Weak acid	Ka
Hydrofluoric acid	5.6×10^{-4}
Formic acid	1.8×10^{-4}
Acetic acid	1.8×10^{-5}

Determine the concentration of the unknown acid and identify the acid based on the Ka and graph.

A) 0.13 M and Hydrofluoric acid
B) 0.13 M and Formic acid
C) 0.032 M and Hydrofluoric acid
D) 0.023 M and Acetic acid

Q328

You are titrating a 0.100 M solution of ammonia (NH_3, $K_b = 1.8 \times 10^{-5}$) with 0.100 M HCl. After adding exactly half of the volume of HCl required to reach the equivalence point, what can you say about the buffer capacity and the pH of the solution?

A) The pH of the solution will be equal to the pKa of NH_4^+, and the buffer capacity is at its maximum.
B) The pH of the solution will be higher than the pKa of NH_4^+, and the buffer capacity is low.
C) The pH of the solution will be lower than the pKa of NH_4^+, and the buffer capacity is high.
D) The pH of the solution will be neutral, and the buffer capacity will be at a minimum.

Q329

The student titrates 15.0 mL unknown concentration of monoprotic acid with 0.0300 M KOH, using a probe to monitor the pH of the solution. The data are plotted producing the following titration curve.

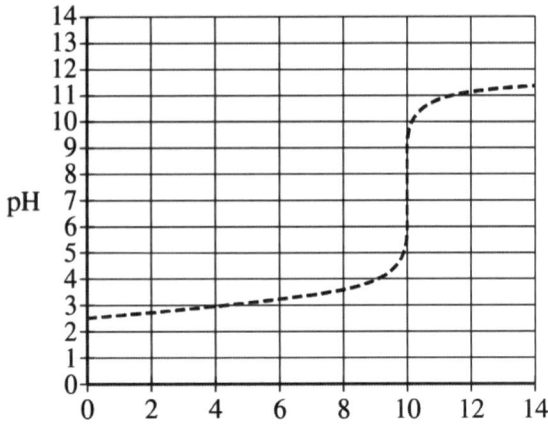

Volume of 0.0300 M KOH added (mL)

Determine the concentration of the monoprotic acid and Ka.

A) 0.0100 M and 6.5 x 10^{-4}
B) 0.0200 M and 4.5 x 10^{-7}
C) 0.0200 M and 4.5 x 10^{-7}
D) 0.0200 M and 6.5 x 10^{-4}

Q330

A student is performing a titration to determine the concentration of an unknown base solution which contains group 1 metal. The student uses 0.400 M sulfuric acid (H_2SO_4) as the titrant and adds it to a solution of the unknown base in an Erlenmeyer flask. The student also uses phenolphthalein as the indicator, which is colorless in acidic conditions and pink in basic conditions. The student records the following information during the experiment:

Initial volume in buret (H_2SO_4)	2.15 mL
Final volume in buret (H_2SO_4)	31.75 mL
Volume of the unknown base in the flask	17.00 mL

Determine the concentration of the base.

A) 0.71 M
B) 0.84 M
C) 1.25 M
D) 1.39 M

Worked solution with answer for Topic 8

		Statement	True	False
	A276	Strong acids completely ionize in aqueous solution, while weak acids partially ionize, meaning they exist primarily as the undissociated form at equilibrium.	v	
	A277	The acid dissociation constant (Ka) is a measure of the strength of an acid, with larger Ka values indicating ~~weaker acids~~ stronger acid due to higher levels of dissociation in solution.		v
	A278	A solution with a higher concentration of hydronium ions (H_3O^+) than hydroxide ions (OH^-) will have a pH less than 7, indicating an acidic solution.	v	
	A279	When calculating the pH of a weak acid solution, the equilibrium concentration of H_3O^+ can be approximated using the initial acid concentration and Ka, assuming the degree of ionization is sufficiently small.	v	
	A280	In pure water at 25°C, the concentration of hydroxide ions (OH^-) is ~~greater than~~ equal to the concentration of hydronium ions (H_3O^+) due to water's self-ionization, leading to a ~~slightly basic~~ neutral solution.		v
	A281	In a titration of a strong acid with a strong base, the equivalence point is reached when the moles of acid equal the moles of base, resulting in a neutral solution with a pH of 7.	v	
	A282	A buffer solution resists pH changes because any added acid combines with the ~~weak acid~~ conjugate base present, preventing significant changes in the pH of the solution.		v
	A283	In a titration curve of a buffer solution, the pH remains relatively stable near the half equivalence point due to the buffer's ability to neutralize both added acid and base.		v
	A284	In salt hydrolysis, the salt formed from a weak acid and a strong base will hydrolyze in water, resulting in a basic solution due to the production of hydroxide ions.	v	
	A285	When a solution of a weak acid and its conjugate base is diluted, the pH of the buffer remains relatively unchanged because the ratio of the concentrations of the weak acid to its conjugate base stays the same, regardless of dilution.	v	
	A286	In a titration of a weak acid with a strong base, ~~the pH at the equivalence point is determined solely by the concentration of the weak acid and is always less than 7, due to the presence of the weak acid's conjugate base.~~ at the equivalence point, the solution contains the conjugate base of the weak acid, making the solution slightly basic, and the pH is typically greater than 7.		v

A287	The Henderson-Hasselbalch equation can be used to calculate the pH of a buffer solution ~~at any point during the titration, including when a strong base has been added beyond the buffer's capacity.~~ when the buffer is functioning, i.e., when the solution contains significant amounts of both the weak acid and its conjugate base. Beyond the buffer capacity, this equation no longer applies.		v
A288	For a polyprotic acid, the second dissociation constant (K_{a2}) is always significantly smaller than the first dissociation constant (K_{a1}) because it is harder to remove a proton from an already negatively charged species.	v	
A289	In a buffer solution, the pH will change ~~more dramatically~~ the least when a strong acid or base is added if the concentrations of the weak acid and its conjugate base are equal, ~~due to the higher sensitivity at this ratio.~~ as this is when the buffer has the maximum capacity to resist changes in pH.		v
A290	In salt hydrolysis, the salt of a weak base and a strong acid will produce a ~~neutral~~ slightly acidic ~~solution because neither the cation nor the anion of the salt significantly reacts with water.~~ as the conjugate acid of the weak base reacts with water to form H_3O^+.		v

A291

A	pH = - log (0.050) = 1.30
B	pH = - log $\sqrt{K_a C}$ = - log $\sqrt{(6.6 * 10^{-4})(0.10)}$ = 2.09
C	[OH⁻] = 0.020 M pOH = - log (0.020) = 1.70 pH = 14 – pOH = 14 – 1.70 = 12.30
D	pOH = - log$\sqrt{K_b C}$ = - log$\sqrt{(1.8 * 10^{-5})(0.25)}$ = 2.67 pH = 14 – 2.67 = 11.33

A292

A	[H⁺] = 0.030 x 2 = 0.060 M pH = - log (0.060) = 1.22
B	pH = - log $\sqrt{K_a C}$ = - log $\sqrt{(1.8 * 10^{-5})(0.20)}$ = 2.72
C	[OH⁻] = 0.040 x 2 M pOH = - log (0.080) = 1.10 pH = 14 – pOH = 14 – 1.10 = 12.90
D	pOH = - log$\sqrt{K_b C}$ = - log$\sqrt{(4.4 * 10^{-4})(0.75)}$ = 1.74 pH = 14 – 1.74 = 12.26

A293

(a)

A : Strong acid + Strong base → Neutral salt + Water
B : Neutral salt + Strong acid → Acidic solution
C : Weak acid + Strong base → Basic solution

| B | < | A | < | C |

(b)
Original pH = 1
$[H^+]$ = M1V1 = M2V2 = (0.10 M)(200 mL) = M2 (300 mL)
M2 = 0.066 M HCl
$[H^+]$ = 0.066 M
pH = - log [0.066] = 1.18
Therefore, the pH of solution B increases when 100 mL of water is added.

A294

(a)
pH = 4.87
$[H^+] = 10^{-pH} = 10^{-4.87} = 1.35 \times 10^{-5}$ M

	$C_2H_5COOH(aq)$	→	$H_3O^+(aq)$	$C_2H_5COO^-(aq)$
Initial	0.150 M			
Change	- 1.35 x 10⁻⁵ M		+ 1.35 x 10⁻⁵ M	+ 1.35 x 10⁻⁵ M
Equilibrium	0.150 - 1.35 x 10⁻⁵ M		1.35 x 10⁻⁵ M	1.35 x 10⁻⁵ M

$Ka = \frac{[H3O^+][C2H5COO^-]}{[C2H5COOH]} = \frac{(1.35*10^{-5})^2}{0.150 - 1.35*10^{-5}} = 1.21 \times 10^{-9}$

(b)
% dissociation = $\frac{1.35*10^{-5}}{0.150}$ x 100 = 0.00900 %

(c)
naMaVa = nbMbVb
(1)(0.1500M) (25.0 mL) = (1)(Mb)(30.0 mL)
Mb = 0.125 M

A295

(a)

$$Ka = \frac{[H_3O^+][C_7H_5O_2^-]}{[HC_7H_5O_2]}$$

(b)

pH = 3.12
$[H^+] = 10^{-pH} = 10^{-3.12} = 7.6 \times 10^{-4}$ M

	$HC_7H_5O_2$(aq)	→	H_3O^+(aq)	$C_7H_5O_2^-$(aq)
Initial	0.0020 M			
Change	$- 7.6 \times 10^{-4}$ M		$+ 7.6 \times 10^{-4}$ M	$+ 7.6 \times 10^{-4}$ M
Equilibrium	$0.0020 - 7.6 \times 10^{-4}$ M		7.6×10^{-4} M	7.6×10^{-4} M

$$Ka = \frac{[H_3O^+][C_7H_5O_2^-]}{[HC_7H_5O_2]} = \frac{(7.6 \times 10^{-4})^2}{0.0020 - 7.6 \times 10^{-4}} = 4.7 \times 10^{-4}$$

A296

(a)

$$pH = pKa + \log \frac{[HCO_3^-]}{[H_2CO_3]} = -\log(4.3 \times 10^{-7}) + \log \frac{[0.50]}{[0.50]}$$
$= 6.37$

(b)

$$pH = pKa + \log \frac{[HCO_3^-]}{[H_2CO_3]} = -\log(4.3 \times 10^{-7}) + \log \frac{[0.25]}{[0.50]}$$
$= 6.07$

(c)

pH of the buffer stays the same because the pH of a buffer solution depends on two factors: the pKa of the acid and the ratio of the concentrations of the conjugate base (sodium bicarbonate) to the acid (carbonic acid). In this case, since the molar ratio of sodium bicarbonate to carbonic acid remains 1:1, the ratio does not change, even if the concentrations of both are doubled. Therefore, the pH remains unchanged as it is determined by the ratio and the pKa, which stays constant.

(d)

	HCO_3^- (aq)	H_3O^+(aq)	→	H_2CO_3 (aq)
Initial	0.50 M	0.010 M		0.50 M
Change	-0.010 M	-0.010 M		+0.010 M
Equilibrium	0.490 M	0		0.510 M

$$pH = pKa + \log \frac{[HCO_3^-]}{[H_2CO_3]} = -\log(4.3 \times 10^{-7}) + \log \frac{[0.490]}{[0.510]}$$
$= 6.35$

(e)

	H_2CO_3 (aq)	OH^- (aq)	$\rightarrow$	H_2O (l)	HCO_3^- (aq)
Initial	0.50 M	0.010 M			0.50 M
Change	-0.010 M	-0.010 M			+0.010 M
Equilibrium	0.490 M	0			0.510 M

$pH = pKa + \log \frac{[HCO3^-]}{[H2CO3]} = -\log(4.3 \times 10^{-7}) + \log \frac{[0.510]}{[0.490]}$

$= 6.38$

(f)

	HCO_3^- (aq)	H_3O^+ (aq)	$\rightarrow$	H_2CO_3 (aq)
Initial	0.10 M	0.10 M		0.10 M
Change	-0.010 M	-0.010 M		+0.010 M
Equilibrium	0.090 M	0		0.110 M

$pH = pKa + \log \frac{[HCO3^-]}{[H2CO3]} = -\log(4.3 \times 10^{-7}) + \log \frac{[0.090]}{[0.110]}$

$= 6.28$

(g)
As the components in the buffer solution increase, the buffer's capacity to resist changes in pH increases because a more concentrated buffer has a larger quantity of the acid and its conjugate base.

A297

(a)

$C_6H_5COOH(aq) + H_2O(l) \rightleftarrows C_6H_5COO^-(aq) + H_3O^+(aq)$

$Ka = \frac{[C6H5COO^-][H3O^+]}{[C6H5COOH]}$

$pKa = -\log Ka = -\log(6.3 \times 10^{-5}) = 4.20$

(b)

$pH = pKa + \log \frac{[C6H5COO^-]}{[C6H5COOH]}$

$= 4.20 + \log \frac{[0.150]}{[0.200]} = 4.08$

(c)

[HCl] = 0.010 mol / 0.500 L = 0.020 M

$C_6H_5COO^-(aq) + H_3O^+(aq) \rightleftarrows C_6H_5COOH(aq) + H_2O(l)$

	$C_6H_5COO^-$ (aq)	H_3O^+ (aq)	$\rightleftarrows$	C_6H_5COOH (aq)	H_2O (l)
Initial	0.150 M	0.020 M		0.200 M	
Change	-0.020 M	-0.020 M		+0.020 M	
Equilibrium	0.130 M	0		0.220 M	

$= 4.20 + \log \frac{[0.130]}{[0.220]} = 3.97$

(d)

$C_6H_5COOH(aq) + OH^-(aq) \rightleftharpoons C_6H_5COO^-(aq) + H_2O(l)$

	$C_6H_5COOH(aq)$	$OH^-(aq)$	$\rightleftharpoons$	$C_6H_5COO^-(aq)$	$H_2O(l)$
Initial	0.200 M	0.020 M		0.150 M	
Change	-0.020 M	-0.020 M		+0.020 M	
Equilibrium	0.180 M	0		0.170 M	

$= 4.20 + \log \frac{[0.170]}{[0.180]} = 4.18$

(e)

In a buffer solution, the weak acid and its conjugate base work together to resist changes in pH. When a small amount of strong acid (like HCl) is added, the conjugate base (sodium benzoate) reacts with the H^+ ions from the acid to form more of the weak acid, thus minimizing the pH change. Similarly, when a small amount of strong base (like NaOH) is added, the weak acid (benzoic acid) donates a proton to neutralize the OH^- ions, forming more of the conjugate base and again minimizing the pH change. This capacity of the buffer to resist pH changes is known as its buffer capacity, and it is most effective when the concentrations of the acid and its conjugate base are comparable.

A298

(a)

$pKa = 5 - \log 1.8 = 4.74$

$pH = pKa + \log \frac{[CH3COO-]}{[CH3COOH]}$

$4.74 = 4.74 + \log \frac{[CH3COO-]}{[CH3COOH]}$

$\log \frac{[CH3COO-]}{[CH3COOH]} = 0$

Thus, the ratio of $[CH_3COO^-]$ to $[CH_3COOH]$ is 1:1.
This means the concentrations of acetic acid and acetate ion are equal in this buffer solution.

(b)

Initial pH: Calculate the initial pH of the 0.100 M CH₃COOH solution before the titration begins.	$pH = -\log \sqrt{Ka\, C}$ $= -\log \sqrt{(1.8 * 10^{-5})(0.100)}$ $= 2.87$
Half-equivalence point: Determine the volume of NaOH needed to reach the half-equivalence point and calculate the pH at this point.	Equivalence point naMaVa = nbMbVb (1)(0.100M)(50.00 mL) = (1)(0.100M)(x mL) x = 50.00 mL Therefore, volume of the half equivalence point is 25.00 mL $pH = pKa = -\log(1.8 * 10^{-5}) = 4.74$

Equivalence point: Calculate the volume of 0.100 M NaOH required to reach the equivalence point. What will the pH be at this point?	Equivalence point naMaVa = nbMbVb (1)(0.100M)(50.00 mL) = (1)(0.100M)(x mL) x = 50.00 mL At the equivalence point, the solution contains only the acetate ion (CH_3COO^-), which is the conjugate base of acetic acid. The pH will be determined by the hydrolysis of acetate: CH_3COO^- (aq) + H_2O (l) ⇌ CH_3COOH (aq) + OH^- (aq) $[CH_3COO^-]$ = 0.00500 mol / (50.00 + 50.00) mL = 0.0500 M $K_b = \frac{K_w}{K_a} = \frac{(1.0 * 10^{-14})}{(1.8 * 10^{-5})} = 5.56 \times 10^{-10} = \frac{x^2}{0.0500-x} = \frac{x^2}{0.0500}$ x = 5.27 x 10^{-6} M pOH = - log (5.27 x 10^{-6}) = 5.28 pH = 14 − pOH = 14 − 5.28 = 8.72
Graph: Sketch a titration curve for the addition of NaOH to the CH_3COOH solution, showing the initial pH, the half-equivalence point, and the equivalence point on the graph.	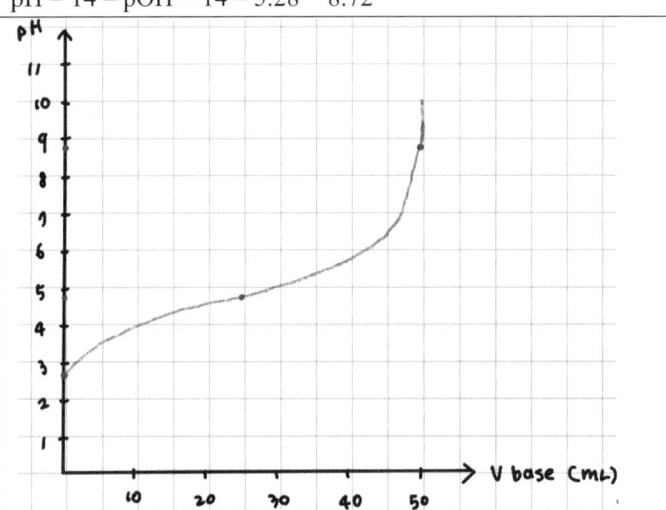

A299

(a)
pKa1 = - log (5.4 x 10^{-2}) = 1.27
pKa2 = - log (5.4 x 10^{-5}) = 4.27

(b)
pH = pKa + log $\frac{[C_2O_4^{2-}]}{[HC_2O_4^-]}$

4.00 = 4.27 + log $\frac{[C_2O_4^{2-}]}{[HC_2O_4^-]}$

log $\frac{[C_2O_4^{2-}]}{[HC_2O_4^-]}$ = - 0.27

$\frac{[C_2O_4^{2-}]}{[HC_2O_4^-]}$ = $10^{-0.27}$ = 0.537

A300

(a)
pH = pKa = 3.17 at half equivalence point
Ka = $10^{-3.17}$ = 6.76 x 10^{-4}

(b)
pH = pKa + log $\frac{[F^-]}{[HF]}$

2.90 = 3.17 + log $\frac{[F^-]}{[HF]}$

log $\frac{[F^-]}{[HF]}$ = - 0.27

$\frac{[F^-]}{[HF]}$ = $10^{-0.27}$ = 0.54

Therefore, [HF] > [F⁻]

(c)
pH = pKa + log $\frac{[F^-]}{[HF]}$

3.40 = 3.17 + log $\frac{[F^-]}{[HF]}$

log $\frac{[F^-]}{[HF]}$ = 0.23

$\frac{[F^-]}{[HF]}$ = $10^{0.23}$ = 1.70

Therefore, [HF] < [F⁻]

A301

(a)
pH of strong acid = - log [H⁺]
pH = - log (0.20) = 0.70

(b)
Added mol of $Ca(OH)_2$ is MV = (0.10 M) (10.0/1000 L) = 0.001 mol
Initial mol of HBr is MV = (0.20 M) (40.0/1000 L) = 0.008 mol
$Ca(OH)_2$ (aq) + 2 HBr(aq) ⇌ 2 H_2O (l) + $CaBr_2$ (aq)

	$Ca(OH)_2$ (aq)	2 HBr(aq)	⇌	2 H_2O (l)	$CaBr_2$ (aq)
Initial	0.001 mol	0.008 mol			
Change	-0.001 mol	-0.002 mol			+0.001 mol
Equilibrium	0	0.006 mol			0.001 mol

After adding 10.0 mL of 0.10 M $Ca(OH)_2$, remained mole of HBr is 0.006 mol.

Molarity of HBr is $\frac{0.006\ mol}{(10+40)mL}$ = 0.12 M

pH = - log (0.12) = 0.92

(c)
pH = 7 at equivalence point because salt from the neutralization of strong acid and strong base is neutral. pH of the resulting solution depends on just water self ionization.

(d)
To find out equivalence point, calculate naMaVa = nbMbVb
(1) (0.20 M) (40.0 mL) = (2) (0.10 M) (x mL)
x = 40.0 mL
After 50.0 mL of 0.10 M calcium hydroxide has been added, 10.0 mL of calcium hydroxide is remained which determine the pH beyond the equivalence point.
(10.0 mL) (0.10 M) = 0.0010 mol
$\frac{0.001\ mol}{(40+50)mL}$ = 0.011 M Ca(OH)$_2$
[OH$^-$] = 0.022 M
pOH = - log [OH$^-$] = - log (0.022) = 1.66
pH = 14.00 – pOH = 14.00 – 1.66 = 12.34

A302

(a)

	CH$_3$COOH (aq)	H$_2$O(l)	⇌	H$_3$O$^+$ (aq)	CH$_3$COO$^-$ (aq)
Initial	0.10 M				
Change	- x M			+ x M	+ x M
Equilibrium	0.10 - x			x	x

$K_a = \frac{x^2}{0.10-x} = 1.8 \times 10^{-5}$
x^2 = (0.10-x) (1.8 x 10^{-5}) = (0.10)(1.8 x 10^{-5}) - - - Assume that 0.10 – x = 0.10 because Ka is very small.
pH of weak acid = - log $\sqrt{Ka\ C}$ = - log $\sqrt{(1.8 * 10^{-5})(0.10)}$ = 2.87

(b)
Added mol of NaOH is MV = (0.10 M) (10.0/1000 L) = 0.001 mol
Initial mol of CH$_3$COOH is MV = (0.10 M) (50.0/1000 L) = 0.005 mol

	CH$_3$COOH (aq)	NaOH (aq)	⇌	H$_2$O (l)	NaCH$_3$COO (aq)
Initial	0.005 mol	0.001 mol			
Change	- 0.001 mol	- 0.001 mol			+ 0.001 mol
Equilibrium	0.004 mol	0			0.001 mol

After adding 10.0 mL of 0.10 M NaOH, remained mole of CH$_3$COOH is 0.004 mol.
Molarity of CH$_3$COOH is $\frac{0.004\ mol}{(10+50)mL}$ = 0.067 M
pH = - log $\sqrt{Ka\ C}$ = - log $\sqrt{(1.8 * 10^{-5})(0.067)}$ = 2.96

(c)
At half equivalence point, pH = pKa = - log Ka = - log (1.8 x 10^{-5}) = 4.74

(d)
To find out equivalence point, calculate naMaVa = nbMbVb
(1) (0.10 M) (50.0 mL) = (1) (0.10 M) (x mL)
x = 50.0 mL

$[CH_3COO^-]$ at equivalence point = $\frac{(0.10\ M)(50\ mL)}{(100\ mL)}$ = 0.050 M

	CH_3COO^- (aq)	H_2O (l)	⇌	CH_3COOH (aq)	OH^- (aq)
Initial	0.050 M				
Change	- x M			+ x M	+ x M
Equilibrium	0.050 – x M			x	x

$K_b = \frac{K_w}{K_a} = \frac{(1.0 * 10^{-14})}{(1.8 * 10^{-5})} = 5.6 \times 10^{-10} = \frac{x^2}{0.050-x}$

x = [OH⁻] = 5.3 x 10⁻⁶ M
pOH = - log (5.3 x 10⁻⁶) = 5.28
pH = 14 – pOH = 14 – 5.28 = 8.72

(e)
After 60.0 mL of 0.10 M sodium hydroxide has been added, 10.0 mL of sodium hydroxide is remained which determine the pH beyond the equivalence point.
(10.0 mL) (0.10 M) = 0.0010 mol

$\frac{0.001\ mol}{(50+60)mL}$ = 0.0091 M NaOH

[OH⁻] = 0.0091M
pOH = - log [OH⁻] = - log (0.091) = 2.04
pH = 14.00 – pOH = 14.00 – 2.04 = 11.96

A303

(a)
Initial pH
For HBr = - log (0.200) = 0.70
For lactic acid = - log $\sqrt{K_a\ C}$ = - log $\sqrt{(1.4 * 10^{-4})(0.200)}$ = 2.28

(b)
The equivalence point volume
naMaVa = nbMbVb
(1)(0.200 M)(30.0 mL) = (1)(0.500 M) (x mL)
x = 12 mL

(c)
half-equivalence point for lactic acid
pH = pKa = - log (1.4 × 10⁻⁴) = 3.86

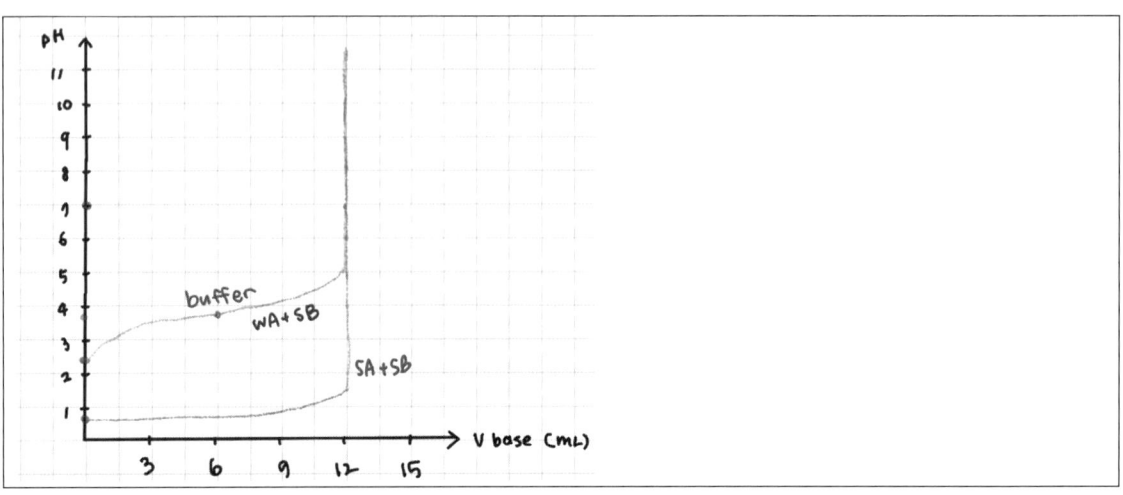

A304

(a)
Initial pH
For HI = $-\log(0.300) = 0.52$
For $H_2SO_4 = -\log(0.600) = 0.22$

(b)
The equivalence point volume
For HI, $n_aM_aV_a = n_bM_bV_b = (1)(0.300\text{ M})(40.0\text{ mL}) = (1)(0.500\text{ M})(x\text{ mL}) \rightarrow x = 24\text{ mL}$
For H_2SO_4, $n_aM_aV_a = n_bM_bV_b = (2)(0.300\text{ M})(40.0\text{ mL}) = (1)(0.500\text{ M})(x\text{ mL}) \rightarrow x = 48\text{ mL}$

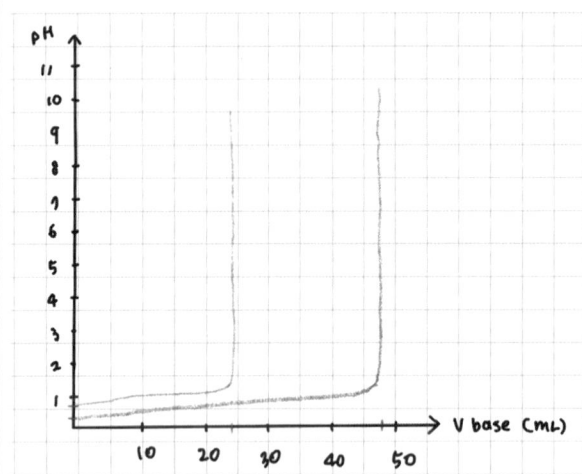

A305

(a)
$n_a M_a V_a = n_b M_b V_b$
(1) (0.100 M) (25.0 mL) = (1) (0.100 M) (x mL)
x = 25.0 mL

(b)
$n_a M_a V_a = n_b M_b V_b$
(2) (0.200 M) (50.0 mL) = (1) (x M) (100.0 mL)
x = 0.200 M

(c)
mol of HNO_3 is (30.0 mL) (0.150 M) = 4.5 mmol
mol of NaOH is (15.0 mL) (0.100 M) = 1.5 mmol

	HNO_3 (aq)	NaOH (aq)	⇌	H_2O (l)	$NaNO_3$ (aq)
Initial	4.5 mmol	1.5 mmol			
Change	- 1.5 mmol	- 1.5 mmol			+ 1.5 mmol
Equilibrium	3.0 mmol	0			1.5 mmol

$[HNO_3] = \frac{3.0 \; mmol}{(30+15) mL} = 0.067$ M

pH = - log (0.067) = 1.18

(d)
$n_a M_a V_a = n_b M_b V_b$
(1) (x M) (35.0 mL) = (1) (0.150 M) (25.0 mL)
x = 0.107 M

(e)
$n_a M_a V_a = n_b M_b V_b$
(2) (x M) (50.0 mL) = (1) (0.200 M) (75.0 mL)
x = 0.150 M

A306

$n_a M_a V_a = n_b M_b V_b$
(2) (x M) (50.0 mL) = (3) (0.100 M) (20.0 mL)
x = 0.060 M

A307

$n_a M_a V_a = n_b M_b V_b$
(2) (0.10 M) (15.0 mL) = (1) (x M) (25.0 mL)
x = 0.12 M

A308

Let's make ICE chart.

	CH_3COO^- (aq)	H_2O (l)	$\rightleftarrows$	CH_3COOH (aq)	OH^- (aq)
Initial	0.10 M				
Change	$-x$ M			$+x$ M	$+x$ M
Equilibrium	$0.10 - x$ M			x M	x M

$Kb = \dfrac{Kw}{Ka} = \dfrac{(1.0 \ast 10^{-14})}{(1.8 \ast 10^{-5})} = 5.6 \times 10^{-10} = \dfrac{x^2}{0.10-x}$

x = 7.45 x 10^{-6} M

pOH = - log (7.45 x 10^{-6}) = 5.13

pH = 14.00 – pOH = 8.87

A309

Let's make ICE chart.

	NH_4^+ (aq)	H_2O (l)	$\rightleftarrows$	NH_3 (aq)	H_3O^+ (aq)
Initial	0.20 M				
Change	$-x$ M			$+x$ M	$+x$ M
Equilibrium	$0.20 - x$ M			x M	x M

$Ka = \dfrac{Kw}{Kb} = \dfrac{(1.0 \ast 10^{-14})}{(1.8 \ast 10^{-5})} = 5.6 \times 10^{-10} = \dfrac{x^2}{0.20-x}$

x = 1.06 x 10^{-5} M

pH = - log (1.06 x 10^{-5}) = 4.98

A310

Let's make ICE chart.

	HSO_4^- (aq)	H_2O (l)	$\rightleftarrows$	H_2SO_4 (aq)	OH^- (aq)
Initial	0.30 M				
Change	$-x$ M			$+x$ M	$+x$ M
Equilibrium	$0.30 - x$ M			x M	x M

$Kb = \dfrac{Kw}{Ka} = \dfrac{(1.0 \ast 10^{-14})}{(1.2 \ast 10^{-2})} = 8.3 \times 10^{-13} = \dfrac{x^2}{0.30-x}$

x = 5.0 x 10^{-7} M

pOH = - log (5.0 x 10^{-7}) = 6.30

pH = 14.00 – pOH = 7.70

A311 (C)

Make ICE table.

	HCOOH (aq)	H$_2$O (l)	⇌	H$_3$O$^+$ (aq)	HCOO$^-$ (aq)
Initial	0.050 M				
Change	- x M			+ x M	+ x M
Equilibrium	0.050 – x M			x M	x M

$K_a = \dfrac{x^2}{0.050-x} = 1.8 \times 10^{-4}$

[H$_3$O$^+$] = x = 0.003 M

pH = 2.52

A312 (A)

Make ICE table.

	CH$_3$NH$_2$ (aq)	H$_2$O (l)	⇌	CH$_3$NH$_3^+$ (aq)	OH$^-$ (aq)
Initial	0.10 M				
Change	- x M			+ x M	+ x M
Equilibrium	0.10 – x M			x M	x M

$K_b = \dfrac{x^2}{0.10-x} = 4.4 \times 10^{-4}$

[OH$^-$] = x = 0.00663 M

pOH = 2.18

pH = 14.00 – pOH = 11.82

A313 (C)

Make ICE table.

	H$_2$SO$_3$ (aq)	H$_2$O (l)	⇌	H$_3$O$^+$ (aq)	HSO$_3^-$ (aq)
Initial	0.070 M				
Change	- x M			+ x M	+ x M
Equilibrium	0.070 – x M			x M	x M

$K_a = \dfrac{x^2}{0.070-x} = 1.5 \times 10^{-2}$

[H$_3$O$^+$] = x = 0.00324 M

pH = 1.49

A314 (B)

Mol of NH$_3$ = (50/1000 L) (0.200 M) = 0.0100 mol

Mol of HCl = (25/1000 L) (0.200 M) = 0.00500 mol

$K_a = \dfrac{K_w}{K_b} = \dfrac{(1.0 \times 10^{-14})}{(1.8 \times 10^{-5})} = 5.56 \times 10^{-10}$

At half equivalence point, pH = pKa = - log (5.56 x 10^{-10}) = 9.26

A315 (C)

Calculate the concentration of acid and conjugate base.

$[CH_3COOH] = \frac{(100.0 \text{ mL} \times 0.250 \text{ M})}{(50.0+100.0) \text{mL}} = 0.167 \text{ M}$

$[CH_3COO^-] = \frac{(50.0 \text{ mL} \times 0.250 \text{ M})}{(50.0+100.0) \text{mL}} = 0.0833 \text{ M}$

$pH = pK_a + \log \frac{[CH_3COO^-]}{[CH_3COOH]} = -\log(1.8 \times 10^{-5}) + \log \frac{0.0833}{0.167} = 4.44$

A316 (B)

Calculate the concentration of acid and conjugate base.

$[C_6H_5COOH] = \frac{(50.0 \text{ mL} \times 0.100 \text{ M})}{(50.0+50.0) \text{mL}} = 0.0500 \text{ M}$

$[C_6H_5COO^-] = \frac{(50.0 \text{ mL} \times 0.050 \text{ M})}{(50.0+50.0) \text{mL}} = 0.0250 \text{ M}$

$pH = pK_a + \log \frac{[C_6H_5COO^-]}{[C_6H_5COOH]} = -\log(6.3 \times 10^{-5}) + \log \frac{0.0250}{0.0500} = 3.90$

A317 (D)

Calculate the concentration of acid and conjugate base.

$[NH_4^+] = \frac{(25.0 \text{ mL} \times 0.300 \text{ M})}{(25.0+75.0) \text{mL}} = 0.0750 \text{ M}$

$[NH_3] = \frac{(75.0 \text{ mL} \times 0.300 \text{ M})}{(75.0+25.0) \text{mL}} = 0.225 \text{ M}$

$K_a = \frac{K_w}{K_b} = \frac{(1.0 \times 10^{-14})}{(1.8 \times 10^{-5})} = 5.56 \times 10^{-10}$

$pH = pK_a + \log \frac{[NH_3]}{[NH_4^+]} = -\log(5.56 \times 10^{-10}) + \log \frac{0.225}{0.0750} = 9.73$

A318 (A)

Calculate the concentration of acid and conjugate base.

$[C_3H_6O_3] = \frac{(100.0 \text{ mL} \times 0.200 \text{ M})}{(100.0+50.0) \text{mL}} = 0.133 \text{ M}$

$[C_3H_5O_3^-] = \frac{(50.0 \text{ mL} \times 0.100 \text{ M})}{(100.0+50.0) \text{mL}} = 0.0333 \text{ M}$

$pH = pK_a + \log \frac{[C_3H_5O_3^-]}{[C_3H_6O_3]} = -\log(1.4 \times 10^{-4}) + \log \frac{0.0333}{0.133} = 3.25$

A319 (A)

A320 (B)

Find out equivalence point.
naMaVa = nbMbVb
(1)(0.100 M)(50.0 mL) = (1)(0.100 M)(x mL)
x = 50.0 mL
Therefore, addition of 30.0 mL of NaOH is before the equivalence point and after half equivalence point.
Make ICE table.

	C_6H_5COOH (aq)	OH^- (aq)	⇌	$C_6H_5COO^-$ (aq)	H_2O (l)
Initial	0.005 mol	0.003 mol			
Change	- 0.003 mol	- 0.003 mol		+ 0.003 mol	
Equilibrium	0.002 mol	0		0.003 mol	
Molarity	$\dfrac{0.002 \text{ mol}}{(50.0+30.0) \text{ mL}}$ = 0.025 M			$\dfrac{0.003 \text{ mol}}{(50.0+30.0) \text{ mL}}$ = 0.0375 M	

$$pH = pKa + \log \frac{[C_6H_5COO^-]}{[C_6H_5COOH]} = -\log(6.3 \times 10^{-5}) + \log \frac{0.0375}{0.025} = 4.38$$

A321 (A)

$pH = pKa = -\log(1.5 \times 10^{-5}) = 5 - \log 1.5 = 4.83$

A322 (B)

A323 (A)

The pH of a strong base is higher than that of a weak base, even at the same concentration.

A324 (D)

The pH of a strong acid is lower than that of a weak acid, even at the same concentration.

A325 (C)

The pH at the equivalence point is determined by the characteristics of the salt produced. In a titration between a strong acid and a strong base, the result is neutral because the resulting salt does not affect the pH. However, in the titration of a weak base and a strong acid, the pH at the equivalence point is acidic because the conjugate acid of the weak base (such as the ammonium ion) is stronger than water, which leads to a lower pH. Therefore, the pH at the equivalence point will be higher for the NaOH solution (as NaOH is a strong base).

A326 (B)

The pH at the equivalence point is determined by the characteristics of the salt produced.
Make ICE table for salt hydrolysis.
First, calculate the concentration of $[CH_3NH_3^+]$ = $\dfrac{0.005 \text{ mol}}{(50.0+50.0) \text{ mL}}$ = 0.05 M

	$CH_3NH_3^+$ (aq)	H_2O (l)	⇌	CH_3NH_2 (aq)	H_3O^+ (aq)
Initial	0.05 M				
Change	- x M			+ x M	+ x M
Equilibrium	0.05 – x M			x M	x M

$Ka = \dfrac{Kw}{Kb} = \dfrac{(1.0 * 10^{-14})}{(4.4 * 10^{-4})} = 2.3 \times 10^{-11} = \dfrac{x^2}{0.05-x}$

$x = 1.07 \times 10^{-6}$ M

$pH = -\log(1.07 \times 10^{-6}) = 5.97$

A327 (B)

First, check the equivalence point (16 mL) to calculate the unknown concentration of the acid.
naMaVa = nbMbVb
(1)(Ma)(25.0 mL) = (1)(0.20 M)(16.0 mL)
Ma = 0.13 M

Second, check the pH at half equivalence point (8 mL) and it is about slightly less than 4.
Calculate the pKa of each weak acids.

Weak acid	Ka	pKa
Hydrofluoric acid	5.6×10^{-4}	$-\log(5.6 \times 10^{-4}) = 3.25$
Formic acid	1.8×10^{-4}	$-\log(1.8 \times 10^{-4}) = 3.74$
Acetic acid	1.8×10^{-5}	$-\log(1.8 \times 10^{-5}) = 4.74$

A328 (A)

At the half-equivalence point in the titration of a weak base (ammonia) with a strong acid (HCl), the concentrations of the weak base and its conjugate acid are equal. This is the point where the buffer system is most effective, and the solution resists changes in pH.

A329 (D)

First, check the equivalence point (10 mL) to calculate the unknown concentration of the acid.
naMaVa = nbMbVb
(1)(Ma)(15.0 mL) = (1)(0.0300 M)(10.0 mL)
Ma = 0.0200 M
Second, check the pH at half equivalence point (5 mL) and it is about slightly greater than 3.

A330 (D)

naMaVa = nbMbVb
(2)(0.400 M)(31.75 – 2.15 mL) = (1)(Mb)(17.00 mL)
Mb = 1.39 M

Topic _9
Thermodynamics and Electrochemistry

*Thermodynamics part is included in Topic 6 in this book

Exam Weighting : 7-9%

Topic 9 Key Point Review

Galvanic cell
- A device that converts chemical energy into electrical energy through a spontaneous redox reaction.
- Anode
  - Site of oxidation (loses electrons); negative electrode.
- Cathode
  - Site of reduction (gains electrons); positive electrode.
- Salt Bridge
  - Maintains electrical neutrality by allowing the flow of ions between the two half-cells.
- Electron Flow
  - From the anode to the cathode through an external circuit.
- Cell Potential (E°cell)
  - The voltage generated by the cell, calculated as: $E°_{cell} = E°_{cathode} - E°_{anode}$
- Spontaneous Reaction: If E°cell > 0, the reaction is spontaneous.

Electrolysis
- A process that uses electrical energy to drive a non-spontaneous redox reaction.
- Anode: Site of oxidation (positive electrode in electrolytic cells).
- Cathode: Site of reduction (negative electrode in electrolytic cells).
- Electron Flow: From the external power source to the cathode and then to the anode.
- Cell Potential (E°cell)
  - The voltage generated by the cell, calculated as: $E°_{cell} = E°_{cathode} - E°_{anode}$
- Nonspontaneous Reaction: If E°cell < 0, the reaction is nonspontaneous.

Faraday's law
- The amount of substance produced at each electrode during electrolysis is directly proportional to the quantity of electric charge passed through the cell.
- 1 Faraday = 1 mole of electrons = 96,485 Coulombs.
- Current (C/sec) x time (sec) x 1/F x
- Current $[\frac{C}{sec}]$ x time [sec] x $\frac{1}{F}$ $[\frac{1 \text{ mol e}}{96485 \text{ C}}]$ x $\frac{(\ ) \text{ mol metal}}{(\ ) \text{ mol e}}$ x $\frac{\text{molar mass of metal}}{1 \text{ mol metal}}$

True/False Questions

Read the following statements carefully and determine whether each one is true or false. Place a tick (✔) in the appropriate box. If the statement is false, correct the incorrect part of the statement.

	Statement	True	False
Q331	In a redox reaction, the substance that is oxidized will have its oxidation number increase, while the substance that is reduced will have its oxidation number decrease.		
Q332	In a galvanic cell, the anode is positively charged, and the cathode is negatively charged.		
Q333	The electromotive force (EMF) of a galvanic cell is always positive under standard conditions.		
Q334	In electrolysis, the flow of electrons is from the cathode to the anode.		
Q335	The process of electrolysis requires an external source of electrical energy to drive a non-spontaneous reaction.		
Q336	In an electrolytic cell, the reduction reaction occurs at the anode, and the oxidation reaction occurs at the cathode.		
Q337	Faraday's law of electrolysis states that the amount of substance deposited or liberated at an electrode is directly proportional to the total charge passed through the electrolyte.		
Q338	If the Gibbs free energy change (ΔG) for a reaction is positive, the cell potential ($E°_{cell}$) for the corresponding electrochemical cell must also be positive.		
Q339	During electrolysis, the amount of product formed at each electrode is independent of the current passed through the system.		
Q340	In a galvanic cell, the flow of ions through the salt bridge compensates for the charge buildup at the electrodes, maintaining electrical neutrality in both half-cells.		

Concept Check Questions

When solving Free-Response Questions (FRQs), it is essential to clearly and accurately explain your reasoning. Make sure to outline the steps in your solution process thoroughly, showing all calculations with appropriate numbers and units. This demonstrates a full understanding of the problem and ensures that your answer is both correct and complete.

Q341
Balance the following redox reaction occurring in acidic solution:

(a)
$Fe^{2+}(aq) + MnO_4^-(aq) \rightarrow Fe^{3+}(aq) + Mn^{2+}(aq)$

(b)
$NO_2^-(aq) + Cr_2O_7^{2-}(aq) \rightarrow NO_3^-(aq) + Cr^{3+}(aq)$

(c)
$MnO_2(s) + ClO^-(aq) \rightarrow MnO_4^-(aq) + Cl^-(aq)$

(d)
$I^-(aq) + HNO_3(aq) \rightarrow I_2(s) + NO(g)$

Q342
Summarize a galvanic cell using the Table.

Anode	
Cathode	
Salt bridge	
External circuit	
Standard cell potential, E°	
Gibbs free energy change, ΔG°	

Q343
Summarize a electrolytic cell using the Table.

Anode	
Cathode	
Salt bridge	
External circuit	
Standard cell potential, E°	
Gibbs free energy change, ΔG°	

Q344
Consider a galvanic cell constructed with the following half-reactions:

Anode (oxidation): $Zn(s) \rightarrow Zn^{2+}(aq) + 2e^-$ $E° = -0.76$ V
Cathode (reduction): $Cu^{2+}(aq) + 2e^- \rightarrow Cu(s)$ $E° = +0.34$ V

The solutions in the half-cells are 1.0 M in Zn^{2+} and Cu^{2+}, and a salt bridge connects the two half-cells.

(a)
Write the overall balanced cell reaction for this galvanic cell.

(b)
Calculate the standard cell potential $E°_{cell}$ for this reaction.

(c)
Explain why the reaction in this galvanic cell is spontaneous and how the sign of $E°_{cell}$ relates to the spontaneity of the reaction.

(d)
What is the role of the salt bridge in this galvanic cell? Explain how the movement of ions through the salt bridge helps maintain electrical neutrality.

(e)
Describe the flow of electrons in this galvanic cell. Which direction do the electrons flow, and why?

(f)
If the concentration of Cu^{2+} were decreased to 0.1 M, how would this affect the cell potential? Use the Nernst equation to explain your reasoning.

Q345
Consider a galvanic cell constructed with the following half-reactions:

Anode (oxidation): $Mg(s) \rightarrow Mg^{2+}(aq) + 2\ e^-$ $E° = -2.37$ V
Cathode (reduction): $Ag^+(aq) + e^- \rightarrow Ag(s)$ $E° = +0.80$ V

The solutions in the half-cells are 1.0 M in Mg^{2+} and Ag^+, and a salt bridge connects the two half-cells.

(a)
Write the overall balanced cell reaction for this galvanic cell.

(b)
Calculate the standard cell potential $E°_{cell}$ for this reaction.

(c)
Explain why the reaction in this galvanic cell is spontaneous and how the sign of $E°_{cell}$ relates to the spontaneity of the reaction.

(d)
What is the role of the salt bridge in this galvanic cell? Discuss how the movement of ions through the salt bridge helps maintain electrical neutrality.

(e)
Describe the flow of electrons in this galvanic cell. Which direction do the electrons flow, and why?

(f)
Calculate the Gibbs free energy change for this galvanic cell.

(g)
If the concentration of Ag$^+$ were decreased to 0.05 M, how would this affect the cell potential? Use the Nernst equation to explain your reasoning.

Q346
Consider a galvanic cell constructed from the following half-reactions:

Anode (oxidation): $Zn(s) \rightarrow Zn^{2+}(aq) + 2\ e^-$ $E° = -0.76$ V
Cathode (reduction): $Cu^{2+}(aq) + 2\ e^- \rightarrow Cu(s)$ $E° = +0.34$ V

The standard cell potential E° cell is calculated as +1.10 V.
The initial concentrations are:
$[Zn^{2+}] = 1.0$ M
$[Cu^{2+}] = 0.01$ M

(a)
Explain the significance of the Nernst equation and how the concentration of ions affects the cell potential.

(b)
If the concentration of Cu^{2+} were increased to 1.0 M, how would this affect the cell potential? Use the Nernst equation to explain your reasoning.

Q347

Consider the following galvanic cell under non-standard conditions:

Anode (oxidation): $Zn(s) \rightarrow Zn^{2+}(aq) + 2e^-$ $\qquad$ E° = −0.76 V
Cathode (reduction): $O_2(g) + 4H^+(aq) + 4e^- \rightarrow 2H_2O(l)$ $\qquad$ E° = +1.23 V

The partial pressure of oxygen O_2 at the cathode is 0.2 atm, and the concentrations of Zn^{2+}(aq) and H^+(aq) are both 1.0 M. Temperature is 298 K.

(a)
Write the overall balanced cell reaction for this galvanic cell.

(b)
Calculate the standard cell potential E°$_{cell}$ for the reaction.

(c)
How would increasing the oxygen pressure to 1.0 atm affect the cell potential? Use the Nernst equation to explain your reasoning.

(d)
Calculate the Gibbs free energy change for the reaction.

Q348

In biological systems, oxygen (O_2) is reduced to water during cellular respiration, while NADH (nicotinamide adenine dinucleotide) is oxidized to NAD^+. Consider the following redox reactions:

Oxidation of NADH : $NADH \rightarrow NAD^+ + H^+(aq) + 2\ e^-$ $\quad\quad E° = -0.320$ V
Reduction of O_2 : $O_2\ (g) + 4\ H^+(aq) + 4\ e^- \rightarrow 2\ H_2O(l)$ $\quad\quad E° = +0.815$ V

(a)
Determine the oxidation number changes for oxygen in the reduction of O_2 to water.

(b)
Write the balanced overall cell reaction by combining the two half-reactions.

(c)
Calculate the standard cell potential $E°_{cell}$ for the overall reaction.

(d)
Calculate the Gibbs free energy change for the overall reaction.

(e)
When the concentration of NADH decreases and while the concentration of NAD^+ increases, will the cell potential increase, decrease, or remain the same? Justify your answer.

Q349

In an industrial electrolysis setup, molten Al_2O_3 is used to extract aluminum metal. The electrolytic cell is supplied with a constant current of 15,300 A, and the aluminum produced collects at the cathode while oxygen gas is released at the anode. The relevant half-reactions are:

Cathode: $Al^{3+}(l) + 3\ e^- \rightarrow Al(l)$
Anode: $2\ O^{2-}(l) \rightarrow O_2(g) + 4\ e^-$

(a)
Write the overall balanced reaction for the electrolysis of Al_2O_3.

(b)
This electrolysis requires an external power source. Explain why electrolysis processes need an external power source, and relate this to the concept of cell potential and Gibbs free energy.

(c)
Calculate the total charge required to produce 2.8 kg of aluminum.

(d)
If the current is 3,000 A, how long would it take to produce 1.4 kg of aluminum?

(e)
Describe the flow of ions in the molten electrolyte and the movement of electrons through the external circuit during electrolysis.

(f)
What is the role of the electrodes in this electrolytic cell? Specifically, explain the role of the anode and cathode in this process.

Q350
A chemistry student wants to prepare I_2. The student has access to the following three reagents: NaCl(aq), F_2(l), and Br_2(g).

Reduction Half reaction	E° (V) at 298 K
$F_2 + 2\ e^- \rightarrow 2\ F^-$	+ 2.87
$Br_2 + 2\ e^- \rightarrow 2\ Br^-$	+ 1.07
$Cl_2 + 2\ e^- \rightarrow 2\ Cl^-$	+ 1.36

Using the data in the table above, write the balanced equation for the thermodynamically favorable reaction that will produce Cl_2 when the student combines two of the reagents.

Justify that the reaction is thermodynamically favorable by calculating the value of E° for the reaction.

Q351

A student is studying an aluminum-air cell, a type of metal-air cell that uses aluminum as the anode. The electrolyte paste contains OH⁻ ions, and oxygen from the air enters through a porous cathode membrane. The relevant half-reactions for the cell are provided in the table below:

Reduction Half reaction	E° (V) at 298 K
$O_2(g) + 2 H_2O(l) + 4 e^- \rightarrow 4 OH^-(aq)$	+ 0.34
$Al(s) + 3 OH^-(aq) \rightarrow Al(OH)_3(s) + 3 e^-$	- 2.31

The overall reaction for the aluminum-air cell is:

$$4 Al(s) + 3 O_2(g) + 6 H_2O(l) \rightarrow 4 Al(OH)_3(s)$$

(a)
Using the data in the table above, calculate the cell potential for the aluminum-air cell.

(b)
A fresh aluminum-air cell is weighed on an analytical balance before being placed in a device. As the cell operates, does the mass of the cell increase, decrease, or remain the same? Explain.

Q352
During the electrolysis of an aqueous solution of copper(II) sulfate (CuSO$_4$), copper metal is deposited at the cathode according to the following half-reaction:

$$Cu^{2+}(aq) + 2\,e^- \rightarrow Cu(s)$$

(a)
If a current of 0.8 A is passed through the solution for 1,5 hours, how many grams of copper are deposited at the cathode?

(b)
What current is required to deposit 4.5 g of copper from a CuSO$_4$ solution in 3.3 hours?

(c)
How long (in minutes) would it take to deposit 27.0 g of copper using a current of 2.8A?

Q353
A silver spoon is to be coated with an additional layer of silver using electrolysis. The electroplating process involves the reduction of silver ions (Ag^+) onto the surface of the spoon.
You want to deposit 5.8 g of silver onto the spoon. The current applied during the electroplating process is 2.3 A. How long (in hours) must electrolysis be carried out to deposit 5.8 g of silver onto the spoon?

Q354
An unknown metal, M, is deposited on the cathode during the electrolysis of a solution containing M^{3+} ions. A current of 2.0 A is applied for 1.5 hours, and 1.940 g of the unknown metal is deposited. Determine the molar mass of the unknown metal and identify the metal.

Q355
A metal N with an unknown molar mass is deposited onto a cathode during electrolysis. The metal exists in solution as $N^{2+}(aq)$, and the reduction half-reaction is:

$$N^{2+}(aq) + 2\,e^- \rightarrow N(s)$$

During electrolysis, a current of 3.0 A is applied for 2.5 hours, and 8.21 g of the metal is deposited on the cathode. Determine the molar mass of the unknown metal and identify the metal.

Multiple Choice Questions

The following questions are multiple-choice.
Choose the correct answer and explain why the other options are incorrect.

Q356
Which of the following best describes the function of a salt bridge in a galvanic cell?

A) To allow the flow of electrons between the anode and cathode
B) To maintain electrical neutrality by allowing the flow of ions between the half-cells
C) To increase the cell potential by allowing the passage of electrons
D) To reduce the activation energy of the redox reaction

Q357
In the electrolysis of molten sodium chloride, NaCl, which reaction occurs at the anode?

A) $Na^+(l) + e^- \rightarrow Na(s)$
B) $Cl_2(g) \rightarrow 2\, Cl^-(aq) + 2\, e^-$
C) $2Cl^-(l) \rightarrow Cl_2(g) + 2\, e^-$
D) $Na(s) \rightarrow Na^+(l) + e^-$

Q358
Which of the following statements about the standard cell potential $E°_{cell}$ is correct?

A) A positive $E°_{cell}$ indicates that the reaction is non-spontaneous.
B) The standard cell potential depends on the concentrations of reactants and products.
C) $E°_{cell}$ is determined by subtracting the reduction potential of the anode from that of the cathode.
D) A galvanic cell operates with a negative $E°_{cell}$.

Q359
Using the Nernst equation, calculate the actual cell potential E_{cell} for a galvanic cell with the following conditions:

Standard cell potential $E°_{cell}$	+ 1.10 V
Anode Zn with [Zn^{2+}]	0.010 M
Cathode Cu with [Cu^{2+}]	1.0 M
Number of moles of electrons transferred	2

A) 1.16 V
B) 1.04 V
C) 1.01 V
D) 1.10 V

Q360
Consider the following galvanic cell reaction under standard conditions:

$$Fe(s) + 2\,H^+(aq) \rightarrow Fe^{2+}(aq) + H_2(g)$$

The standard reduction potentials are:

$$Fe^{2+}/Fe: -0.44\text{ V}$$
$$2H^+/H_2: 0.00\text{ V}$$

The number of moles of electrons transferred in the reaction is n = 2. What is the Gibbs free energy change $\Delta G°$ for this cell reaction?

A) -21.9 kJ/mol$_{rxn}$
B) -42.3 kJ/mol$_{rxn}$
C) -84.9 kJ/mol$_{rxn}$
D) -25.4 kJ/mol$_{rxn}$

Q361
During the electrolysis of molten magnesium chloride (MgCl$_2$), magnesium metal is deposited at the cathode according to the following half-reaction:

$$Mg^{2+}(l) + 2\,e^- \rightarrow Mg(s)$$

If a current of 5.0 A is applied for 4.0 hours, how many grams of magnesium will be deposited?

A) 4.54 g
B) 7.28 g
C) 8.15 g
D) 9.07 g

Q362
Consider a galvanic cell consisting of the following half-reactions:

Anode (oxidation): $Zn^{2+}(aq) + 2\ e^- \rightarrow Zn(s)$ $\quad E° = -0.76$ V
Cathode (reduction): $Ag^+(aq) + e^- \rightarrow Ag(s)$ $\quad E° = +0.80$ V
The standard cell potential $E°_{cell}$ is 1.56 V.

The concentrations in the cell are:
$[Zn^{2+}] = 0.05$ M and $[Ag^+] = 0.001$ M
Use the Nernst equation to calculate the actual cell potential E_{cell} at 280 K.

A) 1.69 V
B) 1.85 V
C) 1.43 V
D) 1.37 V

Q363
During the electrolysis of molten copper(II) chloride ($CuCl_2$), copper metal is deposited at the cathode. You want to deposit 9.5 g of copper using electrolysis. The molar mass of copper is 63.55 g/mol. The electrolysis process is carried out for 2.0 hours. What is the current (in amperes) required to deposit 9.5 g of copper in 2.0 hours?

A) 2.0 A
B) 4.0 A
C) 5.5 A
D) 7.2 A

Q364
The lead storage battery is a common rechargeable battery used in automobiles. The overall cell reaction during discharge is:

$$Pb(s) + PbO_2(s) + 2\ H^+(aq) + 2\ HSO_4^-(aq) \rightarrow 2\ PbSO_4(s) + 2\ H_2O(l)$$

At the cathode, the following half-reaction occurs:

$$PbO_2(s) + 3\ H^+(aq) + HSO_4^-(aq) + 2\ e^- \rightarrow PbSO_4(s) + 2\ H_2O(l)$$

What is the half-reaction that occurs at the anode of the lead storage battery during discharge?

A) $Pb(s) \rightarrow Pb^{2+}(aq) + 2\ e^-$
B) $Pb(s) + HSO_4^-(aq) \rightarrow PbSO_4(s) + 2\ e^- + H^+(aq)$
C) $Pb^{2+}(aq) + SO_4^{2-}(aq) \rightarrow PbSO_4(s)$
D) $Pb(s) + 2\ H_2SO_4(aq) \rightarrow PbSO_4(s) + 2\ H_2O(l)$

Q365
Consider a galvanic cell composed of a zinc electrode in a $ZnSO_4$ solution and a copper electrode in a $CuSO_4$ solution. The half-reactions occurring in the cell are:

Anode (oxidation): $Zn(s) \rightarrow Zn^{2+}(aq) + 2e^-$
Cathode (reduction): $Cu^{2+}(aq) + 2\ e^- \rightarrow Cu(s)$

Which statement is true regarding the mass of the electrodes in this galvanic cell during operation?

A) The mass of both the anode and cathode increases.
B) The mass of the anode decreases, and the mass of the cathode increases.
C) The mass of the anode increases, and the mass of the cathode decreases.
D) The mass of both the anode and cathode remains constant.

Worked solution with answer for Topic 9

	Statement	True	False
A331	In a redox reaction, the substance that is oxidized will have its oxidation number increase, while the substance that is reduced will have its oxidation number decrease.	v	
A332	In a galvanic cell, the anode is ~~positively~~ negatively charged, and the cathode is ~~negatively~~ positively charged.		v
A333	The electromotive force (EMF) of a galvanic cell is always positive under standard conditions.	v	
A334	In electrolysis, the flow of electrons is from the ~~cathode~~ anode to the ~~anode~~ cathode.		v
A335	The process of electrolysis requires an external source of electrical energy to drive a non-spontaneous reaction.	v	
A336	In an electrolytic cell, the ~~reduction~~ oxidation reaction occurs at the anode, and the ~~oxidation~~ reduction reaction occurs at the cathode.		v
A337	Faraday's law of electrolysis states that the amount of substance deposited or liberated at an electrode is directly proportional to the total charge passed through the electrolyte.	v	
A338	If the Gibbs free energy change (ΔG) for a reaction is positive, the cell potential ($E°_{cell}$) for the corresponding electrochemical cell must also be ~~positive~~ negative because $\Delta G = -nFE$.		v
A339	During electrolysis, the amount of product formed at each electrode is ~~independent~~ dependent of the current passed through the system According to Faraday's laws of electrolysis, the amount of substance produced at each electrode is directly proportional to the amount of charge (current × time) passed through the system.		v
A340	In a galvanic cell, the flow of ions through the salt bridge compensates for the charge buildup at the electrodes, maintaining electrical neutrality in both half-cells.	v	

A341

(a)
$5 Fe^{2+}(aq) + MnO_4^-(aq) + 8H^+(aq) \rightarrow 5 Fe^{3+}(aq) + Mn^{2+}(aq) + 4 H_2O(l)$

(b)
$3 NO_2^-(aq) + Cr_2O_7^{2-}(aq) + 8 H^+(aq) \rightarrow 3 NO_3^-(aq) + 2 Cr^{3+}(aq) + 4 H_2O(l)$

(c)
$2 MnO_2(aq) + H_2O(l) + 3 ClO^-(aq) \rightarrow 2 MnO_4^-(aq) + 2 H^+(aq) + 3 Cl^-(aq)$

(d)
$6 I^-(aq) + 2 HNO_3(aq) + 6 H^+(aq) \rightarrow 3 I_2(s) + 2 NO(g) + 4 H_2O(l)$

A342

Anode	The electrode where oxidation occurs.
	In a galvanic cell, the anode is negatively charged because it is the source of electrons.
	The substance at the anode loses electrons (oxidizes).
Cathode	The electrode where reduction takes place.
	The cathode is positively charged in a galvanic cell, as it attracts electrons.
	The substance at the cathode gains electrons (reduces).
Salt bridge	The salt bridge connects the two half-cells and allows the flow of ions to maintain electrical neutrality. It prevents the buildup of charge that would stop the reaction.
External circuit	The flow of electrons from the anode to the cathode occurs through an external wire.
Standard cell potential, $E°$	Positive
Gibbs free energy change, $\Delta G°$	Negative

A343

Anode	The electrode where oxidation occurs.
	The anode is positively charged because it is connected to the positive terminal of the external power source.
	The substance at the anode loses electrons (oxidizes).
Cathode	The electrode where reduction takes place.
	The cathode is negatively charged because it is connected to the negative terminal of the external power source.
	The substance at the cathode gains electrons (reduces).
Salt bridge	Unlike a galvanic cell, an electrolytic cell does not always need a salt bridge, as both electrodes are often placed in the same electrolyte solution.
External circuit	An external power source (such as a battery) is required in an electrolytic cell to force the electrons to move from the anode to the cathode.
	The power source provides the energy needed to drive the non-spontaneous reaction by pumping electrons against the natural electrochemical gradient.
Standard cell potential, $E°$	Negative
Gibbs free energy change, $\Delta G°$	Positive

A344

(a)
Zn(s) + Cu^{2+}(aq) → Zn^{2+}(aq) + Cu(s)

(b)
E° = E°cat − E°an
= (+0.34 V) − (−0.76 V) = 1.10 V

(c)
$\Delta G° = -nFE° = -\left(\frac{2 \text{ mol } e-}{1 \text{ mol rxn}}\right)\left(\frac{96485 \text{ C}}{1 \text{ mol } e-}\right)(1.10 \text{ V})$
= − 212 kJ/mol because 1 V = 1 J / 1 C
Negative $\Delta G°$ indicates that the galvanic cell is spontaneous.

(d)
The salt bridge allows the galvanic cell to operate spontaneously by maintaining electrical neutrality in both half-cells. It balances the charge by allowing the flow of ions:
Cations (positive ions) from the salt bridge move toward the cathode, where reduction occurs, as the cathode gains electrons and develops a negative charge.
Anions (negative ions) from the salt bridge move toward the anode, where oxidation occurs, as the anode loses electrons and develops a positive charge.

(e)
Electrons flow from the anode to the cathode in a galvanic cell because oxidation occurs at the anode. During oxidation, the substance at the anode loses electrons, which are then released into the external circuit. These electrons flow through the wire to the cathode, where reduction occurs. At the cathode, these electrons are accepted by the substance being reduced. This electron flow is what drives the electrochemical reaction and allows the galvanic cell to produce electrical energy.

(f)
According to the Nernst equation : E = E° − (RT/nF) lnQ
If the concentration of Cu^{2+} were decreased, the value of Q increases because Q = $\frac{[Zn^{2+}]}{[Cu^{2+}]}$.
Since lnQ becomes larger, this leads to a larger subtraction from E°, which causes the overall cell potential E to decrease.

A345

(a)
Mg(s) + 2 Ag$^+$(aq) → Mg^{2+}(aq) + 2 Ag(s)

(b)
E° = E°cat − E°an
= (+0.80 V) − (−2.37 V) = 3.17 V

(c)
When ΔG° is negative, it means that the process is thermodynamically favorable, and the reaction will proceed spontaneously. A negative ΔG° corresponds to a positive E°, which also indicates a spontaneous electrochemical reaction.

(d)
The salt bridge plays a crucial role in a galvanic cell by maintaining electrical neutrality and ensuring the continuous flow of electrons, which allows the cell to function spontaneously.

(e)
The electrons generated at the anode (magnesium) flow through the external circuit to the cathode (silver). This flow occurs because the oxidation at the magnesium anode produces electrons, which are then driven toward the silver cathode, where the reduction of silver ions takes place.

(f)
$\Delta G° = -nFE° = -(\frac{2\ mol\ e-}{1\ mol\ rxn})(\frac{96485\ C}{1\ mol\ e-})(3.17\ V)$
$= -612$ kJ/mol because 1 V = 1 J / 1 C

(g)
According to the Nernst equation : $E = E° - (RT/nF) \ln Q$
If the concentration of Ag⁺ were decreased, the value of Q increases because $Q = \frac{[Mg^{2+}]}{[Ag^+]^2}$.
Since lnQ becomes larger, this leads to a larger subtraction from E°, which causes the overall cell potential E to decrease.

A346

(a)
The Nernst equation is significant because it allows us to calculate the cell potential (E) of an electrochemical cell under non-standard conditions (when concentrations of reactants and products are not 1 M, the temperature is not 25°C, or pressure is not 1 atm). The standard cell potential (E°) only applies to ideal conditions, but in real-world applications, concentrations of ions and other factors often differ, which affects the cell's behavior. The Nernst equation helps account for these variations.

(b)
According to the Nernst equation : $E = E° - (RT/nF) \ln Q$
If the concentration of Cu²⁺ were increased, the value of Q increases because $Q = \frac{[Zn^{2+}]}{[Cu^{2+}]}$.
Since lnQ becomes smaller (more negative), the term $-(RT/nF) \ln Q$ adds more to E°, increasing the cell potential E.

A347

(a)
2 Zn(s) + O₂(g) + 4 H⁺(aq) → 2 Zn²⁺(aq) + 2 H₂O(l)

(b)
$E° = E°_{cat} - E°_{an}$
$= (+1.23 \text{ V}) - (-0.76 \text{ V}) = 1.99 \text{ V}$

(c)
According to the Nernst equation : $E = E° - (RT/nF) \ln Q$
If the partial pressure of oxygen (P_{O2}) is increased, the denominator of Q increases, causing Q to decrease. As a result, lnQ becomes smaller (more negative). Since lnQ is more negative, the term $-(RT/nF) \ln Q$ becomes more positive, leading to an increase in the overall cell potential E.

(d)
$\Delta G° = -nFE° = -(\frac{4 \text{ mol } e^-}{1 \text{ mol rxn}})(\frac{96485 \text{ C}}{1 \text{ mol } e^-})(1.99 \text{ V})$
$= -768 \text{ kJ/mol}$ because $1 \text{ V} = 1 \text{ J} / 1 \text{ C}$

A348

(a)
The oxidation number changes from zero to -2.

(b)
$2 \text{ NADH} + O_2 (g) + 2 H^+(aq) + \rightarrow 2 \text{ NAD}^+ + 2 H_2O(l)$

(c)
$E° = E°_{cat} - E°_{an}$
$= (+0.815 \text{ V}) - (-0.320 \text{ V}) = 1.135 \text{ V}$

(d)
$\Delta G° = -nFE° = -(\frac{4 \text{ mol } e^-}{1 \text{ mol rxn}})(\frac{96485 \text{ C}}{1 \text{ mol } e^-})(1.135 \text{ V})$
$= -438 \text{ kJ/mol}$ because $1 \text{ V} = 1 \text{ J} / 1 \text{ C}$

(e)
According to the Nernst equation : $E = E° - (RT/nF) \ln Q$
If the concentration of NADH were decreases, the value of Q increases because $Q = \frac{[NAD+]}{[NADH]^2(PO_2)[H^+]^2}$. Since lnQ becomes larger, this leads to a larger subtraction from E°, which causes the overall cell potential E to decrease.

A349

(a)
$[Al^{3+}(l) + 3\ e^- \rightarrow Al(l)] \times 4$
$[2\ O^{2-}(l) \rightarrow O_2(g) + 4\ e^-] \times 3$
$4\ Al^{3+}(l) + 6\ O^{2-}(l) \rightarrow 4\ Al(l) + 3\ O_2(g)$

(b)
Electrolysis requires an external power source because the reactions involved are non-spontaneous, with positive Gibbs free energy (ΔG > 0) and negative cell potential (Ecell < 0).
The external power source supplies the energy needed to drive the reaction by forcing electrons to flow in a direction that would not naturally occur, enabling the desired chemical transformations.

(c)
$(2800\ g) \left(\frac{1\ mol\ Al}{26.98\ g\ Al}\right)\left(\frac{3\ mol\ e-}{1\ mol\ Al}\right)\left(\frac{96485\ C}{1\ mol\ e-}\right) = 3.00 \times 10^7\ C$

(d)
$\left(\frac{3000\ C}{1sec}\right)(x\ sec)\left(\frac{1\ mol\ e-}{96485\ C}\right)\left(\frac{1\ mol\ Al}{3\ mol\ e-}\right)\left(\frac{26.98\ g\ Al}{1\ mol\ Al}\right) = 1400\ g\ Al$
$x = 5007\ sec$

(e)
Electrons flow from the anode (positive terminal) to the cathode (negative terminal) via the external circuit, while ions flow through the electrolyte to maintain electrical neutrality.

(f)
The anode is the site of oxidation where anions release electrons, and the cathode is the site of reduction where cations gain electrons.

A350

Consider cell potential.

Reduction Half reaction	E° (V) at 298 K
$F_2 + 2\ e- \rightarrow 2\ F^-$	+ 2.87
$Br_2 + 2\ e- \rightarrow 2\ Br^-$	+ 1.07
$Cl_2 + 2\ e- \rightarrow 2\ Cl^-$	+ 1.36

Reaction with Br_2	Oxidation : $2\ Br^- \rightarrow Br_2 + 2\ e-$
	Reduction : $Cl_2 + 2\ e- \rightarrow 2\ Cl^-$
	Balanced overall equation : $2\ Br^- + Cl_2 \rightarrow Br_2 + 2\ Cl^-$
	However, it is impossible because Cl⁻ is prepared not Cl_2.
Reaction with F_2	Oxidation : $2\ Cl^- \rightarrow Cl_2 + 2\ e-$
	Reduction : $F_2 + 2\ e- \rightarrow 2\ F^-$
	Balanced overall equation : $2I^- + F_2 \rightarrow I_2 + 2\ F^-$
	E° = E°cat − E°an

	= (2.87 V) – (1.36 V) = 1.51 V
	Because E° for the reaction has a positive value, the reaction is thermodynamically favorable.

Balanced overall equation : $2I^- + F_2 \rightarrow I_2 + 2 F^-$
Because E° for the reaction has a positive value, the reaction is thermodynamically favorable.

A351

(a)

Reduction Half reaction	E° (V) at 298 K	
$O_2(g) + 2 H_2O(l) + 4 e^- \rightarrow 4 OH^-(aq)$	+ 0.34	Reduction (Cathode)
$Al(s) + 3 OH^-(aq) \rightarrow Al(OH)_3(s) + 3 e^-$	- 2.31	Oxidation (Anode)

E° = E°cat – E°an
= (+0.34 V) – (-2.31 V) = 2.65 V

(b)
In the overall reaction, oxygen gas from the air reacts with aluminum metal to form solid aluminum hydroxide ($Al(OH)_3$):
$4 Al(s) + 3 O_2(g) + 6 H_2O(l) \rightarrow 4 Al(OH)_3(s)$
Aluminum metal is consumed, and oxygen from the air combines with water and aluminum to form solid aluminum hydroxide. Since oxygen is being introduced into the cell (and becomes part of the solid product), the mass of the cell increases as solid aluminum hydroxide forms.

A352

(a)
$(0.8 \frac{C}{sec})(1.5 \text{ hr} \times \frac{3600 \text{ sec}}{1 \text{ hr}})(\frac{1 \text{ mol } e}{96485 \text{ C}})(\frac{1 \text{ mol } Cu}{2 \text{ mol } e})(\frac{63.55 \text{ g } Cu}{1 \text{ mol } Cu})$
= 14.23 g

(b)
$(x \frac{C}{sec})(3.3 \text{ hr} \times \frac{3600 \text{ sec}}{1 \text{ hr}})(\frac{1 \text{ mol } e}{96485 \text{ C}})(\frac{1 \text{ mol } Cu}{2 \text{ mol } e})(\frac{63.55 \text{ g } Cu}{1 \text{ mol } Cu}) = 4.5 \text{ g Cu}$
x = 1.15 A

(c)
$(2.8 \frac{C}{sec})(x \text{ min} \times \frac{60 \text{ sec}}{1 \text{ min}})(\frac{1 \text{ mol } e}{96485 \text{ C}})(\frac{1 \text{ mol } Cu}{2 \text{ mol } e})(\frac{63.55 \text{ g } Cu}{1 \text{ mol } Cu}) = 27.0 \text{ g Cu}$
x = 488 min

A353

$(2.3 \frac{C}{sec})(x \text{ hr} \times \frac{3600 \text{ sec}}{1 \text{ hr}})(\frac{1 \text{ mol } e}{96485 \text{ C}})(\frac{1 \text{ mol } Ag}{1 \text{ mol } e})(\frac{107.87 \text{ g } Ag}{1 \text{ mol } Ag}) = 5.8 \text{ g Ag}$
x = 0.63 hr

A354

$M^{3+}(aq) + 3\ e^- \rightarrow M(s)$

$(2.0\ \frac{C}{sec})(1.5\ hr \times \frac{3600\ sec}{1\ hr})(\frac{1\ mol\ e}{96485\ C})(\frac{1\ mol\ M}{3\ mol\ e})(\frac{x\ g\ M}{1\ mol\ M}) = 1.940\ g\ M$

$x = 51.996$

Therefore, the unknown metal is Chromium.

A355

$N^{2+}(aq) + 2\ e^- \rightarrow N(s)$

$(3.0\ \frac{C}{sec})(2.5\ hr \times \frac{3600\ sec}{1\ hr})(\frac{1\ mol\ e}{96485\ C})(\frac{1\ mol\ N}{2\ mol\ e})(\frac{x\ g\ N}{1\ mol\ N}) = 8.21\ g\ N$

$x = 58.68$

Therefore, the unknown metal is Nickel.

A356 (B)
A357 (C)
A358 (C)
A359 (A)

According to the Nernst equation : $E = E° - (RT/nF)\ \ln Q$

$= (1.10\ V) - \frac{(8.314\frac{J}{mol}K)(298K)}{(2\frac{mol\ e-}{molrxn})(96485\frac{C}{mol\ e-})}\ \ln\ \frac{[0.010]}{[1.0]}$ when $Q = \frac{[Zn^{2+}]}{[Cu^{2+}]}$

$= 1.16\ V$

A360 (C)

A smaller (more negative) standard electrode potential indicates that the substance is more likely to act as an oxidizing agent and lose electrons (undergo oxidation). Therefore, Fe is oxidized at anode.

$E°_{cell} = E°_{cathode} - E°_{anode}$

$= (+0.00\ V) - (-0.44\ V) = +0.44\ V$

$\Delta G° = - nFE° = - (\frac{2\ mol\ e-}{1\ mol\ rxn})(\frac{96485\ C}{1\ mol\ e-})(0.44\ V)$

$= - 84.9\ kJ/mol_{rxn}$ because $1\ V = 1\ J\ /\ 1\ C$

A361 (D)

$(5.0\ \frac{C}{sec})(4.0\ hr \times \frac{3600\ sec}{1\ hr})(\frac{1\ mol\ e}{96485\ C})(\frac{1\ mol\ Mg}{2\ mol\ e})(\frac{24.31\ g\ Mg}{1\ mol\ Mg})$

$= 9.07\ g\ Mg$

A362 (C)

According to the Nernst equation : $E = E° - (RT/nF)\ \ln Q$

$= (1.56\ V) - \frac{(8.314\frac{J}{mol}K)(280K)}{(2\frac{mol\ e-}{molrxn})(96485\frac{C}{mol\ e-})}\ \ln\ \frac{[0.05]}{[0.001]^2}$ when $Q = \frac{[Zn^{2+}]}{[Ag^+]^2}$

$= 1.43\ V$

A363 (B)

$$(x \frac{C}{sec})(2.0 \text{ hr} \times \frac{3600 \text{ sec}}{1 \text{ hr}})(\frac{1 \text{ mol e}}{96485 \text{ C}})(\frac{1 \text{ mol Cu}}{2 \text{ mol e}})(\frac{63.55 \text{ g Cu}}{1 \text{ mol Cu}})$$
$$= 9.5 \text{ g Cu}$$
$$x = 4.0 \text{ A}$$

A364 (B)

A365 (B)